Luminos is the Open Access monograph publishing program from UC Press. Luminos provides a framework for preserving and reinvigorating monograph publishing for the future and increases the reach and visibility of important scholarly work. Titles published in the UC Press Luminos model are published with the same high standards for selection, peer review, production, and marketing as those in our traditional program. www.luminosoa.org

A

[signature: Philip E. Lilienthal]

B O O K

The Philip E. Lilienthal imprint
honors special books
in commemoration of a man whose work
at University of California Press from 1954 to 1979
was marked by dedication to young authors
and to high standards in the field of Asian Studies.
Friends, family, authors, and foundations have together
endowed the Lilienthal Fund, which enables UC Press
to publish under this imprint selected books
in a way that reflects the taste and judgment
of a great and beloved editor.

Rules of the House

Rules of the House

Family Law and Domestic Disputes in Colonial Korea

———

Sungyun Lim

中

UNIVERSITY OF CALIFORNIA PRESS

The publisher and the University of California Press Foundation gratefully acknowledge the generous support of the Philip E. Lilienthal Imprint in Asian Studies, established by a major gift from Sally Lilienthal.

The publisher and the University of California Press Foundation also gratefully acknowledge the generous support of the Association for Asian Studies in making this book possible.

University of California Press, one of the most distinguished university presses in the United States, enriches lives around the world by advancing scholarship in the humanities, social sciences, and natural sciences. Its activities are supported by the UC Press Foundation and by philanthropic contributions from individuals and institutions. For more information, visit www.ucpress.edu.

University of California Press
Oakland, California

Suggested citation:
Lim, S. *Rules of the House: Family Law and Domestic Disputes in Colonial Korea*. Oakland: University of California Press, 2019. DOI: https://doi. org/10.1525/luminos.60

Library of Congress Cataloging-in-Publication Data

Names: Lim, Sungyun, 1977–author.
Title: Rules of the house : family law and domestic disputes in colonial
   Korea / Sungyun Lim.
Description: Oakland, California : University of California Press, [2018] |
   Includes bibliographical references and index. | This work is licensed
   under a Creative Commons CC-BY-NC-ND license. To view a copy of the
   license, visit http://creativecommons.org/licenses. |
Identifiers: LCCN 2018030657 (print) | LCCN 2018032111 (ebook) | ISBN
   9780520972506 (ebook) | ISBN 9780520302525 (pbk. : alk. paper)
Subjects: LCSH: Women—Legal status, laws, etc.—Korea—20th century. |
   Domestic relations—Korea—20th century. | Korea—History—Japanese
   occupation, 1910–1945.
Classification: LCC KPA2467.W65 (ebook) | LCC KPA2467.W65 L56 2018 (print) |
   DDC 346.51901/509041—dc23
LC record available at https://lccn.loc.gov/2018030657

28 27 26 25 24 23 22 21 20 19
10 9 8 7 6 5 4 3 2 1

CONTENTS

ILLUSTRATIONS

ACKNOWLEDGMENTS

In the long time it took me to complete this book, I have incurred intellectual and material debts to many. I am happy to acknowledge some of them here.

I have benefited greatly from scholars who have generously provided academic guidance along the long trajectory of this project. First of all, I thank my teachers at Berkeley, whose teachings and influences I have come to appreciate more and more over the years. Andrew Barshay had the insight to see a project even before there was one and provided patient guidance. Irwin Scheiner taught me how to think with precision, while Wen-hsin Yeh inspired me to explore with imagination. Mizuno Naoki, formerly of the Center for Humanities at Kyoto University, was a generous and resourceful adviser during my research in Japan and provided critical guidance in archival research. Lee Seung-yup supplied crucial help in gathering archival material used in this book. Jung Ji Young of Ewha Womans University has been the de facto mentor of the project from its inception and introduced me to relevant scholarship in Korea. John Duncan graciously hosted me at the UCLA Center for Korean Studies during my year as the Korea Foundation postdoctoral fellow. Namhee Lee, Chris Hanscom, and Jennifer Jung-Kim were generous to welcome me into their vibrant intellectual community.

I presented earlier versions of the manuscript at various venues and received many invaluable comments. For this I thank the Center for Korean Studies at UC Berkeley, the Research Institute of Korean Studies at Korea University, the Nam Center for Korean Studies at the University of Michigan, the Center for East Asian Studies at the University of Chicago, the UCLA Center for Korean Studies, the Department of Women's Studies at the University of Maryland–College Park, the Research Institute of Comparative History and Culture at Hanyang University, the Center for East Asian Studies at Stanford University, and multiple annual meetings of the Association for Asian Studies. I thank all who were present at these events, especially the panel organizers and discussants: Mike Shapiro, Jun Uchida, Kyu Hyun Kim, Ken Wells, Jun Yoo, Seung-kyung Kim, the late Nancy Abelmann, Sinwoo Lee, Hannah Lim, Tadashi Ishikawa, Susan Burns, Kyeong-hee Choi, Jooyeon Hahm, David Ambaras, Hong Yang-hee, and Yoshikawa Ayako.

The History Department at the University of Colorado Boulder has been a warm and invigorating intellectual community to develop this project in, and its generous help and guidance has been crucial in completing the book. Marcia Yonemoto has been a wise mentor and a generous colleague and has answered many desperate calls for help in all matters personal and professional with utmost generosity. She has read and commented on multiple versions of this manuscript since its roughest stage and made it infinitely better. Many colleagues also kindly read and commented on earlier versions of the manuscript, many of them on numerous occasions. For this I thank Marjorie McIntosh; Mithi Mukherjee; John Willis; Céline Dauverd; Miriam Kingsberg Kadia; Fredy González; Liora Halperin, now of the University of Washington; Martha Hanna; Myles Osbourne; Samanthis Smalls; Henry Lovejoy; Lil Fenn; Peter Wood; and Vilja Hulden. Elissa Guralnick provided expert editing advice through three writing workshops that I was fortunate to be part of.

I received helpful advice on earlier versions of the manuscript during the long revision process. First of all, I thank the faculty advisers and participants at the SSRC Korean Studies Junior Faculty Workshop for their helpful advice: the late Nancy Abelmann, Nicole Constable, Hae Yeon Choo, Jiyeon Kang, Jaeeun Kim, Seo Young Park, Deborah Solomon, Dafna Zur, and Maria Gillombardo. A manuscript workshop with the Global Korea series at the University of California Press also gave me the opportunity to receive timely advice during the last stage of the revision process. I thank the Academy of Korean Studies for funding the workshop. I thank Barbara Molony and Jun Yoo for their invaluable comments. I thank John Lie for accepting this book to be part of his series. I also thank two anonymous reviewers of the manuscript, whose insightful comments saved me from many errors. Any remaining errors are, of course, solely mine. Kathryn Ragsdale generously shared her talent through multiple revisions of the manuscript. Reed Malcolm, Archna Patel, and Francisco Reinking are credited for deftly moving the book through the publishing process. The Center for Korean Studies at the University of California, Berkeley, has provided a subsidy for this book to be included in the Luminos program, for which I am very thankful.

The Japan Foundation Doctoral Research Fellowship funded the initial part of the research for this book. The Korea Foundation Postdoctoral Fellowship and the Center for Humanities and the Arts Faculty Fellowship at the University of Colorado Boulder funded valuable time away from teaching, which was crucial to completing the book.

My friend Yi Soojung of the National Museum of Modern and Contemporary Art in Korea generously shared her expertise in obtaining permission to use the cover image of this book. I also thank the copyright holders represented by Woonwoo Art Gallery for their permission to use this image.

Chapter 4 of this book is a modified version of a previously published article, "Affection and Assimilation: Concubinage and the Ideal of Conjugal Love in Colonial Korea, 1922–1938," *Gender and History* 28, no. 2 (2016): 461–79, and it is included here with the permission of the publisher.

Lastly, my most heartfelt thanks go to my family. My late father has taught me the joy not only of intellectual pursuit but also of hiking, which has been a source of great joy and sanity. He probably never imagined that I would end up in the foothills of the Rockies when he took me hiking every weekend in Seoul, but I am sure he is happy that I am putting those skills to good use here. My mother supported me over the years with help of every kind, but I thank her most for teaching me by example that behind the most conventional package of a person can lie the most unconventional kind of life. Kwangmin has stood by me through all my endeavors with unwavering support and has influenced me in deeper ways than I would sometimes like to admit. Seungjae has shouldered well the burden of having an academic mother and has given me only joy in return. I hope in my next project I can take his advice to include more maps.

Introduction

In 1912 a lawsuit was waged over a woman's right to own and bequeath property on her own accord. The woman, who was now dead, had remarried in her widowhood with a three-year-old son. To her new marriage she brought 200 *wŏn*, with which she purchased nine parcels *(majigi)* of rice paddy. It was this land she bequeathed to her two sons: four parcels to the son from her previous marriage and the rest to the son of her second marriage. The plaintiff, who seems to have been a creditor of the second son, sued the first son, demanding that he hand over his parcels. He denied the first son's claim to the land, arguing that the widow did not have the right to leave property to her son from a previous marriage: "According to Korean custom, it is a certain fact that a wife does not have any legal capacity; she cannot meddle at all with matters of property while the husband is living and must absolutely submit herself to the husband."[1]

Many aspects of this case are surprising to the modern reader. The life choices of this deceased woman defy contemporary notions about what was possible for a common Korean woman at the turn of the twentieth century. She chose to remarry instead of remaining single in chaste widowhood, and she was able to bring her son into her second marriage. She also exercised a significant degree of property rights, buying land with her own money and gifting it on her own accord. The Japanese judges of the High Court of Colonial Korea (Chōsen kōtō hōin), against the expectations of modern readers accustomed to assumptions about the abject status of women in premodern Korea and their even worse status under Japanese colonial rule, surprisingly defended the property rights of the woman. The judges' statement read, "There is no law or Korean custom that bans a woman with a living husband from buying property with her money and bequeathing it to her children." Comments that were most severely damaging to women's property rights came not from the colonial judges but from the Korean plaintiff, with his confident claim that "Korean custom" categorically denied any property rights to women and prescribed "absolute submission" of wives to husbands.

This 1912 case exposes a gap between what we have come to believe about women's legal status under Japanese colonial rule and how women were dealt with in practice. In the following pages I explore the transformation of women's legal rights in the creation of the small patriarchal family that emerged out of Japanese imposition of the household system during the Japanese colonial period. This transformation is visible to us in records of women's active participation in civil lawsuits.

THE DEBATE OVER *HOJUJE* ABOLITION

Many of the assumptions about women under Japanese colonial rule that have become conventional knowledge in South Korea were created in the late 1990s, finding wide currency in the heated public debate to abolish the household-head system *(hojuje)* installed by the Japanese, beginning with the implementation of their version of the household-registration system (K: *hojŏk;* J: *koseki*) in 1909.[2] The debate in South Korea that culminated in the 2003 National Assembly decision to abolish the old registry system homed in on the colonial origin of that system, which had been obfuscated during the postwar years in South Korea. Formulated in the Japanese metropole, the household system was disseminated throughout Japan's colonies as the administrative foundation of the Japanese Empire and its family-state ideology. It met diverging fates in different territories as the empire was dismembered after Japan's defeat in World War II: it was abolished in the Japanese homeland under U.S. occupation as a culprit in wartime mobilization and dismantled in North Korea as a vestige of feudalism, but it was embraced in South Korea as "Korean tradition," against strong opposition from women's groups for its discriminatory orientation.[3]

The debate that emerged in the late 1990s and early 2000s framed the household-head system anew, as not simply an issue of gender discrimination but also an issue of colonial legacy. The colonial origin of the registry came as a surprise to many Koreans, and this new angle of discourse provoked an explosive response during the time of heightened anti-Japanese sentiment in South Korea in the 2000s.[4] Pundits began pitting the registry's colonial legacy squarely against the claim to "tradition" that was the core of the argument of the system's proponents. "Many think that *hojuje* is our Confucian tradition," one critic pointed out, "but in fact it was a product of Japanese "spiritual invasion *[sasang ch'im'nyak]*."[5] The sex-discrimination aspect of the registry, they argued, also was a colonial imposition rather than Korean tradition. Revisionist histories of family culture in the Chosŏn dynasty and scholarship on the family-state ideology of wartime Japan added academic support to the argument that misogynistic family culture was not Korean tradition but a product of Japanese colonial rule.

After the abolition of the household-head system, the old registry was replaced with a new registry *(kajok kwan'gye tŭngnokpu)* in 2008 that was based on the individual but still fell short of solving all problems. One issue highlighted in the public debate over the old registry was the suffering that it imposed on the fast-growing number of nonnormative families in ever-changing Korean society. The tribulations of divorced mothers, in particular, struck a chord in Korean society: under the old system, a divorced mother, even if she had full custody of her child, could not exercise full parental rights because of the restrictions of the registry, with its basis in patrilineal principles that never severed the parental rights of the father. For any official business such as school registration, a mother had to produce the family register of her child's birth father, where the child was registered as his child. Similar problems continued even after the old registries were abolished, since the residential registry *(chumin tŭngnokpu)* continued to register family members under their relationship to the "head of the household" *(sedaeju)*. As residential registries are routinely required for all official business, from school registrations to job applications, nonnormative families have been particularly concerned with the exposure of their private family lives through these registries. "I remarried so that I could give my children a proper family, but my children are stigmatized on the registry as 'coresident *[tong'gŏ'in]*,'" as if they are not part of the family," lamented one woman in a 2015 article about the new family-relations registry.[6]

The continued struggles of families in South Korea with the idiosyncratic features of the family registry aptly illustrate the long legacy of a household system that even abolishment could not undo. Although the new system aimed to overhaul the patriarchal hierarchy and the patrilineal principles of the old system, it could not shake fully free of some of the major features of the old family registry: the privileging of familial relationships in defining one's personal identity and the primacy of the patriarchal nuclear family unit as the underlying organizing (albeit now hidden) principle of official registration.

Even more significant for contemporary Korea than the Japanese imposition of a household-registry system was the larger realm of practice of which that system was a part, for it is there that the enduring legacy of Japanese colonial rule truly lies. The Japanese made the small patriarchal family the official administrative unit in Korea and the basis of their family-law regime. The Japanese imposed a new boundary around the household and exercised exclusive power in administering the newly defined family unit. This, rather than the strengthening of patriarchal power, was the significant innovation in the Japanese colonial household system. That Korea was strongly patriarchal before the onset of colonialism is no secret. As we have seen earlier and as will be repeatedly evident, it was Korean men who pushed to strengthen patriarchal customs when the colonial household system threatened to weaken their position by dissolving the traditional lineage system, or the traditional patrilineal descent group.[7] A quantitative gauge of patriarchal power therefore would be the wrong means to assess change in the family system in this period: the impact of the Japanese household system becomes pronounced only when we look at it as a contest between two family systems that were both patriarchal.

This contest between two patriarchal family systems produced particular gender dynamics in the colonial legal system. Koreans were not passive receptors of these colonial family policies. Korean men, as noted, actively pushed back against the colonial household system. Nor were Korean women passive victims of the colonial legal policies; they actively participated in the colonial legal system in an effort to claim their rights and to protect those rights through official channels. Furthermore, to expand their rights in Korea, they at times pushed to expand the application of Japanese laws to Korea. The colonial state, in turn, eagerly mobilized women's—and other reform-minded Koreans'—desire for legal integration to promote the colonial goal of assimilation.

FAMILY LAW AND JAPANESE ASSIMILATION POLICY

The reason why colonial family laws were accepted as tradition in post-1945 South Korea was that the Japanese legal system fundamentally relied on Korean customs to adjudicate family matters between Koreans. While most of the Japanese Civil Code was transposed through the Civil Ordinances in Korea (*chōsen minjirei*, 1912), a small but significant exception was the rules governing family matters. To the family affairs of Koreans and cases between Koreans the courts applied "Korean custom" *(chōsen kanshū)*, a noncodified and loosely defined set of family customs produced through surveys of customs and inquiries conducted by the Office of the Governor General (also known as the Government General [Sōtokufu]).[8] The Japanese, in other words, operated a hybrid legal system in Korea, where a single legal system applied different laws depending on the litigants involved: Japanese litigants were subject to Japanese laws, and Koreans to Korean customs. This process, intended to lead to the ultimate goal of a legally integrated Japanese Empire, was premised on the concept that the various legal spheres would be integrated as the "level of the peoples" *(mindo)* was raised.[9] Following this logic, the exemptions to the Japanese Civil Code were incrementally diminished over the period of colonial rule. The exception for family matters, which followed precedents in European colonies, seems to have been devised to serve other objectives as well. For one, relying on Korean customary laws was useful for maintaining stability in the colony as well as for appeasing the local elite, to whom continuity (however deceptive and fleeting) was appealing.

Applying different laws to different nationals in Korea required maintaining a division between those who belonged to the Japanese metropole, that is, were citizens of Japan, and Koreans, who were colonial subjects. This was one of the key roles of the household registers.[10] The household-registry system, thus, was more than just an administrative system of identity registry; it also was a system for the verification of national belonging within the expanding empire and, thereby, a critical part of the colonial legal system.[11] The "original place of registry" *(honseki)* in the registry functioned as a de facto marker of nationality, as moving the *honseki* was not allowed until the end of Japanese rule—despite demands for change as practical needs mounted for both Koreans and Japanese.[12]

The organization of civil laws through the utilization of family customs also, significantly, helped the colonial government manage the tension created by its goal of assimilation *(dōka)* and the continuing reality of discrimination. This tension was most intensely felt by the Japanese on the colonial ground.[13] Following the example of European empires, the Japanese presented their colonial rule as designed to "civilize" the colonized population. At the same time, according to the Japanese ideology of assimilation, the gap between the colonizers and the colonized was to be bridged by imperial benevolence, as subjects in the colony received the same benevolent rule as those in the metropole. The maintenance of separate legal spheres in Korea therefore served a dual purpose. On the one hand, it preserved the myth of colonial difference, which posited that the colony was backward and needed to emulate the progressive metropole that was always ahead. On the other hand, the distance between the family laws of the colony and the metropole furnished reasons for the project of assimilation with its premise of the potential for the colony to be integrated with the metropole, thereby realizing the ideal of integration in the Japanese Empire at large.

This tension between the need for separation and the ideal of integration often was palpable in the course of colonial administration, as illustrated by the following disagreement between two Japanese colonial officials in Korea. Both Oda Mikijirō and Tateishi Shūichi were engaged in legal preparations for a reform of Civil Ordinances in advance of the 1918 Common Law (Kyōtsūhō) and the 1922 Household-Registration Law (Kosekihō).[14] Oda sought to include as many of the local family customs as possible, while Tateishi pushed to extend the Japanese Civil Code to Korean family matters:

> One day, Mr. Oda asked me, "Do you know why the British Empire was so successful in its colonial policy? It was because it respected the natives' customs and mores. In order to retain Korea as an eternal colony, we should respect their customs and retain their mores as they exist today." To that, I replied, "If we are content to keep Korea as an eternal colony, I agree. But I don't think Korea should be left a mere colony; I think that it should be 'made into Japan *[naichika]*' as soon as possible."[15]

Tateishi's position aptly illustrates the logic behind Japanese assimilation policies: extending Japanese family law to Korea was equivalent to making Koreans become Japanese, thereby making Korea an inseparable part of Japan. In contrast, if colonized Korea were to retain its own family customs, it would remain a Japanese "colony," an entity separate from the Japanese family state.

Since the separation of legal spheres in civil matters was predicated on the differences in family customs between Korea and Japan, attempts at reform of these family customs naturally had implications for the colony's status within the empire vis-à-vis the metropole. The process of legal assimilation was to be realized through a gradual expansion of the matters to which the Japanese Civil Code applied and a concomitant shrinking of exemptions where Korean customs applied. The first of these assimilatory reforms was a series of reforms in 1921–22, when numerous family-law matters, such as the legal age of marriage, divorce, parental rights and sponsorship, and regulations on family councils *(shinzokukai)* became subject to the Japanese Civil Code. The second occurred in 1939 (implemented in 1940), when adoption and family names were made subject to the Japanese Civil Code, a reform widely known for the Name-Change Policy (Sōshi Kaimei).

The process of incrementally expanding the application of Japanese legal codes to replace Korean customs is a process that I call *legal assimilation*. Specifically, legal assimilation meant incrementally extending Japanese legal codes in a carefully orchestrated process, whereby local customs were manipulated to slowly accommodate the laws from the metropole. I thus am expanding the definition of assimilation from the more conventional usage that refers to a unilateral erasure of the colonized's culture by the colonizer, encapsulated in terms such as "national annihilation policy" *(minjok malsal chŏng'ch'aek),* which has been treated as synonymous with "assimilation policy" (K: *tonghwa chŏngch'aek;* J: *dōka seisaku).*[16] This more strident definition of assimilation dominated the earliest scholarship on colonial family laws, wherein these laws were understood to be a product of Japanese "distortion" of Korean family customs.[17] By my definition assimilation was a process whereby the systems of colonized territories were integrated into the larger system of the empire. Although the system of the metropole became the template for such accommodations, the process did not result in a unilateral erasure of one culture by another; the end result, rather, was a restructuring of the metropole as well as the colonies. Much recent scholarship on the Japanese Empire in fact redefines assimilation in a similar fashion: Takashi Fujitani's recent work has reconsidered the "forced assimilation policy" as a radical process of inclusion of the colonial populations, which meant a fundamental reshaping of the Japanese Empire as a whole.[18] Janet Poole also has depicted the later wartime period as involving a radical reimagining by Korean intellectuals of the Japanese Empire as a whole, including a redefinition of the relationship between Korea and the Japanese metropole.[19]

Structural integration of the colonial legal sphere into that of the metropole through civil- and customary-law reforms led to the structural transformation of Korean families themselves, as the structure of society changed from lineage-based to one based on small families. This, I argue, was the most enduring effect of colonial assimilation efforts on the Korean family. Through legal assimilation and the implementation of the Japanese family system, traditional lineage groups in Korea that privileged kinship ties lost legal recognition in favor of the household, the new unit of family. In the traditional lineage system, defined by kinship ties, the rights of each lineage member varied relationally. Degrees of kinship ties as well as their pertinent rights followed traditional lineage laws (chongpŏp) rather than the status laws defined by the new colonial state.[20] In contrast, the colonial state emphasized the boundary of the family and clearly distinguished the family members inside of the household from those outside. With the household system, the colonial state tried to redefine the relationship between the family and the state, by claiming the exclusive right to define family boundaries and personal status.[21]

The scholarship on colonial family laws has in fact moved in the direction of acknowledging the local accommodations made by the colonial institution in the process of producing the customary laws. Hong Yang-hŭi has argued that rather than a straightforward distortion of Korean customs, the customary laws were derived through a more complex mechanism whereby the Japanese family system (ie-seido) was transplanted (isik) in Korea in the name of "Korean custom."[22] In the process the Japanese actively utilized existing Confucian family culture to accommodate the patriarchal Japanese family system. Yi Sŭng-il, on the other hand, has further emphasized the fluid interaction of the colonial legal system and practices on the ground, arguing that the shifting customary laws in Korea reflected not just the unilateral expansion of Japanese laws but also the changing practices among Koreans.[23] Most recently, Marie Seong-Hak Kim has argued that, unlike the European counterparts that the Japanese customary laws were modeled after, the customary laws in colonial Korea (and Japan) were "bureaucratically invented" in the legal system. The invention process was directed by individual judges' pragmatic decisions to "accommodate evolving practices" rather than a premeditated colonial policy to distort and control.[24] Building on this trend to emphasize the power of the colonial society in shaping colonial laws, I show how the Koreans who litigated at the colonial courts understood and utilized the laws. As a result, rather than focusing on the colonial legalists, I concentrate more on the evolving legal consciousness of the colonized Koreans, which left a lasting legacy in the postcolonial years in family law.

Considering the Japanese colonizers' efforts to utilize Korean customs requires, of course, understanding the sources of those customary laws in the Chosŏn dynasty, but I also consider the transition from the Chosŏn dynasty to Japanese colonial rule as a significant enough break to warrant a serious investigation of the colonial legal system on its own. The Japanese colonial legal system not only left a significant legacy, the full extent of which is yet to be fully explored, but also provided a unique space where continuing patterns of familial conflict played out.[25] Unlike Chŏng Kŭng-sik, who has challenged the colonial distortion thesis by pointing to existing precedents of patrilineal succession practices before the colonial period, I agree with Yang and Hong that the colonial legal system had a significant and lasting role in rigidifying the existing patriarchal biases from "cultural norms" into "legal norms."[26] Emphasizing the break, however, does not mean that I read this transition as a quantifiable trajectory toward modernity or a gain or loss of women's rights, as some have implied.[27] Rather, my focus is to see how women's rights were redefined from one patriarchal system to another.

The civil disputes that are the central source for this book are a direct product of the reconfiguration of the family and the redistribution of family property under Japanese colonial rule. As the lineage system was weakened, exclusive property rights of the household head were strengthened in its stead. This in turn strengthened the property rights of certain women in opposition to the rights of lineage elders, leading to a heightened number of civil disputes. The gendered conflicts over family property were byproducts of colonial legal policy.

CUSTOMARY LAWS AND TRADITION

Scholars of colonial law in other areas of the world, interrogating the ways in which the colonial propaganda of legal modernization intersected with local customs, also similarly highlight the particular articulation of the modern and the traditional in colonial legal regimes. In some cases, the colonized people embraced certain customs deemed backward by the colonial state as a tactic of resistance; in other cases, colonized people seemingly usurped modern measures to bolster traditional existing power relations. As Martin Chanock has elucidated, battles over customary laws in colonial courts often masked an underlying struggle over socioeconomic issues recently reconfigured by colonial economic conditions.[28] Tamara Lynn Loos, in her examination of the Siamese case, notes how the enforcement of monogamy at the turn of the twentieth century inspired some individuals to embrace polygyny, not only as part of their tradition but also as a critical component of an alternative modernity.[29] Mytheli Sreenivas, in her examination of colonial India, examines how the argument for expanding women's property rights was hijacked by men who wanted to expand their own rights as heads of nuclear families.[30] Within the Japanese Empire, Chen Chao-ju has examined how the Taiwanese marriage custom of *simpua* (little daughter-in-law) was subject to multiple reconceptualizations under Japanese colonial legal discourse.[31] These studies illuminate the deeper socioeconomic context of legal struggles fought over old customs—often hidden behind the rhetoric of modernity.

For the case of Korea, I propose that assimilation, rather than being perceived as a cultural assault of the colonizer on the colonized, was to a significant degree disseminated and accepted as the universal direction of progress. The particular family laws imported in the process, in other words, were perceived not only as Japanese customs but as laws of the empire with a universal value: the Civil Code of Japan became the Civil Code of the Japanese Empire. Whether or not it indeed really promoted universal values in the colony is beside the point. What is important is that to Koreans, the universal values written into the Japanese Civil Code, albeit limited, were as much as they could achieve in terms of legal progress under Japanese colonial rule. From this perspective I seek to show how assimilation could be desirable for some colonized people, as assimilation often meant the dissemination of progressive legal rights in the colony. The colonial legal system was an important arena in which the colonized people's desire for civilization and the colonial state's desire for assimilation met. These legal changes, I argue, unfolded not necessarily through coercion but through affective mobilization of Koreans, who responded to reforms with proactive consent motivated by a yearning for progress. The colonial legal system became a forum for Korean women to pursue their desires for an ideal family: from a widow's desire to have her rights strengthened to a daughter's desire to have a share in inheritance to a New Woman's desire for a love marriage.[32] Through adjudication of these mundane familial conflicts, the colonial state intimately impacted the family life of colonized Koreans. In other words, separate legal spheres maintained in the Korean colony ended up producing a strong desire among some sectors of Koreans for legal assimilation.

Instead of political rights such as suffrage that were denied to the colony, women's demands for rights often were articulated within the framework provided by efforts for legal assimilation. It was thus that the desires of some Koreans provided a useful and effective basis for the Japanese colonial state to mobilize its imperial subjects to implement the colonial household system. Yet legal assimilation and its mechanisms also were identified with modernization and progress. After the liberation in 1945, the processes of modernization—formerly directed toward assimilation—quickly shed their colonial origins to form the basic foundation of family law in Korea.

Much previous scholarship has focused on detecting whether Japanese colonial laws were accurate or distorted representations of Korean customs, begging the question of how to define Korean customs when in fact there was not a uniform set of customs across local and class boundaries before the colonial use of customary laws. I argue that there was no pure form of Korean customs to be rescued from alleged colonial distortions and, instead, read the laws and the legal discourse as dynamically changing throughout the colonial period, serving as sites where the evolution of the mutual understanding and identities of Koreans and Japanese are recorded. The resulting customary laws had the power to influence not only how Japanese understood Koreans but also how Koreans understood themselves. The legal definition of Korean customs was not necessarily a true reflection of the customs in practice, but it still had the power to affect their practice.

WOMEN IN THE COLONIAL LEGAL SYSTEM

The colonial legal archive contains numerous examples of proactive and ingenious uses of the legal system by Korean women. Through examination of women's roles in domestic disputes in the colonial courts, I highlight the complex gender dynamics manifest under the colonial regime. Contrary to what their doubly victimized position under Korean patriarchal Confucian culture and Japanese patriarchal modernity would lead us to believe, Korean women under Japanese colonial rule actively participated in the colonial legal system to claim and defend their rights. The majority of the cases that directly involved hammering out the specifics of Korean customary laws had women involved as litigants: among the 156 cases collected in the *Chōsen kōtō hōin hanketsuroku* (Records of verdicts in the High Court of Colonial Korea), which directly concerned Korean family customs, 93 had women as the litigating party. Cases with female litigants concerned a wide range of issues, from marriage, divorce, adoption, and inheritance to disputes over property transactions. The dominant presence of women in these civil cases challenges us to think about women's position in the legal system during the colonial period. These records show not only how active colonized Korean women were in the colonial courts but also how women's legal rights were central in the civil disputes that concerned Korean family customs.

The high visibility of women in the colonial courts does not necessarily prove that women enjoyed a high level of legal rights. What it does prove—beyond the fact that they had sufficient rights to bring lawsuits to court—is that women's legal rights were heatedly contested in the colonial courts. This also suggests that many women found the colonial courts to be their main recourse. The evidence challenges the dominant notion about Korean women under colonial rule: that they were helpless and passive victims.[33] Their prominence in colonial civil courts had more to do with the changing dynamics of gender relations under the new colonial legal regime than with preexisting "evil customs" of misogyny among Koreans or the patriarchal nature of the Japanese legal system. If anything, the heightened visibility of women at the courts represented a certain strengthening of particular legal rights for women. While the household system under the Japanese strengthened the rights of the household head, it did so even where the household head was a woman. The colonial legal system also provided official backing for certain rights that had previously been relegated to private and customary handling, presumably to the detriment of certain women. Such women and their volatile position reminds us of the widows of British India and the rite of sati. Gayatri Spivak, in her examination of these sacrificial, or rather sacrificed widows, suggests that more widows may have burned on the pyre in Bengal because widows in that region had inheritance rights.[34] The familial anxiety wrought by a changing colonial legal regime is hidden in the imperialist and colonial reading of the sacrificed women, who are made illegible by both the imperialists, who read them only as victims of customs, and the male Indian nationalists, who read them as admirable and willing practitioners of Indian tradition. The widows in the Korean colonial civil case records are subject to a similar fate: they are constantly viewed as helpless victims of backward Korean customs (to be saved by the modern Japanese laws) or victims of the colonial laws that deprived of them of the rights they allegedly enjoyed in the precolonial era. Korean women in the colonial civil courts thus also need to be examined as subjects on an "ideological battleground" of interpretation.

The civil disputes that I analyze in *Rules of the House* often show how gendered conflict over family property unfolded at odds with the Japanese colonial laws, a perspective previous scholarship privileging the Korea-Japan dichotomy has downplayed. Often Korean men and their patriarchal interests, rather than Japanese laws, were the opponents of Korean women's struggle to have their customary rights acknowledged. Challenging previous scholarship that emphasized patriarchal biases of the Japanese colonial laws over the existing patriarchal biases of Korean customs, what I present in *Rules of the House* makes clear that the issues of women's rights were in a complex, and often complicit, relationship with the colonial power. Colonial law, armed with the state's power as well as the discourse of civilization, effectively wedged itself between colonized men and women: oftentimes colonial law benefited Korean women's rights in unexpected ways, and Korean men struck back strongly for patriarchal interests.

The antagonistic relationship between Korean men and women is prominent in close readings of the litigants' arguments. Rather than following the decisions and the judges' explanations for making those decisions, on which previous scholarship has predominantly focused, I consider the litigants and the arguments they presented in court. Through close readings of their arguments, I expose the patriarchal biases of the male litigants, as well as the legal world of the female litigants who tried to disrupt such patriarchal jurisprudence. Through the variety of arguments—and the world views that informed them—that created and recreated notions about Korean customs and Korean women's place in them, I show that colonized Koreans were active participants in the discursive production of colonial knowledge about Koreans and their family customs. The case records are part of the colonial archive along with other forms of information, such as customs-survey reports, newspaper and journal articles on Korean customs and mores, and novels that deal with Korean family matters. Korean litigants—in addition to the Japanese or the Korean collaborators powerful enough to control the customs-survey process—also were among the producers who shaped the contours of the colonial perception of Korean family customs. In this sense, I agree with the notion that "colonial texts are not 'reflections' of colonial relations but are 'constructive' of them, and . . . therefore require us to attend to the 'configurations' of the archive itself."[35]

In *Rules of the House* I also seek to break new ground in the study of women and gender in Korean history by illuminating an underrepresented group of women in the field of women's history. In doing so I hope not merely to expand our under-standing of a new group of women but also to suggest a more radical view of how modernity impacted colonial Korean society. With a few exceptions, previ-ous studies of women in colonial Korea have focused predominantly on either the educated and privileged class of New Women or the working-class "factory girls."[36] This artificial separation of certain groups of women from others has resulted in discussions of the impact of modernity as a contained phenomenon within a cer-tain stratum of society or strictly within the cultural realm. The court cases that I examine here reveal that previously underrepresented groups of women, such as widows and concubines, in fact can be found at the forefront of colonial legal transformations, participating in the modern legal system side by side with the more typical New Women and thus also at the forefront of the experience of colo-nial modernity.

OVERVIEW OF THE BOOK

The following chapters trace the trajectory of the household system as it was estab-lished in Korea under Japanese colonial rule. The account necessarily begins by considering the traditional customs on which that system was based, in particular the lineage system that emerged during the late Chosŏn dynasty. The story that then follows is of the process by which the lineage system was replaced by the colonial household system and the different legal issues that contributed to that system's articulation.

In chapter 1 I examine how the late Chosŏn emergence of the patriarchal family system in the form of the lineage system reconfigured women's inheritance rights. In the seventeenth and the eighteenth centuries, as families abandoned partible inheritance in favor of primogeniture, daughters' inheritance rights were replaced by those of mothers, and the rights and status of widows without heirs became increasingly precarious.

Chapter 2 brings us to the beginning of colonial rule and examines widows' lawsuits over inheritance rights against in-law family members in the colonial courts. Contrary to the conventional notion that Korean women lost many legal rights under the colonial legal system, widows' rights were largely protected in the colonial civil courts. This was a coincidental result of the colonial legal system: as the Japanese were trying to implement the new family unit of the household, the widows who embodied its boundary received legal protection. The customary rights of widows to inherit the family headship worked hand in hand with the colonial household system and functioned to weaken the ties of the traditional lineage system. Under the colonial legal system, widows gained official backing for their customary rights against the abusive extortion efforts of their in-law family members. The victory of widows was not without its limitations, since the inheri-tance rights recognized for widows proved only temporary.

Chapters 3 and 4 deal with the 1920s and 1930s, when various reform discourses on family law emerged and fiercely contended with one another. Popularly referred to as the Cultural Rule (Bunka Seiji) period and widely seen as a period of relaxed colonial policies, this period was also a time of incomplete assimilation, flanked on either side by the two major assimilatory reforms in the Civil Ordinances in 1921–22 and in 1939. The era saw intense contention between two contradictory forces: the need for separation and the desire for assimilation. In chapter 3 I examine the reform discourses over inheritance rights that emerged in the 1920s and the 1930s "age of progress," as the colonial state's goal of dissolving the lineage and clarifying the boundary of the household was advanced through manipulating discourses that equated assimilation with progress. The debate over inheritance reforms focused around expanding women's rights through granting daughters the right to inherit. Couching this in the language of progress, the Government General tried to implement son-in-law adoption in Korea, a measure that drew widely divided responses from the colonized Koreans. While many Korean women enthusiastically supported the measure, the backlash from the conservative elite was significant enough to cause postponement of the measure until 1940. When son-in-law adoption eventually was implemented in 1940, it was with a significant compromise with the principles of Korean lineage and, as a result, denied daughters the right to become female household heads independently of husbands. The compromise with the Korean lineage laws continued into the postcolonial period, marginalizing daughters in inheritance and failing to check the power of household heads.

In chapter 4 I examine reform discourses about the conjugal relationship in the 1920s and 1930s and show how the universal ideal of conjugal love, which was gaining increasing popularity at the time, converged with the colonial state's goal of legal assimilation. Through a wide range of divorce and inheritance cases that hinged on the definition of a conjugal relationship, I show that the legal definition of a female spouse in this period came to be defined increasingly by affective companionship. While some wives demanded expanded rights to divorce when their marriages did not fulfill the ideal of affective marriage, some concubines demanded inheritance rights on the ground that they had fulfilled the role of an affective spouse. Making affective companionship a primary and necessary definition of a female spouse ended up stripping both wives and concubines of their rights to economic independence and incorporated the conjugal relationship into the colonial household system. The ideal of affective marriage, therefore, eventually served the assimilation of the Korean family into the Japanese family system.

Chapter 5 examines the reform discourse in the 1940s following the Civil-Ordinances Reform of 1939 (implemented in 1940) and the persistence of its influence in postcolonial reforms. The new Civil Ordinances, notorious particularly for the Name-Change Policy, aimed at completing the assimilation of Koreans to Japanese under wartime exigencies yet ended up maintaining and fossilizing what had been deemed unique features of Korean family customs, spawning a continuing production of scholarly discussion of Korean family customs and how to reform them. These discourses left an important legacy, which was to naturalize the direction of assimilatory reforms as a rational and progressive solution to the inevitable worldwide trend toward family dissolution. Despite strong anti-Japanese sentiments in the immediate wake of liberation, legacies of the discourses on the 1940s reforms exerted a strong influence on the new Civil Code of South Korea in 1960. Hiding behind the facade of recapturing Korean tradition, much of the direction of colonial-era reforms toward strengthening the patriarchal small family and instating son-in-law adoption as a way to expand daughters' inheritance rights made its way into the new Civil Code.

I close the book with a conclusion, where I summarize my key points and consider the ramifications of the long life of the household system in South Korea until the recent abolition of the household-head system *(hojuje)* in 2005.

A NOTE ON SOURCES

Rules of the House makes use of a wide range of primary sources written in Japanese and Korean. The largest number of primary sources are drawn from the collection of civil cases in *Chōsen kōtō hōin hanketsuroku*. These cases provide a privileged window not only into everyday life struggles over family matters during the colonial period but also into the active participation of colonized Korean women in the colonial courts. The thirty-volume collection has records of around 2,000 civil cases, 156 cases among which are categorized under "Korean Civil Ordinances," indicating that they dealt with Korean family matters to be adjudicated according to Korean family customs and not the Japanese Civil Code. The number of these cases may not seem high, and they certainly were a very limited portion of all family-related cases decided in the local and appellate courts, but these cases had influential power in the colonial legal system. Unlike local and appellate court cases, some of which received media attention in sensational newspaper articles, reports of these cases were distributed through official routes, monthly through the *Shihō Kyōkai Zasshi* (Journal of the Judicial Association), as well as in other government notices and circulars. The cases concerning the Civil Ordinances were especially important because Korean customary laws were uncodified and the High Court's decisions functioned as important precedents. The court system in the Korean colony was a direct import of the metropolitan counterpart, consisting of tertiary court levels, the local courts, the appellate courts, and the High Court (Chōsen Kōtō Hōin). Judges were drawn from among both Japanese and Koreans, with Koreans being assigned mostly to the local court–level and civil cases. There were about 250 Korean judges and 50 Korean prosecutors during the Japanese colonial period.[37] Korean judges were allowed to rule on cases only in which both plaintiff and defendant were Korean and were excluded from the High

Court bench, indicating the importance that the Japanese Government General placed on the decisions of the High Court and their potential impact.[38] Indeed, the only cases cited as precedents and related reference in High Court decisions were previous decisions of the High Court of Korea and the Supreme Court of Japan (Daishin'in).

In addition to the High Court records, *Rules of the House* makes use of a variety of related material, including journals, newspapers, and novels, written in both Japanese and Korean. The legal journal *Shihō Kyōkai Zasshi* was published by the Judicial Association (1921–45), the official organization for colonial judicial officials and specialists, including judges, prosecutors, and lawyers; it published, for their reference, official notices, administrative inquiries, all legal decisions from the Chōsen High Court, and academic essays on various legal matters. The association also had the right to issue formal agreements *(ketsu'i)* on inquiries from the courts on matters of Korean customs: their official agreements were acknowledged as customary laws.[39] The picture that emerges from these sources is much messier than the collected statements of judges on civil-case decisions would lead us to believe.

Korean-language newspapers and journals of the time also reflect high public interest in legal matters. Newspapers carried copious accounts of legal events, ranging from dry reports on pending legal reforms, in both Korea and the Japanese metropole, to sensational reportage on civil disputes over matters such as divorce, concubinage, and parental rights. Novels also provide a valuable source of insight into popular understanding. These novels, commonly serialized in Korean-language newspapers, are a repository of the common-sense legal knowledge that was easily available to the reading public and show what their authors imagined, at least, to be the popular level of legal knowledge at the time.

Widows on the Margins of the Family

In 1898 a man submitted an appeal to the Ministry of Legal Affairs (Pŏppu), deny-ing an accusation of widow rape against his son. The plaintiff, Chŏng Tong-il, had paid a hundred coins to a man so that his son could marry the man's widowed daughter-in-law. Soon after the wedding the widow's natal family severely rep-rimanded the father-in-law for the marriage and demanded the widow's return. Back in her natal home, the widow was rebuked for having defiled her chastity; "unable to bear the shame," she eventually committed suicide. The widow's family, in turn, sued the plaintiff's son for "raping the widow," and he was imprisoned. In his letter of appeal, Chŏng pleaded that his son was innocent and should not be charged with rape when the widow had come willingly to the wedding site.[1]

This case raises many questions about the situation of women, widows in partic-ular, at a point in 1890s Korea when change was imminent, but the consequences of centuries of social, economic, and ideological developments still prevailed. Widow chastity was an important moral virtue for elite women in the Chosŏn dynasty from early on.[2] By the end of the Chosŏn dynasty, with the increased competi-tion between elite families, widow chastity became a "public indicator of the moral level" of the family.[3] In the increasing competition for official recognition, widows were pushed to perform more drastic acts, usually suicide, to prove their virtue.[4] In her study of a widow suicide case from the early nineteenth century, Jungwon Kim has argued that widows' virtue became a "highly vulnerable asset" for the family as well as the women themselves in the period; to protect the honor of herself and the family, a widow would commit suicide at the slightest slander against her chastity.[5]

Widow chastity, or the prescription that widows remain unmarried, was abol-ished, formally at least, in 1894 as part of the Kabo Reforms of 1894–96 undertaken in the Chosŏn court by the pro-Japanese cabinet.[6] Under the strengthened influence of the Japanese during the Sino-Japanese War, former pro-Japanese reformers of the Kapsin Coup in 1884 were brought back into the cabinet from exile in Japan and were able to implement many of the reforms that they had failed to implement before. In addition to various measures to reform Korea in the model of Meiji Japan, many institutional reforms were implemented to at once modernize Korea and optimally prepare Korea to be a Japanese protectorate.[7] The reforms that were undertaken during this period therefore are a good indicator of which Korean customs were considered backward as well as an impediment to Japanese control. Social institutions that were considered the basis of *yangban* elite power, therefore, were targeted for reform.[8] The abolition of the ban on widow remarriage was one of these, together with the abolition of early marriage, the discrimination of offspring of concubines *(sŏja)*, and slavery.[9] Women's status by then had become a "yardstick for the civility of an entire country" in Korea as well.[10] Mistreatment of widows, or women in general, was considered a marker of backwardness, and a particularly Asian backwardness at that. Customs like the ban on remarriage of widows, for example, often were criticized in the same terms as the notorious practice of sati in India; the news of its abolition by the British was well known around Asia, including in Korea.[11]

Another key goal of the Kabo Reforms was to establish and expand new institutions. The appeal letter introduced at the opening of the chapter is part of a collection of letters addressed to the Ministry of Legal Affairs, a judicial institution created by the reforms that served as a kind of appellate court. The head of the Ministry of Legal Affairs received letters requesting revocation of decisions handed down in the local courts administered by local magistrates.[12] In 1894 the Korean court had established the Ministry of Legal Affairs as the sole administrative apparatus for legal matters. Judicial matters were to be handled by the Provisional Court of the Department of Justice (Pŏppu amun kwonsŏl chaep'anso).

Despite the Kabo Reforms, however, the practices surrounding widow chastity persisted, and the collection of appeal letters addressed to the Ministry of Legal Affairs contains a set of cases filed under the category of "widow rape" *(kŏpkwa)*. "Rape" was a serious crime according to *Taejŏn hoet'ong* (1865), the Chosŏn legal codes, and a perpetrator could receive punishment of up to a sentence of death.[13] The fact that people understood widow rape to be a uniquely punishable offense seems to suggest that, even after the Kabo Reforms, widow chastity still was regarded as a prized act of morality. In fact, the details of the 1898 case reveal a wide spectrum of attitudes toward widow chastity: while the natal family seems to have been so attached to the ideal of chastity that they drove their daughter to suicide, the father-in-law seems to have considered it a mundane matter to sell his daughter-in-law in marriage for profit.

The case reveals much about what was considered normative, acceptable, and transgressive. We can detect, for example, that the widow remained with her husband's family and that it was not considered particularly criminal for the husband's family to arrange her remarriage and even collect a dowry in the process. But we also can detect that marrying off a widowed daughter-in-law was not considered an honorable act and that it could earn criticism from the widow's natal family. The widow's natal family seems to have had the recourse of claiming her back. We also can see that the virtue of widow chastity was still a viable ethical norm and that families thought that their reputation relied significantly on proper adherence to virtue by the women of the family. It also is clear that an accusation of rape could be far more than a matter of sexual offense.

Most of the cases concerning widows mentioned in the appeal letters to the Ministry of Legal Affairs involved attempts or actual incidents of rape or abduction, both of which were considered serious crimes in the Chosŏn dynasty. Accused men often pleaded their innocence by saying they had entered into sexual relations with a widow with her consent or sometimes even with the assistance of a matchmaker. These men often rebutted the charges of rape with accusations that the in-laws were trying to sell off their widowed relative to another bidder. While these cases are filed under "widow rape," upon closer examination they often are not at all about the moral prescription of female chastity against immoral outbursts of male desire. In many instances the sexual offense came under official scrutiny only because of the violence of widow suicides, which often grew out of what was essentially an economic conflict. Those accused of raping a widow often were men who had gotten on the wrong side of the in-laws by providing an insufficient amount of money for the widow. In one of the cases, a daughter-in-law was threatened with rape by her brother-in-law when she refused to obtain money from her natal family.[14] A survey of the cases involving widows among the appeal letters show that behind the issue of rape or remarriage there existed a common and deeper problem: the tension over family property between the widow and her in-laws.[15]

Although the case is filed under "widow rape," we are unlikely ever to find out whether this widow was indeed married off against her will, or if she was a willing bride protesting against the familial censure against a new marriage. The same goes for other widows who appear in the collection of letters to the Ministry of Legal Affairs, mostly as corpses. These dead widows remind us of Bhuvaneswari's suicide in Gayatri Spivak's "Can the Subaltern Speak?"[16] As in the case of Spivak's dead woman, our dead widow likewise could be viewed in widely different subjectivities: a defiled widow, a willing (and perhaps not so chaste) bride, and even an abject victim of the brutal prescriptions of Confucianism. Yet, just like the early nineteenth-century widow in Jungwon Kim's study, this widow seems to have killed herself in protest. Whatever the real story was, suicide seems to have been used by the widow as what Kim calls a "premeditated strategy" to express her anger and protect her honor.[17] In a world where Confucian ethics, which idolized widow chastity, still had great currency, some chaste widows found suicide their only and last recourse to expose the truth of the violence to which they were subject.[18]

Still, it was not so much the Confucian prescription of widow chastity to which widows fell victim but their marginalized position in a virilocal marriage system. They were victims of a land-based property regime that largely deprived women of access to property ownership. In *Dowry Murder* Veena Talwar Oldenburg shows that the practice of dowry murder in India, where a woman could be murdered for insufficient dowry, was a product of British imperialism, which had transformed the Indian economy to favor men over women, both in the labor market as well as in property ownership.[19] In the process dowry was redefined from movable property voluntarily given to women in marriage by natal families for provision and as a mark of status to "groom price," where the bride's family paid the groom's family to compensate for the (perceived) inferior economic (earning) power of the bride. In short, dowry murder was not a cultural problem but an economic one. Oldenburg's case inspires us to rethink the argument that Korean women were victimized by Confucianism (or by the culture-as-culprit thesis, in Oldenburg's term) in a whole new way. In other words, women's marginalization in the family was not from cultural or ideological transformation per se ("Confucianization") but rather from the socioeconomic transformation of family that reconfigured property relations and concentrated land property in the hands of sons (and later in the hands of the eldest son) as the lineage system matured.[20]

The case thus illustrates the precarious position of widows at the end of the Chosŏn period. In their marginal place in the family, many widows seem to have been perceived as burdens, and even threats, to family viability. Accordingly, they were subject to extortion, threats of expulsion from the family, or pressure to remarry (or sold in marriage in exchange for monetary compensation). Whatever the specifics of individual cases, these dead widows seem to have been pushed to the limits of their existence by numerous converging desires: the widow's desire to protect her honor, the natal family's desire to maintain the widow's chastity, and the marital family's desire to decrease the financial burden of keeping the widow.

By the late nineteenth century, where we encounter the corpse of the raped widow, the Korean family system and ideology had effectively pushed widows to the margins, where they had to negotiate between the impossible ideal of widow chastity and the realities of their position in the marital family. What does the case of these dead widows tell us about the state of widows' and women's position in the family at the end of the Chosŏn dynasty? What is the process through which widows became so marginalized in the family system? In the following I examine the reconfiguration of family practices in marriage customs, living arrangements, ancestral rites succession, and property inheritance in the seventeenth century that increasingly marginalized women's claim to family property. I also show that, in addition to this slow transformation of inheritance practices, the patrilineal principle that became the official principle of family arrangement of the court from the beginning of the Chosŏn dynasty made women's, and especially widows', right to family property a precarious one, susceptible to continuous challenges. Revealing sources for our purposes lie in accounts of litigation, where economic conflicts dating from the beginning of the Chosŏn dynasty were exposed and resolved. The fault line increasingly came to be between married-in women (who were widowed) and those linked through agnatic ties.

THE EMERGENCE OF PATRILINEAL FAMILY PRACTICES

Confucian ideology was highly prescriptive when it came to matters of family, and it was instrumental in transforming family practices in the Chosŏn dynasty, when it became the official ideology of the court. According to Confucian teachings, a proper family should be organized on strict hierarchical principles, where the wife was always to submit to the husband's guidance. A woman was taught to adhere to the "Three Followings [Samjong Jido]," which meant that she should follow her father when young, her husband upon marrying, and her son in widowhood. Marriage was to be strictly virilocal: a woman married into a man's family, signifying a wife's submission to a husband's ways. The wife had significant restrictions in legal rights as well. She was expected to submit her rights over property to her husband while married, and she had no right to divorce her husband; the husband, on the other hand, could divorce the wife on seven legitimate grounds (ch'ilgŏ ji ak), which included jealousy and failure to produce children.[21] In inheritance families were to exercise primogeniture: the firstborn son inherited the right and obligation to perform the ancestor rites and with that the right to inherit the dominant portion of the family property.

It was another couple of centuries after the initial round of reforms by the court before the lineage system became fully fledged as a result of steps initiated by the elite.[22] Scholars largely agree that this happened sometime around the mid-seventeenth century after the Imjin War (also known as the Hideyoshi Invasions, 1592–98). It was then that lineages became larger and began enforcing lineage-securing practices such as virilocal marriage, primogeniture in inheritance of the ritual heirship, and the exclusion of daughters and privileging of firstborn sons in property inheritance. As early as the mid-sixteenth century, some families began abandoning partible inheritance and setting aside property to compensate for ancestral rites that were becoming increasingly elaborate. At the same time, families began allotting more inheritance to the sons (and later, the eldest sons), who began to take on more responsibility in carrying out rites.[23] As the ideal of conducting ancestral rites for four generations of ancestors spread among the ruling class of yangban, agnatic kin who congregated to perform the rites became more organized, with stronger leadership and systematic lineal succession. Lineage groups thus formed were designated the "small lineage" (sojong), as opposed to the "large lineage" (taejong), which referred to all descendants sharing a common lineage seat (pon'gwan), the purported geographic site of the lineage's origin.[24]

These changes came about slowly across families but, by the eighteenth century, were normative expectations for elite yangban families. In the late eighteenth and the nineteenth centuries, the conspicuous practice of Confucian rites spread even to the lower levels of the middle-status class *(chung'in)* and to wealthy merchants.[25] This affected family makeup and dynamics, strengthening the powers of patrilineal heirs against other elders. Chŏng Chi-yŏng (Jung Ji Young), for example, detects a declining number of women household heads in household registers, even among commoners, in the eighteenth century.[26] The status of household head increasingly came to be passed on directly to sons rather than to widowed wives, reflecting a shift in ritual inheritance and the accompanying public recognition and status given to the ritual heir.[27]

VARIATIONS IN FAMILY PRACTICE

Evidence suggests that even after the principle of virilocal marriage became established as the norm, modified forms of uxorilocal marriage customs, a remnant from the preceding Koryŏ dynasty (918–1392), continued for centuries. In the Koryŏ dynasty the wedding took place in the bride's house, where the bride continued to live after the wedding, while the groom had a variety of options: he could live with the bride in her natal home, return to his home and visit the bride occasionally, or the couple could move away from both homes to set up a separate residence, typically to follow his posts.[28] As marriage was utilized to form ties of alliance and patronage, upper-class men commonly married multiple women and rotated among their respective houses.[29] Despite continued efforts by the Chosŏn court to reform marriage customs to implement *ch'inyŏng* (C: *qinying),* the wedding rites at the groom's house, such change initially was resisted by the yangban elite families. King Sejong (r. 1418–50), for instance, conducted all the royal weddings in *ch'inyŏng*-style to be an example to his court officials, but to no avail.[30] By the sixteenth century, what is called a "half-virilocal marriage" *(pan-ch'inyŏng)* was practiced widely among the yangban elite. A half-virilocal marriage entailed a wedding ceremony at the bride's house, after which the couple would move to the groom's house. As time went on and the custom of virilocal marriage spread, women increasingly moved into their husband's families' home, but it was not rare for them to postpone the departure until they were comfortably settled into the marital relationship with a number of children. Many couples chose to extend the period in the bride's house for quite a long time, one year on average but sometimes longer.[31] Although the time the couple lived in the bride's family was gradually shortened, a nineteenth-century record still shows a bride joining the groom's family six months after the wedding. The record includes no sign that this practice was unusual; therefore, it would be safe to assume that this delayed move was perfectly acceptable.[32]

While uxorilocal marriage was still in practice, daughters had equal rights to inheritance as well as an equal share of the obligation to support natal parents in old age and also the responsibility of carrying out ancestral rites.[33] Even when a daughter was expected to marry out of the house, it was not uncommon for part of the household property to be inherited by her to then be passed on to her descendants. Records indicate that yangban-class women had rights over separate property that they inherited from natal households and passed on; records show men reporting among the property they inherited property that originated with a maternal grandmother.[34]

VIRILOCAL MARRIAGE AND THE RECONFIGURATION OF FAMILY PROPERTY

Virilocal marriage significantly impacted a woman's position in the family: while she lost standing in her natal family, she gained a new standing in her marital family. Upon moving to her husband's house, the bride lost all the familiar surroundings and support that she had grown up with. Prescriptive literature for women aimed to suppress women's emotional attachment to their natal parents, while asking that they transfer their feeling of filial piety to their parents-in-law.[35] Popular didactic stories of women sacrificing themselves for natal parents from the Koryŏ dynasty disappear in the Chosŏn dynasty. Instead, women gained a new strong and stable status in the marital family as mother of the future heir, as well as mistress of the inner quarters and overseer of the preparation of ancestral rites, the significance of which grew steadily in the late Chosŏn period. By the mid-seventeenth century, as laws of lineal succession were followed by more yangban families, wives' status in the family was strengthened in comparison to that of daughters.

Even with their newly gained status in the marital house, wives' rights paled in comparison to the increasing rights of sons. As agnatic principles became more pronounced under the lineage system, the patrilineal line from father to children (increasingly sons rather than daughters) became emphasized, and legal rights over family property also began to reflect this change. Beginning in the sixteenth century, adoptees, who used to be chosen from outside of the lineage, increasingly were chosen exclusively among agnatic kin.[36] Also, an increasing number of sons inherited directly from their deceased fathers rather than waiting until their widowed mothers passed away. In other words, wives slowly lost rights to directly inherit from their husbands. Such a move was first initiated by the Chosŏn court itself: as early as 1411 the court began to let sons directly inherit from their deceased fathers, bypassing widowed mothers.[37]

Daughters' rights accordingly were diminished. As the virilocal marriage custom spread, daughters were excluded from ancestor-rites succession, which traditionally was a shared responsibility of all children. Often the performance of rites rotated among the houses of sons and daughters. Such a sharing of obligations supported the practice of partible inheritance, which included daughters.[38] But as daughters began marrying out and living farther away from the natal household, ancestral rites increasingly became the obligation of sons and then increasingly that of the eldest son.[39] As ancestral rites became more formalized and onerous, inheritance increasingly came to be considered a compensation for their economic burden. As virilocal marriage practices made sharing the obligation to carry out ancestral rites more difficult, more and more families began to excuse sons-in-law from ancestral rites duties, and sons-in-law, in turn, excused themselves from inheriting from a wife's natal family, yielding their share to her siblings, who would carry out the rites.[40] From the mid-sixteenth century, families began to replace daughters' inheritance in immovable property with dowries of movable property.

CONFLICTS OVER WIDOW RIGHTS

The principle of virilocal marriage affected widows as well. As the virilocal principle was strengthened, virilocal residence came to be expected even in widowhood. Although widows seem to have commonly returned to their natal families or remarried during the Koryŏ dynasty, widows in the Chosŏn dynasty were expected to remain in the marital family, never to remarry. The notorious ban on widow remarriage—meant only for upper-class women—was promulgated as a rule in 1485, when sons of remarried widows were banned from sitting for the civil examinations.[41] Widows therefore were forced to keep their chastity for the sake of their sons' future prospects and to maintain the status of themselves and their marital families. To encourage widow chastity and to assist the livelihood of chaste widows, the court allowed a chaste widow to retain part of her husband's rank land as *susinjŏn* (land to preserve chastity), but that practice was abolished as early as 1466; this was an indication, not of the diminished importance of widow chastity, but rather of a strengthened expectation of it, as it indicates that the court expected the marital family to support the widow.[42]

On the other hand, such a strong obligation to remain chaste also resulted in stronger rights for widows despite Confucian agnatic principles. Traditionally, since the Koryŏ dynasty, widows had rights to own and manage their husbands' property until the ritual heir had matured enough to assume the duties.[43] Widows also, in the meantime, had ritual rights and the obligation to carry out ancestral rites. The same logic applied when a widow had no sons and an heir had to be adopted. Such a widow still enjoyed usufructuary rights over her husband's estate and had the prerogative to select an heir.[44] As a *ch'ongbu* (eldest daughter-in-law), a widow could move into the lineage's main house and take over possession of the land and slaves set aside for the support of ancestral rites. In terms of ritual succession, *ch'ongbu* had precedence over a husband's nephews.

While remaining customs of uxorilocal marriage practices enabled women to enjoy certain rights that they lost in the late Chosŏn period, there is not a neat storyline by which women's standing in the family consistently diminished from

Koryŏ to late Chosŏn. The trend toward virilocal marriage and lineage formation formally and forcefully initiated at the outset of the Chosŏn dynasty meant increasing tension over women's property rights. Legal records show that women were subject to challenges to their property rights from marital relatives all throughout the Chosŏn dynasty, albeit with differing degrees of intensity.

Although legal records mainly represent (often extreme) violations of norms, and thus are not the optimal source for deducing norms, they nonetheless provide a rich source of information about what was considered ideal, "normal," and transgressive. Records of lawsuits or criminal investigations provide us with a vantage point on how family norms were practiced in everyday life. These records, far more than the ideals laid out in the prescriptive literature, tell us about the actual rules for customs that people adhered to, just as sources like diaries provide glimpses into customs-as-practices rather than customs-as-ideals. Actual family practices are useful not only to see how things were different in reality from prescriptions but also in showing the boundaries of what was considered acceptable, if not ideal. Similar contrasts between ideal and practice also are employed by legal anthropologists in distinguishing between law-as-text and law in everyday life.[45]

Even though many records remain about legal disputes that were civil in nature, the Chosŏn dynasty legal system, in accordance with the legal culture of China, did not have civil laws separate from penal codes.[46] Not only was there no separation of civil matters from penal matters, but there were no codes written for civil matters, except for procedural laws for such disputes. Also, most of today's civil matters were in general considered outside of the judicial concern of the state. Legal administration of the state was focused on adjudicating criminal matters, and therefore only penal codes were compiled.[47]

This is not to say that civil conflicts were ignored by the state. As economic relationships became more complex in the late Chosŏn dynasty, legal codes had to accommodate a growing number of conflicts between private parties of a civil nature when those parties appealed for official adjudication. *Sok-taejŏn,* a legal code compiled in 1746 to complement the original codes of *Kyŏngguk taejŏn,* included eleven new categories of codes, among which were "Listening to Disputes [*Chŏngri:* Procedural laws]" and "Land Registers [*munki*]," to address the growing number of civil litigations. Since family order was deemed a critical foundation of the Confucian world order, some family matters that may seem private to the modern reader were very much at the center of state interest. Failure to marry off a daughter by the age of thirty, for example, was deemed criminal and was a subject of direct state intervention.[48] Yet the focus of adjudication in civil disputes was not delineation of rights but conflict resolution, even though validation of rights was what happened in the end and what the litigators sought.[49]

Confucian ideology influenced what sort of cases came to court as well as how they were adjudicated. Civil lawsuits were discouraged under Confucian legal culture. Lawsuits with monetary objectives were perceived as indications of selfish intentions and symptomatic of disharmonious relationships. The ideal of the Confucian state, therefore, was to have no lawsuits *(musong)*. Even in criminal matters ritual propriety played an important role in adjudication. In noncriminal matters lodging lawsuits against one's elders or superiors was discouraged and could warrant the death penalty regardless of who was at fault. One of the major concerns of the state was breaches of propriety. For example, when a grandson became entangled in a lawsuit for selling a family property without the permission of his grandmother, he lost the case not because he was not the legitimate owner but because he had breached propriety by bringing a lawsuit against his elder. The majority of civil cases concentrated on issues considered acceptable in terms of maintaining Confucian social order: disputes over property boundaries and cultivation rights, slaves (especially those who had run away), and gravesites. In such a legal culture, where it was considered inappropriate for family members to lodge lawsuits against one another, it was rare for familial conflict over property to appear in official legal records. Indeed, one result in some cases was for both the plaintiff and the accused to be penalized for disrupting harmony.[50]

Despite such limitations, a number of records remain where widows came forward to accuse their in-laws of taking away property that they had inherited from their late husbands. In some cases, widows even sued their natal families for property.[51] These cases show several implicit concepts about family-property ownership in the Chosŏn dynasty. One was the principle of "separate family, separate property" *(pun'ga pyŏl'jae),* by which lineage elders had limited rights over the property of family members living in separate households.[52] Another was that women, especially as heads of their own households, had certain rights to property. Women also had rights over separate property that they inherited from their natal families and also independent ownership over property and wages that they earned. Despite the Confucian sense of propriety that encouraged submission to elders in all things, such concepts of property ownership remained strong and provided bases for property litigations throughout the Chosŏn dynasty.

Married-in women who were not mothers of heirs (i.e., sons) posed a unique threat to the agnatic lineage system. Cho Ŭn traces how even as early as the fifteenth century, the Chosŏn court tried to limit women's place in the family inheritance regime to their status as mothers; a widow, for example, no longer directly inherited from her husband if she had children who could inherit on her behalf.[53] This meant that a new concept of property ownership emerged in the Chosŏn dynasty, whereby property ownership became collectively held by the patrilineal kin group, access to which depended on one's membership in that kin group and was stratified depending on one's standing within it. Membership was restricted to agnatic kin, and one's standing followed the agnatic principles that defined one's share of obligation in the performance of ancestral rites. Widows without children, therefore, posed a unique challenge in the inheritance regime, especially because they were expected to remain in the marital family. Since they lacked children who could inherit in their stead, they had to be given some inheritance rights, albeit provisional, to ensure the flow of property to the next generation to an adopted heir; yet, as they were denied lineage membership, they were forever outsiders. Changes in widows' property rights, therefore, serve as a barometer of the transition in property ownership from being individually based to being collectively based in the agnatic lineage.[54]

As patrilineal principles grew stronger in the Chosŏn dynasty, a widow's position in the family became an ever more volatile one: she was not quite a member of the agnatic kin group, but she held significant ritual and property rights as the key figure protecting the patrilineal line.[55] It was thus that widow rights, that is, ch'ongbu-gwŏn, became a common source of conflict between women and marital family members. Families struggled to restrict widows' property rights to keep control over family property within the hands of agnatic kin. In 1466 chastity land, the rank land of a late husband that a widow was allowed to keep to support her during widowhood, was abolished.[56] A widow was now expected to be supported by her sons or her husband's family. Exercises of property rights that would have been unremarkable in the Koryŏ dynasty were considered preposterous in the newly evolving lineage system: a widow selling family property under her management would cause great alarm to her husband's brothers. In some cases, younger brothers-in-law resented the widow and deprived her of inheritance or even expelled her from the house. In 1488 a dispute broke out in the royal family when a younger brother usurped the ritual heirship of his elder brother's widow. Although the court reprimanded the younger brother for harming propriety by expelling his sister-in-law, it also took his side and acknowledged him as the legitimate ritual heir. The court concluded that customary widow rights were too strong and contradicted patrilineal principles, eventually declaring that the widow should not be allowed to succeed to ritual heirship unless her husband had already succeeded as the ritual heir.[57] In 1554 an official restriction also was placed on whom a widow could adopt as her husband's heir: adopted heirs had to be chosen strictly from among agnatic kin. A widow thus could not adopt from her natal family and the previous exception for adopting toddlers from outside of a family was banned. Often, especially when she had only daughters, a widow would postpone adopting an heir, creating tension with her in-laws, whose main interest was in securing an heir for the family line.

Cases of widows who died without children serve to reveal in stark relief the emerging concept of kasan, or family property, in late Chosŏn. Family property was not new, for it had been a source of controversy even earlier in the Chosŏn dynasty. Records of a series of litigations over such properties remain from the sixteenth century. These cases show that, as the concept of family property spread, even property of married-in women came to be folded into the collective property of the marital lineage. In 1560 two families, Choe and Son, went head-to-head over a piece of property that had been inherited from a Choe daughter who had married into the Son family. Her property, which had been inherited by her adopted daughter from her natal family (another Choe), had passed to her son-in-law and was about to be inherited by a nonrelation (the son-in-law's second wife and son). In sending one of its daughters as an adoptive daughter to the Son family, the Choe's had attempted to maintain control over the property given in marriage, but the plan fell apart when the adoptive daughter also died without leaving children. When the Son family attempted to pass the property that was originally from the Choe family to one of the descendants of the Sons, technically cutting all traces of Choe ties to the property, the Choes went to court but were able to reclaim only half of the property; the rest was divided among all Son progeny, including those unrelated to the Choes.[58] In 1583 a lawsuit was lodged from the opposite direction, from a marital family against the natal family of a dead woman. This dispute over an inherited slave broke out between the Yi and Kim families. When a Kim daughter died without children, her natal father retrieved the family slave given to her in marriage and gifted him to one of his other children. In response to this, the dead daughter's adopted son brought suit against the Kim family, citing his rights to inheritance as the ritual heir.[59] In both of these cases, the woman's family lost control of the property granted to a daughter in marriage, as it had become increasingly difficult to retrieve such property when a daughter died without children. This was a sharp departure from Koryŏ dynasty conventions.

In the Koryŏ dynasty, when a woman died, her property was enjoyed by her spouse until his remarriage or death, upon which point the property was returned to the woman's natal family. This custom was observed until the early Chosŏn dynasty, when, in King Sejong's reign, debates flared over whether a widower had an obligation to return property when he remarried. Eventually, it was decided that when the widower died, one-third of the property (from the deceased wife's family) was to be given to the ritual heir born of the second wife (who presumably would continue to observe ancestral rites for the deceased first wife), and two-thirds of the property was to be returned to the natal family. A woman, however, could keep her husband's property only when she maintained chastity. By 1548 the court ordered that in cases where a child born of a second wife bore the obligation to continue the ancestral rites, he or she could inherit all of the first wife's property.[60]

By the late seventeenth century, inheritance rights of the ritual heir were further strengthened. A case from 1696 between the widow Yu and the adopted ritual heir shows how much a widow's rights over family property had diminished. When the widow Yu tried to pass on part of the family property to her five daughters, citing her deceased husband's verbal testament on his deathbed, the ritual heir sued her, citing his rights as the ritual heir.[61] The widow eventually won the lawsuit, but such resistance on the part of the ritual heir to partible inheritance and to inheritance by daughters, as well as the extent of the ritual heir's exclusive rights to inherit family property, is a stark contrast with the practice of bilateral and partible inheritance common during the sixteenth century.

As property given in marriage was increasingly difficult to retrieve, it is easy to understand why daughters were given an increasingly smaller share of property that had any lasting value, such as land or slaves. Land inheritance to married-out daughters seems to have begun diminishing sometime in the sixteenth century, a trend more pronounced during the late seventeenth century. Slaves, especially wet nurses, continued to be provided to daughters of wealthy families, but they were given without formal papers, presumably so that they could easily be retrieved when need be. This also made disputes more difficult for the natal families when conflict did break out, because they lacked documentary evidence.[62] By the late seventeenth century, when virilocal marriage and agnatic principles had become more established, married-in women brought with them dowry that was valuable but not worth much more than what they could themselves consume.

By the end of the Chosŏn dynasty, then, a family-property regime had developed that pushed women to the margins of the family in terms of rights of access to family property. As daughters, they were largely excluded from family inheritance, except for some movable valuables received as dowry. As married-in women, they lost direct inheritance rights to their husband's rank land or other forms of property. As widows, they had indirect rights over family property as the mother of the ritual heir, but without sons they were in a precarious position: expected to remain chaste (unmarried) and stay in the marital house, yet unable to own property in their own name. As the eldest daughter-in-law (ch'ongbu), a woman had provisional rights over family property, but she had to turn over her rights as soon as a ritual heir was secured.

CONCLUSION

I have outlined the long process through which patrilineal principles were entrenched in family practices, especially customs that governed marriage and inheritance. While virilocal marriage and agnatic inheritance increasingly marginalized women's rights to family property, it also maintained widow rights, which led to inevitable contradictions. While widows were indispensable in ensuring the stable succession of heirs and property along patrilineal lines, the fact that these women married into the family from outside, as nonagnatic members, posed a threat to the desire and principle to limit access to family property to agnatic kin. As we have seen, widow rights had an inherently ambivalent relationship with patrilineal family principles and were a source of familial conflicts from the beginning of the Chosŏn dynasty.

The ambivalent and controversial nature of widow rights were what lay behind the dead widow bodies from the 1890s that we encountered at the beginning of this chapter. Yet it would be incorrect to see these women as helpless victims of strident Confucian prescriptions for widow chastity. More accurately, I would argue, they were active agents using suicide as the strongest and loudest legal voice available to them to advocate for their innocence, and as such were successors to the widows who appear in legal cases of the Chosŏn dynasty. Forceful female litigants again emerge in legal records in the Japanese colonial period, which began just a few years later. The pattern of familial conflict over widows during the colonial period, moreover, was similar to that from the Chosŏn dynasty. The continuity of such patterns dispels the popular perception that colonial rule dramatically changed (for better or for worse) Korean families and the lives of women. What was changed was merely the legal venue that widows used to claim and defend their rights.

What is significant, these cases show, is how similar family conflicts were treated differently under the two different legal systems. While the widows in the nineteenth century were invariantly depicted as victims of moral crimes or experienced loss of propriety, the widows from colonial courts presented themselves as bearers of certain rights for which they demanded recognition. Also, while the power of widows' positions, shown in the nineteenth-century letters, was contingent on their moral authority (that is, the chastity or propriety that they derived from being reputable members of their families), the rights of widows in the colonial period cases were independent of any moral qualities. Rather than reflecting any drastic change in consciousness (in what was, after all, a short ten-year span), these changes reflected the different cultures of judicial process within which widows operated.

2

Widowed Household Heads and the
New Boundary of the Family

With the beginning of Japanese colonial rule, many things about women and their position in the family were transformed. At the base of the legal structure implemented in the colonies and the status of women within it was the family system that had developed in Japan in the Meiji era. Ordained in the Meiji Civil Code (1898), the formal framework of the Japanese family system *(ie-seido),* or the household system, embodied the Japanese political ideology of the family state, which literally, figuratively, and ideologically captured the Japanese citizenry into one large big national family under the paternal authority of the emperor. It is this family system that the Japanese tried to transplant in colonial Korea through the colonial legal system and the household registry.

The impact of the colonial transformation of the traditional family system was complex for the colonized, especially for some of the women and widows who occupied a marginal position in society and found new opportunities in the volatile legal environment that colonial rule engendered. The Japanese family system had a transformative effect in Korea, as it did in Japan, specifically by creating an official boundary around the unit of household, which weakened the traditional lineage system. The new administrative unit of the household restructured family relations; each household was an administrative unit as well as a legal unit, firmly placed under the administrative authority of the household head. These were made manageable and legible to the state through the household registry *(koseki).* The operation of the modern colonial legal system systematized adjudication processes, cutting the operative power of the cultural and customary authority of family elders and significantly boosting certain women's standing in legal struggles against family elders. Widows, whose position in the family had long been threatened, found an official and systematized route to have their pleas addressed.

In this chapter I examine the impact of the colonial household system through records of civil cases that involve widows and their customary rights. Rather than resort to suicide to express their resentment, as did those widows from the late nineteenth century we encountered in the previous chapter, widows under Japanese colonial rule proactively utilized the colonial legal system to claim their customary rights over property and often won. Yet these victories had their limitations. Since strengthened widow rights were an accouterment of strengthened household-head rights, widows' rights still were vulnerable once a male heir was secured through adoption. A widow's house headship remained temporary, as a later case we examine at the end of the chapter illustrates through one widow's vain attempt to make her tenure as household head permanent.

JAPANESE FAMILY POLICIES AND THE COLONIAL LEGAL SYSTEM

The Ordinances on Civil Matters (Chōsen Minjirei) promulgated in 1912 extended the Japanese Civil Code in its entirety in Korea, with the important exceptions of family and inheritance matters, which were designated to be ruled according to Korean custom.[1] Family customs thus were meant to play a prominent role in the colonial civil-law regime. An immediate problem, however, was that Korea lacked any codified set of customary laws. Following the tradition of Chinese legal culture, Korea had long left most civil matters to be dealt with privately, handled by local magistrates only when they were considered harmful to public order.[2] Without a tradition of private law, there also was no history of customary law formation.[3] To fill this gap, the Japanese conducted customs surveys to collect material to determine Korean customs in practice. The result, published later in 1912 as Kanshū chōsa hōkokusho (Customs-survey report), was used in the colonial courts as a reference on Korean customs in conjunction with additional surveys and inquiries, though these by no means were sufficient to cover all matters that came to the colonial civil courts. In addition, the discrepancy between the civil-law regime in precolonial Korea and the Japanese Civil Code meant that there was bound to be some adjustment, if not outright distortion, of customs in the process of their becoming customary law.

For leadership in the colonies, the operation of a customary law regime served some important political objectives. As with Taiwan, the governor general of Korea answered directly to the emperor, bypassing the Japanese Diet. Establishing colonies as separate legal spheres ensured political ease of control and enabled a flexibility that facilitated the transition to colonial rule. The Japanese authorities were concerned that applying foreign laws to private affairs, such as family matters, might cause too much disruption to local society. As a latecomer to empire building, the Japanese were positioned to take cues from other colonizers, such as the British, German, and the French, who applied local customs in matters of family and religion.[4]

That keeping Korea as a separate legal sphere was the main objective of the customary laws is proven by the fact that locating the Korean difference in family matters was not always part of the plan. The choice to do so was derived from a long and rather haphazard process. Japanese influence on Korean legal matters began with protectorate rule in 1905, even before Korea was formally annexed to Japan in 1910. Rescinding the unequal treaties and thus severing the Western countries' ties to Korea was crucial to Japan's monopolization of Korea—a fact of which the Japanese resident general, Itō Hirobumi, was acutely aware.[5] Itō recognized a pressing need for a proper system of civil law in what he saw as a still chaotic legal system in Korea. As the first step toward legal reform, Itō formed a system of legal advisers. Judges and lawyers from Japan were invited to local regions in Korea to "advise and assist" the Korean administrator-judges in legal matters. Korea's 1895 efforts to modernize the judicial system during the Kabo Reforms by implementing new judicial procedures had fallen far short of what had been achieved in the Japanese legal system.[6] Civil cases and criminal cases remained undivided, and local administrators doubled as judges. Without any legal or administrative authority, however, the Japanese legal advisers had limited means of directly implementing reforms of the local courts.

For the reform of the framework within which these courts operated, Itō, with a background in law and having himself been a significant contributor to the writing of the Japanese Constitution, envisioned a civil law for Korea separate from the Japanese Civil Code. To write such civil law, Itō included among the legal advisers he invited to Korea Ume Kenjirō (1860–1910), a prominent civil-law scholar who had participated in the writing of Japan's Civil Code.[7] In Japan Ume had been a member of the Enactment Faction (Dankō-ha) and had supported a Civil Code based on universal principles rather than Japanese customs. Yet in Korea he supported a Civil Code more agreeable to local customs. What is notable is that, unlike the customary law regime enacted later in 1912, Ume's plan was to produce separate laws for commercial matters in Korea based on its customs but extend Japanese family laws to Korean family matters. Accordingly, Ume's customs surveys concentrated on customs concerning land, such as ownership, transactions, land tenure, and tenancy.

The sudden shift of Japan's Korea policy in 1909, following a whirlwind of events, turned the legal policy on civil laws in Korea on its head. In 1907 King Kojong's attempt to publicize his discontentment with Japanese control failed at the Hague Convention. In the aftermath of this incident, the Japanese forced King Kojong's abdication and assumed control over legal and diplomatic matters in Korea. Following the assassination of Itō Hirobumi by An Chung-gǔn, a Korean nationalist, the Consignment of Judicial Power in November 1909 nullified the need to write new civil laws for Korea. Japan discarded its plan to keep Korea as a protectorate and signed the Annexation Treaty in 1910 to formally colonize Korea.[8] Ume's original plan came to naught, and, shortly after, in August 1910, Ume himself died from typhoid fever.

Despite the tumult of the times, legal reforms after 1910 were carried out with smooth continuity under the supervision, in part, of the same legal experts already on the ground since 1906. They were joined by many legal specialists newly recruited after 1910 with attractive pay and benefits.[9] Shifting away from Ume's original plan, the overall direction of reform was toward legal assimilation, whereby the new modern Japanese laws and legal system would be implemented almost wholesale in Korea. Korean exception became confined to the area of family matters, thereby giving family customs a more prominent role in defining the Korean difference.

Legal reform in Korea was later remembered by its implementers as a smooth and optimistic march toward progress. One judge, Yamaguchi Sadamasa, reminisced in 1940 about how ecstatic he had been over the transfer of legal matters in 1909: his decision to come to Korea, which was an ambitious career gamble for a young legalist, had finally paid off. The happy sentiment was shared by many, and the Japanese legalists celebrated the occasion with various festivities. At the old site of Kyŏnghŭi Palace they held a sports meet (daiundōkai) and a costume ball, where they dressed up as British and German officers and European ladies; they also marched in a costume parade.[10] The Government General installed a modern court system modeled on Japan's own in 1909, even with similar court names, and began implementing divisions between judicial and administrative duties as well as between penal and civil matters.

The colonial civil-court system, formalized in 1912, had three levels, consisting of eight local courts, three appellate courts (fukushin hōin), and a High Court (kōtō hŏ'in). Litigating parties commonly had legal representatives or lawyers, either Korean or Japanese, although even at the highest level of the High Court some cases were litigated by the plaintiffs or defendants themselves.[11] Lawsuits were quite expensive; one had to pay the lawsuit filing fee of 3.50 wŏn. If one hired a scribe, which seems to have been the common practice, one paid an additional 5.00–6.00 wŏn, bringing the total to around 10.00 wŏn. Considering that an average female factory worker's monthly earnings were around 12.00 wŏn, filing a lawsuit must not have been undertaken lightly.[12] The filing fee, moreover, was only part of the challenge. A scene in Kim Tong-in's short story "Yakan jaŭi sŭlp'ŭm" (Sadness of the weak, 1919) provides a sense, albeit fictional, of the economic realities of a lawsuit for a person of modest income. In this story a young female student is impregnated by her employer and sues him for compensation. As an orphan from a poor, rural family, putting herself through school by working as a live-in tutor in an affluent household, she can afford a lawsuit only because she receives an unexpected severance payment from the employer's wife. Her limited monetary power, however, inhibits her from hiring a lawyer, which proves to be a critical disadvantage against the defendant, who hires a very eloquent professional.[13]

INVENTED CUSTOMS

Much ink has been spilled about how accurate or distorting the survey process was for Korean family customs. This process was very much influenced by the Japanese-introduced household system in addition to the logic of customary lawmaking. Countering the conventional understanding that the survey distorted, or "misinterpreted," Korean custom, scholar Yi Sŭng-il more recently has argued that the changes in customary law merely reflected the natural change of customs themselves under colonial rule.[14] Marie Seong-hak Kim has argued that the colonial survey process of customary laws was inadvertently a process of the "invention of tradition." Owing to their invented nature, Kim notes, the customary laws of colonial Korea lacked the critical component of customary laws in European cases: communal consensus. Since customary laws were produced through judicial processes in a very short period compared to the long historical processes through which European customary laws were created, Koreans themselves ironically were marginalized in the creation process of the very customs that they supposedly embraced. It was not surprising that Korean litigants commonly claimed that the Korean customs cited as the basis on which the colonial courts adjudicated were inauthentic. What was happening was that Korean custom (Chōsen kanshū) was not exactly what Koreans were practicing customarily, but rather a set of customs artificially created by the colonial judicial system through a process of replies (kaitō) and bulletins (tsūchō).[15]

In fact, the way that surveys were designed made a certain distortion unavoidable. Customs that the Koreans observed were not customary laws per se, and the very process of systemizing them into customary laws entailed codifying practices that previously lacked uniformity and communal agreement. Yet the surveys assumed that there already were uniform customs among Koreans, though this was far from the truth.[16]

That the surveys used as key sources textual material such as old legal codes from the Chosŏn dynasty and China contributed to the confusion.[17] Using textual sources in customs surveys meant the risk of equating law-as-text with custom-as-practice. Especially in the premodern Korean context, where legal codes often functioned as ideals rather than norms, it was problematic to consider these as sources for customary laws. Codes on civil matters from premodern Chinese traditions reflected more the reality of the ideal than the reality of practice—should rather than is—and thus probably were not an optimal source for customary laws, indigenous as they may have been. Using written records as sources for customary law meant that customs that were being weakened could be revived. This might explain why some Koreans seemed exasperated by the customs that the Japanese colonial court decided to acknowledge, such as widow rights. Since the Japanese relied on old Chosŏn legal code books as a source, widow rights may well have been a dying practice, upheld on paper because of the moral purpose (e.g., widow chastity) it was serving. That also would explain why some of the customs listed on the *Kanshū chōsa hōkokusho* seem contradictory to one another: some customs were text-derived, and others may have been derived from practice.

In the process of compiling the *Kanshū chōsa hōkokusho,* local variations were erased. Korean customs were not nationally homogeneous. In institutionalizing a set of customary practices known as Korean customs, some customary practices inevitably had to be excluded and ignored. If certain customs were found to be in conflict with the overall framework of colonial law, they were not incorporated into the colonial legal system even if they fit a broad definition of national customs. For instance, even though concubinage was a widespread practice, customs related to concubines were not acknowledged as part of the customary law.[18] Instead, concubines were banned from household registries in 1915.[19] It thus was the practice of the colonial court not only to pick and choose among diverse customs but also to exclude those Korean customs that did not fit into the colonial legal scheme, replacing them with alternatives that usually were comparable to articles from the Japanese Civil Code. The end product was a nationalized version of customs that was new and alien to many Koreans.

Biases built into the survey process contributed to the problem of confusion. Local interviewees, for example, were drawn from the ranks of local notables, presumably with a penchant for customs that benefited them more than others (the younger generation, the poor, and women). In one customs survey, for example, all interviewees were men between forty and seventy years of age. They also seemed to have status: reports duly noted their occupations, most of which, such as "former head of township" or "member of Confucian student organization *[chang'ŭi]*" seemed honorary, but probably held a certain currency of local power.[20]

But beyond the design or method of the surveys, it was also the framework that proved problematic. The customs surveys operated on the assumption that the household system was already in practice, although the surveys were conducted before the household system was firmly established; this pushed the customs-survey process in the assimilatory direction. The survey questionnaires reveal that the household *(ie)* that formed the basis of status in the Japanese Civil Code was assumed to be in practice in Korea. While survey results detected that there was a complex and varying definition of the boundary of the family in Korea, questions such as "Is there a house that a son must enter?" simply assumed that households existed in Korea and differences existed only in procedural matters. Yet later reports drawn from local surveys conducted occasionally to supplement the *Kanshū chōsa hōkokusho* show that a continuing discrepancy existed in the legal framework of the household and the actual lived realities of family life. A 1919 report, which was conducted to determine the applicability of *inkyo* (retirement of the household head) in Korea, showed that Koreans preferred terms like *chǒnga* and *kajang* rather than *inkyo* or *koshu,* showing that the Korean sense of a *ka* and its head was different from the Japanese sense of a household and its head *(koshu).*[21] Given the built-in biases of the customs-survey process itself, accurately surveying customs in practice was a flawed project from the beginning. In other words, the boundary of the household that often played a definitive role in deciding family matters was a Japanese legal concept imposed not only on legal matters but also, from the beginning, on the process of surveying local customs.[22]

WIDOWS CONTEST THE HOUSEHOLD

Throughout the colonial period, there were 72 High Court cases that involved widows as litigants, most of which concerned widows' property rights. This was around 3 percent of all civil cases (2003 in total), but 30 percent of all cases concerning family matters and 40 percent of the 156 cases categorized under "Korean Civil Ordinances" (Chōsen Minjirei), the colonial civil laws that concerned Korean customs. Although this number may not seem high, these were just the cases that made it to the highest level of courts and thus a fraction of all the cases adjudicated in the local courts. The High Court cases are significant, moreover, because these decisions had wide-ranging impact as precedents.[23] They were disseminated through official notices to the local courts and, after the Judicial Association was established, to all legal professionals through their monthly journal, *Shihō Kyōkai Zasshi* (Judicial Association journal).[24]

Widows' lawsuits uniquely illuminate the impact of the Japanese legal system on Korean families. Widows who were household heads literally embodied the boundary between the new colonial household and the lineage and thus often found themselves in a crossfire between the interests of the lineage and the interests of the colonial state. The new household regime, combined with clarified legal rights under the modern colonial legal system, meant that Korean women, especially widows, found themselves unexpected beneficiaries in the colonial legal system. Although such gains were not gains for all women, or for women's rights in particular, they demonstrate that the workings of colonial laws had a complex influence on women's status and legal rights under the colonial legal system: at the very least, the new colonial legal system breached the old system just enough so that some women were able to utilize it to their gain in unexpected ways.[25]

In January 1917, for example, two civil cases reached the High Court of Colonial Korea, one over the management rights of a piece of land and another over the ownership of harvest from that land. The land had been owned by a man who died in 1914, leaving behind a young wife and an infant son, who also died shortly after. The cases involved the widow, named Yi Se-sǒn, and the older brother of the deceased, Ko Sǔng-hwan. When Yi's husband passed away, Ko took charge of her husband's land and refused to give her any harvest from that land, prompting her to sue him. Yi argued that she had the customary right to retain her late husband's property and manage it until she found a suitable adoptee to inherit the household. Ko, on the other hand, argued that in the event a woman was widowed without an heir, it was "Korean custom to have a close (male) relative in the lineage [J: *monchū*; K: *munjung*] manage the property," as women were dependents and had no rights over property, according to Korean custom. Yi won both cases in both the local and appellate courts, but Ko took the case to the High Court.[26]

Rather than demonstrating a sudden amnesia about what existing customary rights were for widows, this case, and many other cases over widow rights in the early years of the Japanese colonial period, more likely represented a continuity of conflicts and disagreements over widow rights. As we have already seen in chapter 1, widows' positions in marital families were increasingly threatened during the late Chosŏn dynasty, as the property regime came to favor land property, and daughters were excluded from inheriting land. By the end of the Chosŏn dynasty, widows, it seems, were victimized by contradictory standards: they were expected to remain single yet were subject to being sold in remarriage—sometimes against their will. The colonial civil courts merely provided a new venue in which these conflicts were enacted.

This case is notable because it shows how conflicts that were not new in themselves played out differently in the colonial legal system. First of all, the widow Yi pursued her own lawsuit. In a very similar case from 1906, before the onset of Japanese colonial rule, a widow's brother-in-law appealed on her behalf against a cousin-in-law who had taken the land title *(chŏndap munkwŏn)* previously owned by her late husband.[27] The cousin-in-law had persuaded the widow to entrust the household's land title to him. Land titles, during the Chosŏn dynasty, were a critical proof of ownership.[28] Since the widow's son was still young and the document needed safekeeping, the widow had agreed. Seven years later, when her cousin-in-law had not given her any of the harvest, the widow realized that she had been deceived and appealed to her brother-in-law for help. It is significant that the widow from 1906 did not directly put forth the lawsuit herself, unlike the widow Yi, who did.[29]

A more striking difference in the colonial legal system, perhaps, was how matters of widow rights became the subject of official legal attention, and civil lawsuits such as these became opportunities for the colonial legal system to clarify customary rights. The High Court sided with the widow Yi in the 1917 case. It refuted the brother-in-law's claim that Koreans categorically denied property rights to women. As a widow and now the household head of her family, Yi, the judges stated, had the right to inherit her late husband's property and manage it until she adopted an heir. Such decisions would later be used as precedents in rulings when similar cases emerged.

Widow rights themselves were not an invention of the colonial legal system. As explained in chapter 1, widows had special customary rights in Korea before the colonial period. An eldest daughter-in-law *(ch'ongbu)* of the family had a special ritual standing, and, in cases where the family head died without an heir, the daughter-in-law was eligible to continue the ancestral rites and adopt an heir to continue the family line. To suppress the remarriage of widows, the Chosŏn court allowed widows to keep their husband's rank land as "chastity land" *(susinjŏn)*. Yet these rights were continuously challenged at court, for they clashed with the principle of patrilineality, as the trend toward exclusive agnatic inheritance grew stronger after the seventeenth century. An inheritance regime that flowed through bilateral lines gave way to an inheritance regime that gave rights exclusively to agnatic kin. A long tradition of partible inheritance also gave way to primogeniture, further marginalizing daughters' inheritance rights in the family. Widow rights seem to have been uneven and weakening, especially among commoners, by the late nineteenth century.

There are several likely reasons why widow rights were acknowledged under the colonial legal system as legitimate Korean customs. First of all, widow rights served a practical purpose in the legal system by filling an important gap necessitated by the colonial household system. In the household system, where the household head had an important legal capacity, succession needed to happen immediately after the household head's death. Therefore, there always needed to be a designated heir in any given household. In the absence of daughters' inheritance rights, having a widow as the backup heir was a necessary provision for households that lacked sons as heirs. Yet the strong tradition of agnatic inheritance in the Korean family system, centuries old at this point, dictated that family property had to pass into the hands of agnatic kin and denied widows permanent inheritance rights. The administrative need for a backup heir, yet the customary resistance to giving widows full inheritance rights, produced colonial widow rights that were neither full inheritance rights nor an outright lack of rights.

Parts of the *Kanshū chōsa hōkokusho* do give credence to the argument of the brother-in-law who denied independent property rights for women. Item 5, "Are There Restrictions in the Wife's Legal Capacity?," notes, "In Korea, the wife must be absolutely obedient to the husband . . . and in all legal transactions (contracts, lawsuits, and other important legal actions) must receive permission from the husband." Item 132, "What Kind of Rights Does the Husband Have over the Wife?," notes again that the husband's power over the wife is mightily large and that the "wife must always receive permission from the husband in all legal matters."[30]

Yet widows and their rights and status were another matter. Descriptions from the *Kanshū chōsa hōkokusho* show the ambivalent and vague nature of widow rights. Item 164, "What Happens When There Is No Legally Assumed or Designated Heir to the Household Head?," clearly states that the widow of the household head had the right to choose the heir when the household head died without one: "When the household head dies without an heir to conduct ancestral rites, an heir needs to be chosen, which amounts to nothing less than the action of adopting a son after the death of the adoptive father. *The person to decide the adoption is the wife* [that is, the widow]. If there is no wife, then this responsibility falls on the mother [of the deceased household head]. If neither of these persons is alive, then the lineage association is to decide the adoption."

Yet custom was more equivocal about the inheritance of property. Item, 168, "Who Can Become the Property Heir?," states,

> When the household head [koshu] (except for a female household head) dies, the heir to the property is the same as the heir to the ancestral rites, others who can perform the ancestral rites, or the deceased's brother. A daughter cannot become an heir to property. The heir has to be someone within the house; someone [living or registered] in another house [take ni oru mono] cannot become a property heir. . . . When there is no son, [one can] either have the wife accept [ukuru] the portion of inheritance or choose an adoptee and have him accept the adoptive father's portion of inheritance, but the custom is inconsistent on this point. . . . If the deceased family member does not have a son and if the deceased is the eldest son, the inheritance is passed on [shōkei] to his father. If he is a younger son, the property is passed on to his wife. If the [deceased] family member is not married or is a daughter, the inheritance is passed on to the father.[31]

In other words, according to the Kanshū chōsa hōkokusho, when there was no suitable heir, the widow could "receive" property. But the description itself was conflicted: the widow could receive property, but, as a woman, she could not become heir to property. Because the purpose of these descriptions was to clearly designate heirs, it established the widow as the last resort for passing on the family property when there was no heir but made sure that she had only temporary rights over the property until an heir was chosen. The Kanshū chōsa hōkokusho also states elsewhere, "People do not acknowledge retirement of a household head in Korea, but when a widow household head has adopted an heir for the deceased male household head, the adoptee, of course, becomes the household head, and the widow who had been the household head [retires and she] and her family members become his family members."[32]

Since the Japanese also wanted to maintain the household as the only legal unit of family, widows were critical to keeping the property within the household and preventing the property from being subsumed into the main house, thereby obliterating the particular household. The problem was that there was no legally defined tenure of a widow in the household-head position. Widow rights were acknowledged, but the contours of their rights were not clearly delineated. This ambiguity not only subjected widows to vulnerability but was bound to cause problems and, indeed, became a source of contention as well.

THE COLONIAL REGIME RECONFIGURES THE HOUSEHOLD

Widow cases show that more than Korean customs, it was the new household framework that determined the outcome of lawsuits. The colonial household system implemented through household registration thus deeply affected family life in colonial Korea. The civil-registration system was introduced in 1909, and the

Civil-Registration Law (Minsekihō) required all Koreans to register by household units under the name of the household head (J: *koshu;* K: *hoju*). Also noted in the registers were the address of the family and the names and dates of status changes of all family members, such as births, deaths, marriages, divorces, adoptions, and recognition of (the paternity of) children born out of wed-lock.[33]

To be sure, family registration itself was not new in Korean history; it was the legal function of it that was new to Koreans. Records of registering king's subjects in household units date as far back as the Three Kingdoms period. The Koryŏ and Chosŏn courts also required subjects to register with the state. The purpose of the Chosŏn dynasty family registers was to clarify personal status for the yangban elite and to levy corvée and head taxes on commoners.[34] The unit of the family registered was the unit of coresidency, including family members but also any relatives, slaves, or hired hands that shared the residence. The term, head of the household *(hoju),* also was in use since the Chosŏn dynasty, but the role of the household head was entirely different from that recognized by the colonial registry: in the Chosŏn dynasty the household head was simply a representative of the family responsible for paying the household tax to the state authorities.[35] Rather than a position of authority, the household head performed an administrative function. Therefore, taking on the duties of the household head in the place of an ailing father or an aging mother could even be considered an act of filial piety.[36] Surveys from as late as the 1920s show that Koreans had a concept of *chŏn'ga* (passing on the family), meaning passing on the position of *hoju*, or *kajang*, to a younger family member when the older *hoju* had grown too old to properly perform the administrative role.[37] The Kwangmu Registry, a reformed household registry put in place shortly before the onset of Japanese rule between 1896 and 1907, as part of Kojong's efforts at strengthening the court administration, did not change much in these regards. The objective of reflecting the lived reality of the family was strengthened: the focus was on accurate depictions of who lived within the family, regardless of their relations.[38] In short, although previous forms of household registries existed in Korea, their function was an administrative identification of the household composition, with the household head serving merely to represent the family.

The Japanese-installed household registry differed from previous Korean versions in some significant respects. First, it imposed a particular family structure rather than accurately reflecting existing coresidence patterns, as the Kwangmu Registry, for example, had aimed to do.[39] In the Japanese-installed system, the household head and family members were registered, while other unrelated coresidents—such as servants, who had been registered in the Kwangmu Registry—were excluded. Patriarchal principles and primogeniture also were imposed for inheritance of the position of the household head. Unlike in the previous Kwangmu Registry, the ability of an eldest son to divide his household from the parents' household was restricted; as a result, within the first few years of the

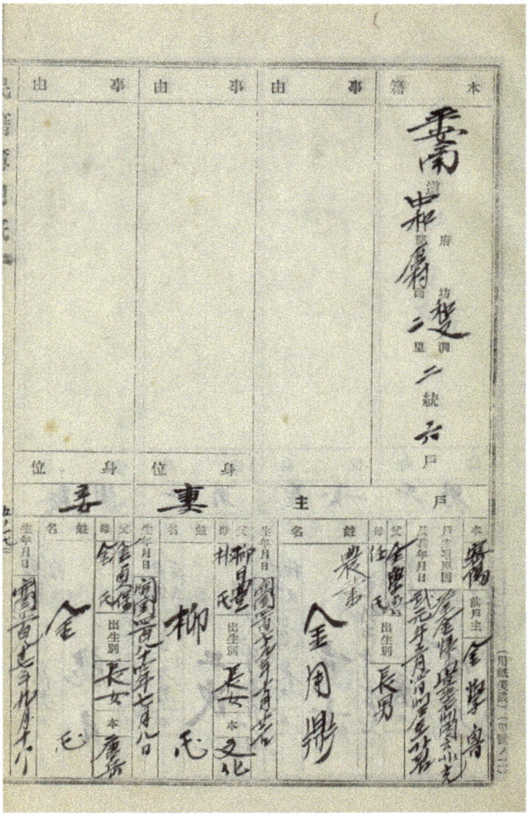

FIGURE 1. A page of a household register with a wife and a concubine. From Ariga, "Kosekini kansuru jikō."

Household-Registration Law's promulgation, families were restructured to follow the newly normative structure of the patrilineal stem family.[40] The household registry recorded the personal status of all residents in a household unit under the administrative authority of the household head, whose position was inherited according to principles of primogeniture and patrilineal succession. The household head held both legal and economic power, with the authority to approve all status changes of family members, such as marriages, divorces, and the registration of births, as well as the right of an individual to claim a larger portion of family property in inheritance. Validation of family status changes that used to be in the realm of the family and the community were now moved to the realm of government administration. Through the Japanese-installed household registry, the relationship between the state and society was reconfigured, and the Japanese colonial apparatus inserted itself into the private space of the family.[41]

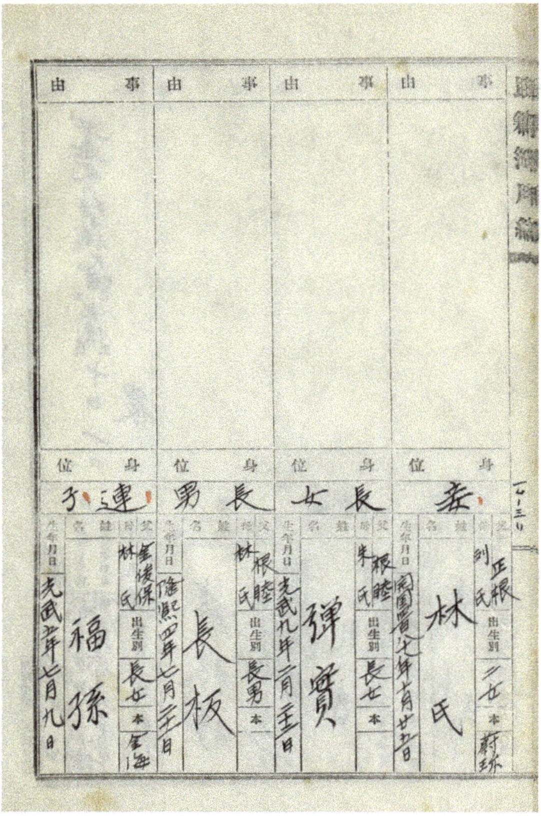

FIGURE 2. A page of a household register with a concubine and a daughter she brought in. From Ariga, "Kosekini kansuru jikō."

In addition, the registry officially transformed the definition and boundary of the family. The household that was registered was not a simple reflection of the actual coresident family. It privileged the definition of family that centered around consanguinity, that is, relations by blood organized around the principle of patriarchal hierarchy. The collection of household registers from 1913, gathered presumably in preparation for the 1918 Common Law (Kyōtsūhō) and the 1922 Household-Registration Law (Kosekihō), shows that there was a significant gap between the proper household that the colonial state was trying to enforce and the actual lived realities of Korean families.[42] Among the registers collected for their peculiarities were those of households with both a wife and a concubine, households with *tsureko* (children from a wife's previous marriage), households headed by a widow living with a daughter and a son-in-law, and households of

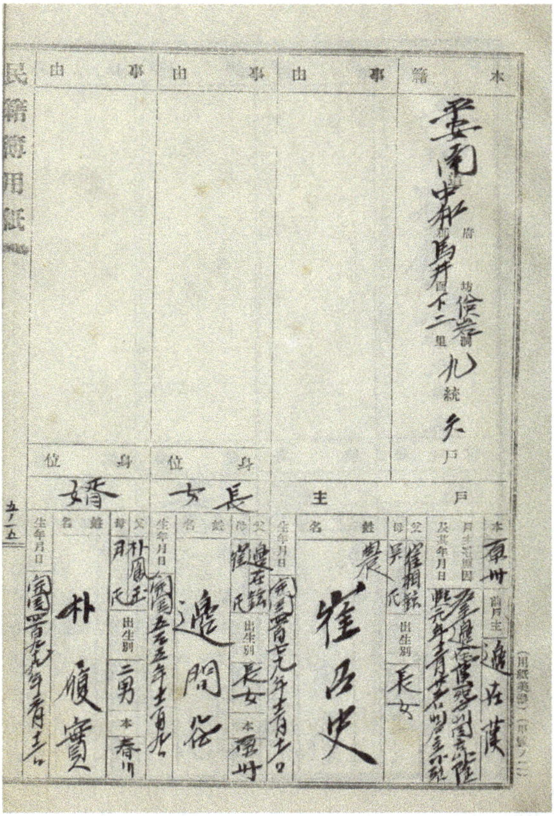

FIGURE 3. A page of a household register with a widowed household head and her daughter and son-in-law. From Ariga, "Kosekini kansuru jikō."

monks, a group of unrelated people who yet shared one residence and economy.[43] These were all groups of people coresiding in one household, reported by those people themselves as a household, that nonetheless were considered by the colonial state unfit to be considered as proper households. Clearly, the household in the registry was meant to be more than just a reflection of the lived reality: it was an abstract legal concept imposed on the lived reality. In fact, this concept of a household unit was the first instance of the extension of metropolitan family law into Korea, even before Korea was formally colonized.[44]

It was the new boundary of the family that most critically determined the outcome of many of the cases that involved widow rights. In the previously mentioned case from 1917, the brother-in-law, Ko, lost the case because his claim to be a family member of the widow was denied by the judges. According to the appellate court

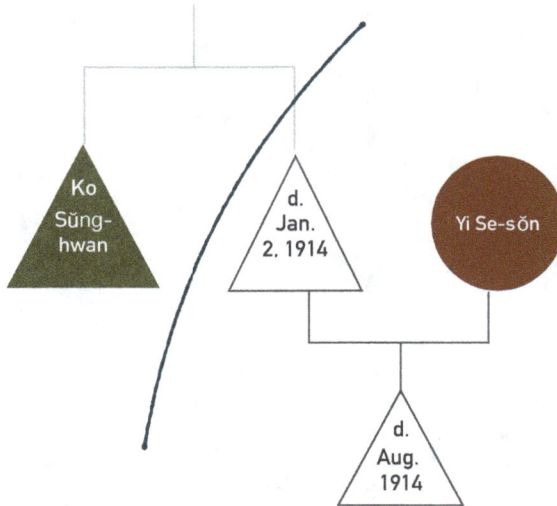

FIGURE 4. A diagram of the Yi Se-sŏn case.

judge, Yi Se-sŏn, the widow, was the only family member left to inherit the property until a suitable heir was found. To this, Ko adamantly protested, "According to
Korean custom, brothers are one body and are of one family regardless of whether
they live together. It is also without question that the brother's wife is one family."
To this, the High Court judge noted, "Once a household is divided, the household
head of the divided house and his family members are not family members of the
main house. . . . Therefore, it was right for the original decision to not acknowledge
that defendant [Yi Se-sŏn] is plaintiff's [Ko's] family."[45]

The judge was subtly but surely changing the definition of family from kinship to the legal unit of registration. The new household implemented through
the colonial registration system thus clashed with the traditional family system
in Korea, which had placed a strong value on consanguinal ties. The principle
of the Ordinances on Civil Matters that decreed family issues in Korea were to
be dealt with according to Korean customs did not stop the colonial state from
imposing this new boundary of the family in Korea. This and similar decisions
articulated a new boundary of the family: one defined by the Civil-Registration
Law, whereby the boundary of the family was circumscribed to correspond to the
boundary of the household. All informal family ties were deemed legally irrelevant. In the process widow rights, perhaps unbeknownst to the litigants themselves, were strengthened as the claims of in-law relatives were curtailed along the
household boundary.

The case of Yi Se-sŏn, therefore, shows how widows benefited inadvertently as
the placeholders of the boundary between the household and the lineage. In this,

as in all the cases where widows' property rights were upheld, what was really being confirmed was the legal boundary of the household. Upholding a widow's right to inherit the household property directly enforced the boundary of the household. Traditional rights of the widow in this way found new support from the colonial regime. The protection of a widow's right to her deceased husband's property may have been one of the most striking ways in which the Koreans learned about the everyday consequences of the household system. In the previously mentioned case, the appellate court stated, "Even though the plaintiff argues that there were customary rights *for a household head* to manage the property for a widow when her husband dies without an heir, the husband in question died after he had divided his household from the plaintiff's household, and therefore the plaintiff has no such rights to claim."[46]

With the establishment of the new boundary, the legal rights of relatives outside of the household boundary also were denied. Customarily legitimate but informal family titles were suppressed in favor of the new legal terms dictated by the household-registration system. To Ko's claim of rights as a "lineage relative," the colonial court responded with another term, "household head," the legally recognized position in the household with prerogatives over family property. In other words, the colonial court was denying legal recognition to property claims based on lineage ties rather than household membership. The widow's right to inherit her dead husband's property and the brother's failure to extend his power over that property protected the boundary of the household. The competing definitions of family boundary offered by Ko and the colonial court not only reveal a wide disjuncture between the colonial law and the local customs of the colonized but also show that these differences were constantly (and sometimes covertly) negotiated to facilitate the colonial system. Even though family matters were to be ruled by Korean customs, certain Korean customs were discarded, ignored, or drastically modified to fit the Japanese legal framework and Japanese objectives.

To stress the new boundary around the household, judges on the High Court sought help from a different customary concept: "separate register, separate property" (J: *besseki yizai;* K: *pyŏlchŏk yijae*). Originally, this was merely a term that designated a separated house, very similar to the Japanese legal concept of *bunke* (divided house) or *bunseki* (separated registry). In legal documents from the Koryŏ and Chosŏn dynasties the concept *pyŏlchŏk yijae* was used to discourage separating a register and dividing a house when the parents were alive.[47] Yet the term in the High Court was used to mean something different and prescriptive: if they had a separate register, their property was also separate. Cases that drew on this principle followed exactly the same logic as the Yi Se-sŏn case and show that the colonial court was consistent in its effort to enforce this new legal boundary of the family. As early as 1911, the judges stated that, according to the Korean custom of "separate register, separate property," a relative outside of the household could not inherit the household property. This case also involved a male relative of the husband's family protesting the widow's inheritance of her deceased husband's property.[48]

In another case that also cited this principle—the 1913 case of Chŏng In-su versus Yi Tong-sik— the court ruled that Chŏng could not inherit from his grandfather's concubine, Madam Chu (Chu-jo'i), because she was registered in a separate household register from his. Her property instead was passed on to Yi, her nephew, whom she had designated as her heir.[49] This decision also curtailed an existing family tie, that between a mother and a child, prescriptively imposed between a father's spouses and his offspring. Chŏng In-su based his claim to inheritance on his perceived, or culturally prescribed obligation, to support Mme. Chu in her old age, reflecting traditional family sentiments. To this claim the High Court judge replied that he was not a family member of the widowed concubine. In fact, under colonial law Chŏng no longer had the obligation to care for his grandfather's concubine. Under the new law, which encouraged monogamy, adding concubines to the household registers was banned, and the familial relationship of the concubine with her husband and his proper wife's children was officially severed. As such, this new legal condition gave concubines like Mme. Chu the opportunity to free themselves from the husband's family, allowing them to become heads of their own household. They were then free to bequeath their property to whomever they designated, someone they could trust to honor their souls with annual ancestral rites. For Mme. Chu, that was not Chŏng In-su, her "grandson."

HOUSEHOLD AND PROPERTY OWNERSHIP

Redrawing the family boundaries had a larger implication than just reorganizing the family system. It also meant drastically restructuring property relations within Korean society, shifting land from communal ownership to ownership by individual heads of households. When the colonial land surveys compelled landowners to register their land with the colonial administration, it enforced the concept of individual ownership that denied customary rights such as surface or tenancy rights, causing great confusion and distress to tenants who had enjoyed long hereditary rights of tenancy and cultivation over the land.[50] Because this new colonial definition of property ownership meant that there was only one owner per parcel, many families were thrown into chaos by the need to delineate the prerogatives of the lineage heir. Once the heir of the core family was declared to be the land's sole owner, traditional restraints on his ownership (especially in terms of selling or mortgaging the land) also became ineffective. As is shown in the following cases, the family patriarch became no longer able to claim rights to property owned by members of his family who lived outside of his household, even if the traditional norms had prescribed otherwise.

One of the areas where the new colonial property ownership wreaked particularly serious havoc was that of ritual estates (wit'o), agricultural lands set aside by the lineage to fund ancestral rites, the managerial rights to which were granted to the heir of the main family. While the colonial government nominally continued to acknowledge the communal ownership of such land by the lineage, this principle sat awkwardly within the overall structure of individual ownership that precluded any restrictions by customary rights of communal ownership.

This conflict was visible in the following cases from the 1910s concerning burial sites as well. Burial-site cases were categorized separately among Korean custom-related cases in the High Court decisions. The perception was that burial sites had a special customary status that marked them as different from other landed properties. Indeed, the litigants involved in burial-site cases did cite a special set of customs that constrained the general concept of property ownership under the colonial legal system. There were customary distances between grave sites that needed to be observed, which varied according to the buried person's status, both social and familial. Problems arose when the owner of a burial site did not own all the extra space that custom designated as the necessary space to be left empty. When another person who owned within this extra space buried his own relative in it, a conflict would break out with the owner of the first burial site, who would protest that the second person was violating his customary rights. At heart, this was a conflict between customary rights and personal ownership. Invariably, the colonial court ruled in favor of the latter. If the owner of the first burial site did not own all the customary land around the burial site, he could not protest another person's use of this land.[51]

In 1911 the High Court heard a particularly messy case concerning a grave site.[52] This case between two family members shows how traditional familial propriety or customary rights had lost ground to the claims of individual ownership instituted by the new colonial regime. More pointedly, it shows how the new focus on exclusive ownership functioned to curtail the customary claims of lineage that had spanned family boundaries. Within the framework of exclusive ownership of property, the customary rights of the core lineage family over other families based on ritualistic grounds were no longer sanctioned. This case involved the plaintiff—a second nephew of the accused—burying his father on land that the accused claimed as his. The accused went to the police, claiming that there was an "unidentified body" in his land. Failing to find the person who had buried the body, the police exhumed it. The plaintiff was suing to have the body reburied at the site. As it turned out, the burial site was part of a larger patch of land that the plaintiff's great-grandfather had given to his younger brother, the accused's grandfather. While agreeing that the land was given to the ancestor of the accused, the plaintiff argued that the burial site itself was a "shamanistic ground [ŭmsaji]" and therefore excluded from the gift. Arguing that the injunction that had forbidden anyone from owning this shamanistic ground was now lifted, he stated that it should be returned to its rightful heir—himself—as he was the great-grandson of the original owner. The accused, meanwhile, denied any such customary restrictions on the land. One can assume that before the institutionalization of registered ownership, customary propriety binding these two relatives would have prevented the accused from exhuming the body of a second cousin buried on his land. After all, the deceased second cousin of the core family would have had a ritualistically higher position. Stating that there were no such customary restrictions based on the plot's being a "shamanistic ground," the colonial court upheld the accused's right of ownership. Since the accused had the right to decide whom to bury in his land and since he had done all he could to find the person who had buried the unidentified body, his decision to exhume was deemed entirely justified.

Owing to similar complications, further cases concerning communal ownership were presented in front of the courts in 1915 and 1916, including two cases of lineage members who had sold their communal land without the consent of other lineage members.[53] In both cases the lineage members had registered the communal land under their names as individual property and conducted the sales with proper seals and documents. Although the High Court acknowledged the communal nature of both pieces of land, there was little that the court could do to prevent these individuals from claiming the communal lands as their own beyond rebuking the individuals for foregoing the customary process of consulting the other members of the lineage before the sale.

The new land-registry system, launched after the land surveys that the Japanese colonial state conducted between 1910 and 1918, also strengthened household-head rights over property, curtailing any kinship ties or cultural convention that attempted to override such rights. In the sense that both systems strengthened household-head rights, the property cases over ancestral burial grounds were similar to widow cases like that of Yi Se-sŏn. Putting widow cases in the context of such other cases thus challenges us to evaluate widows' victories in inheritance cases within a larger picture. The victories of widows, it seems, did not particularly mean that the colonial courts were extending women's property rights per se. Rather, the colonial court was showing a consistent and marked preference for upholding the new household boundary and protecting the colonial household against the extended reaches of the lineage. As with the aforementioned land-ownership cases, the women triumphed in court only because the denial of their claims would have meant a threat to the boundary of the household unit.

The new household unit, therefore, had dual functions: limiting the authority of the patriarch over the extended kinship and defining a new boundary around the household that was enforced by and legible to the colonial state. In other words, although it preserved a certain collectivity of the family unit, the Japanese colonial state did so by significantly disrupting the existing collective unit of the lineage. Although both family systems strongly espoused patriarchy, there were crucial differences in their definitions, especially in terms of family boundaries, giving rise to strong conflicts between the two systems. Therefore, the critical impact of the

Japanese Civil Code in colonial Korea was not that it strengthened or weakened the patriarchal ideology but that it enabled the colonial state to define the boundary of the family on its own terms. In this way Japanese colonial family law forged a new relationship between Korean families and the colonial state as the state tried to get rid of the competing object of loyalty, the lineage. With the new family law, lineage power was weakened, making the resultant colonial household much more directly accountable to the state.

Interestingly, this imposition of the household boundary on informal reaches of kinship also existed in Japan, even before the Meiji Civil Code was promulgated. One 1878 case from Japan suggests that the household had a similar effect of curtailing larger kinship ties. This case, which occasioned a Japanese Supreme Court (Daishin'in) decision on July 27, 1878, involved a civil suit between Arabe Ryūji and his father, Arabe Heizaemon, over the issue of household inheritance.[54] In 1858 Ryūji separated his household registry *(koseki wo waketa)* as an older son; in 1878 Heizaemon retired as the household head and passed the household on to his younger son, Heijū. A year later, however, Heijū passed away without a son, leaving the family scrambling to find an heir. When Heizaemon passed on the inheritance of the household to Kama, his daughter and Heijū's sister, Ryūji objected, saying that his son, Koji, was the rightful heir. Ryūji argued that only sons could be household heads; daughters could be made heirs only when there were no suitable sons. The Supreme Court, however, backed Heizaemon, ruling that Ryūji, as a member of another household, had no right to meddle in the Heijū household's business of deciding an heir—neither could Ryūji send Koji, his proper son *(chakushi)* and an eligible heir to his own household, to another household.

The case touched on many issues of central concern within the contemporary debate in Japan over family law (e.g., issues of daughter inheritances, household boundaries, and divisions of a household). While the principle of inheritance was formulated to support the prerogatives of the household head, its enforcement in practice did not necessarily result in the strengthening of the collectivity principle. Instead, by strengthening the enforcement of the household boundary (i.e., when the boundary of such a family violated the boundary of the household), it could have the opposite effect. This was partly related to the state's desire to prevent the hasty division of households by families to avoid military conscription. But the most striking aspect of this particular case was the state's desire to implement its own version of the family boundary, as recorded in the household registers, rather than acknowledge the nebulous ties of kinship claimed by the litigants. In this way, even as the Meiji state was struggling to reconcile various visions of the Civil Code, it ensured that old informal and private ties of kinship would be regulated by the administrative boundary of the family that matched the official household register legible to the state. Thus, the boundary of the family came long before the principle of household collectivity or the authority of the household head, which became increasingly important after the promulgation of the Meiji Civil Code in 1898.

The implementation of the household system strengthened the household boundary against claims of kinship authority from outside of the household. In many lawsuits widows could take advantage of the strengthened boundary of the household and inherit family property (ownership or management) over in-laws. Such decisions were not inspired by the need to expand widows' rights at large, let alone women's rights. The following section analyzes civil lawsuits in which widows were involved to show that many of the widows' victories were a double-edged sword: as these decisions strengthened household-head rights they weakened widow rights because widow rights, as well as the rights of all the household members, were subsumed by the strengthened rights of the household head.

With the strengthening of the individual rights of the household head, widows became more vulnerable to the actions of the male heir. It became almost impossible, for one thing, to cancel an adoption, because that would mean disinheriting a household head. Also, personal influence over the adopted son, which used to be culturally acceptable, became defunct under the colonial legal system. A case in 1912 illustrated the precarious status of a widow under the colonial household system. On May 28, 1912, a lawsuit erupted over a property sale that a widow had made.[55] The plaintiff, Pak Chi-yang, was the adopted heir of the household and claimed that the property that had been sold was his. The accused, Choe Chong-u, claimed that he had obtained the property from the widow of the household, Madam Chu. Choe argued that although Pak had been adopted as the heir, the widow later disinherited *(ri'en)* him, so he had no rights to the inheritance. In the first trial, Choe won. The local court acknowledged the fact that Madam Chu had disinherited Pak and that he therefore had no rights to said property. In his appeal Pak argued that, according to Korean custom, once he had become the household head, the elders of the household could not disinherit him. The inheritance thus was legitimate according to Korean custom, and the decision of the local court was mistaken. Moreover, he added, "Madam Chu was merely a concubine [*hwachŏp*— literally, flower concubine, i.e., a young concubine of an older man], and did not have the authority of a household elder to disinherit the adopted heir." The High Court accepted Pak's argument. It ignored the accusation that Madam Chu was a concubine—she was probably a wife of remarriage—but conceded that even if she were a proper household elder, she had no rights to disinherit Pak once he had succeeded to the household headship.

This case demonstrated how the High Court specifically tried to strengthen household-head rights through stabilizing the household-head position. The decision contradicted the court's own decision on a different case in the same year. In 1912 the High Court permitted a family to disinherit an adoptee who had succeeded to the household headship on the grounds that the adoptee was chosen from the wrong generation of agnatic kin, violating Korean customary laws of adoption.[56] Although the Korean custom of *somok* stipulated that the adoptee had to be from one generation below the inheritor, the family chose an adoptee

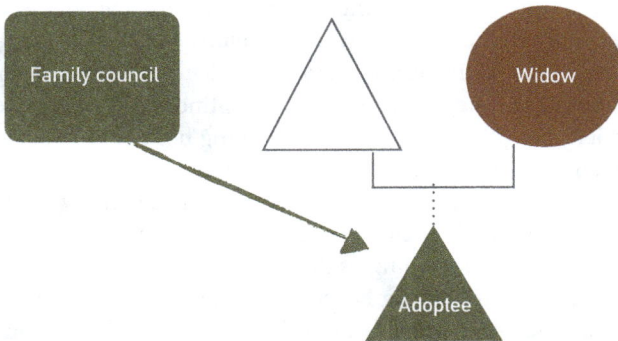

FIGURE 5. A diagram of the 1933 case, where the widow refused to adopt an heir.

from the same generation. The High Court stated that the ban on disinheriting an adopted heir once he had succeeded as household head was not an established custom at the time. Also, to acknowledge an exclusive right for the household head over which even the household elder had no influence was definitely a transformation of Korean custom. The court acknowledged not only that the household head shared his ownership with no one but also that he had full legal authority over the household property without having to answer to any other authority in the family. This, one could say, was a covert assimilation of Korean inheritance custom to Japanese custom. And, as a result, the property rights of the household head were strengthened. More important, widows and other elders of the household were further constrained from exercising power over the household property. Unlike her Chosŏn dynasty counterparts, who exercised moral authority over the household head, whether he was her descendent or adopted, the widow of the colonial period had no such recourse; she was cut off from the household property once she selected the heir and passed the household-head position on to him. In other words, even though the widow's right to designate an heir was a powerful one, once the heir was chosen, she had no power over the heir or the household property.

Not all widows were resigned to this disadvantageous position. In October 31, 1933, the Chōsen High Court delivered a decision on a lawsuit that a widow had brought against the family council that arranged an adoption for her.[57] The widow argued that she did not acknowledge the adoption and therefore it was invalid. The family council's side argued that it had to act only because the widow was negligent about arranging an adoption. The widow claimed that her deceased husband left her a testament telling her specifically not to adopt; she was merely respecting her husband's death wish. The head of the family council argued that, according to Korean custom, it was the widow's obligation to adopt a male heir to carry on the ancestral rites, and the husband's testament prohibiting the adoption, therefore, was invalid. The widow then pointed out that the adopted heir designated by the family council was a frivolous spender who was bound to ruin her family business. If the family business were ruined and the family turned out into the streets, how would the ancestral rites be continued? This was precisely why her husband left the will, she emphasized, warning her not to adopt an heir. Did a widow in Korea have the choice not to adopt an heir? Benign as it sounded, the widow's query revealed the critical ambiguity in customary widow rights in colonial Korea: the widow household headship was supposed to be temporary, but there was no explicit rule regarding its duration.

Claiming that she was obeying her husband's testament, what the widow was really doing was utilizing a loophole in the legal system to claim permanent ownership of her husband's estate. In the end, the widow won the case and was able to dissolve the unwanted adoption, though she was not given permanent rights over the estate. The court merely concluded that the widow's refusal to accept the heir in accord with her husband's testament could not be interpreted as a "willful refusal to adopt." The High Court dodged the demand to pass a clear decision on the matter, but the case revealed the heart of the problem with customary widow rights. The lineage's interest (represented by the family council) and the widow's interest were put into deadlock by the temporary nature and the obscure boundary of widow rights. The legal limbo that the colonial court chose is understandable, because the colonial court itself was put in a quandary. Widow rights were something to be phased out (as its conceptual basis was in the lineage system), but without daughter's rights to the household headship, abolishing widow rights could only strengthen traditional lineage power.

CONCLUSION

I have examined how the new unit of the family installed through the household registers functioned to strengthen customary widow rights. Contrary to what conventional understanding would suggest, and also contrary to the experience of some widows subject to utter mistreatment because of an absolute lack of power, many widows were successful in having their customary rights acknowledged in the colonial court system. These widows actively fought and won against their in-law relatives who claimed in the colonial courts that Korean custom denied any inheritance rights to women. The colonial court system and the customary laws created through this system, in fact, benefited the widows subject to diminishing rights under strengthening patrilineal lineages on the eve of Japanese colonial rule.

Yet I argue also that strengthened widow rights were accompanied by strengthened household-head rights. Even though the 1912 Ordinances on Civil Matters seemed to acknowledge Korean custom in family matters, this acknowledgment happened only in the context of the household system that had been implemented in 1909. The household system already significantly redefined the family boundary and affected how Korean family custom was interpreted and applied in the colonial courts. As a result, widows who could become and remain household heads benefited, but those widows who passed the household-head position to adoptees too soon sometimes felt mistreated. The strengthened household-head rights meant that the traditional authority of mothers who could challenge household-head rights was denied. Once the heir assumed the household-head position, there was no one in the house who could disinherit him. The problem with widow rights was mostly from their poorly defined nature. A widow's right to ascend to household headship was only temporary, good only until she designated an heir to whom to pass on the position and the household property. Much contention thus arose because when this adoption needed to occur was not clearly defined. Indeed, the frequency of cases concerning widow rights seems to attest to the unstable nature of widow rights in the context of a modern property regime where clear property relations were key. Eventually, the colonial state tried to solve this problem by replacing widow inheritance with daughter inheritance, the issue to which we turn in the following chapter.

Arguing for Daughters' Inheritance Rights

On December 7, 1939, the *Tonga Ilbo* reported on a sensational lawsuit between a mother-in-law and a daughter-in-law filed at the Pusan Local Court. The dispute was over an estate involving a large sum (200,000 *wŏn*) left by the recently deceased Yi Kwang-uk. Following Yi's death, his daughter-in-law, Pak Rae-gyŏng, a "chaste widow since young," as it was noted, had arranged a posthumous adoption for her deceased husband to inherit the large estate and carry on the family line. Yi's widow, Kim Su-rae, had mortgaged part of the estate to store away some cash, while filing suit against Pak for arranging an adoption without her approval. She argued that it was her right as the widow to arrange an adoption. In a short interview quoted at the end of the article, readers were treated to the opinions of the two widows: Kim asserted that her husband never had any intention to arrange an adoption and, since they had a daughter, she would rather adopt a son-in-law; Pak stated that it was her right as the daughter-in-law of the family to arrange an adoption, and Kim's refusal to adopt an heir was a scheme to take over the estate, which violated the law as well as Korean custom.[1]

Given the age of the widow Kim, which was forty-two, much younger than the deceased husband (eighty) and even younger than her daughter-in-law, who was forty-four, we can easily assume that she was a second wife. Although the daughter-in-law, Pak, was right about her customary right to adopt an heir for her husband, the fact that she was unable to do so for so many years until Yi died tells us that Kim perhaps was right about the deceased husband's unwillingness regarding such an adoption. What is also intriguing is Kim's statement that she would rather adopt a son-in-law as an heir. At this point in 1939, son-in-law adoption, a Japanese custom, was not yet an option for Koreans. The Civil-Ordinances Reform, which enabled son-in-law adoption, had been barely promulgated in November 1939, to be implemented in February 1940.[2] Yet the article does not explicitly question the viability of this option. It shows that by the late 1930s the anticipation that son-in-law adoption would be imminently available in Korea was so widespread that it was natural for the widow to consider it a viable possibility. At the same time, the tone of the article aptly captures the image of the widow in the late 1930s. Noting that widows were enthralled by lawsuits over dividing property, "even before all the funeral processions were over," it depicted the widows as greedy and litigious.

REFORM DISCOURSES UNDER CULTURAL RULE

What should we make of the derogatory image of widows that emerged in the public media of the 1920s and 1930s? I would argue that it derived from discourses for expanding women's rights that developed in ways that championed daughter's rights over widows' rights. As daughters' inheritance rights emerged as a progressive cause for reforming family law in the 1920s and 1930s, among both the Japanese and some reform-minded Koreans, the inheritance rights of other women, such as widows, and different routes to expand women's rights over property were suppressed.

The 1920s were a period of reform in colonial Korea. As the new "Cultural Rule" proposed in the aftermath of the March First Movement ushered in less restrictive colonial policies, Koreans were allowed a larger public space in the form of a public press. This venue was embraced by cultural nationalists as a forum for advocating reforms, in the belief that such reforms (or reconstruction, as Yi Kwang-su would have it), were necessary for a stronger nation.[3] As the 1920s progressed, Korean-language newspapers played a central role in disseminating ideas about national reforms and enlightenment.[4] Matters of family customs, such as concubinage, early marriage, and widow chastity, were key targets for reform. At the same time, new ideas about women and family, such as women's rights, romantic love, and sexuality were entering Korea and competed with reform ideas laid out by the nationalists and the colonial state.

The new Cultural Rule was part of a larger shift in principles of colonial management under the cabinet of Japanese prime minister Hara Kei. The shockwave of the March First Movement, coupled with the new diplomatic climate under the Washington Treaty System, pushed the Japanese metropole to propound a policy for more liberal colonial management. In the legal sphere Hara Kei promoted "Extending Home Rules" *(naichi enchō shugi),* promising colonial subjects the benefit of legal treatment equal to that of metropolitan subjects while trying to constrain the power of governor generals that lay outside the purview of the diet.[5] Legal assimilation had both practical and ideological goals. On the ideological side it would realize the colonial promise of *isshi dōjin,* granting equal benefits of the rule of the law to all colonial subjects.[6] On the practical side legal assimilation would facilitate legal transactions between colonial territories and simplify colonial management by reducing customary exceptions. Facilitating better legal transactions between colonial territories also meant that it would be easier to form familial ties across the metropole-colony divide, another significant component of integrating the colony and the metropole, thereby achieving *naisen yūwa,* harmony between Japan and Korea.[7]

In this new political environment, the Government General launched a series of legal reforms. In 1918 the Japanese government had promulgated the Common Law (Kyōtsūhō) that laid out terms of correspondence between different legal spheres in the Japanese Empire. A few years later, in 1922, the Household-Registration Law (Kosekihō) was promulgated to reform the Korean family registry to conform more closely to its counterpart in Japan. The registry took on a new legal function: it now served to officiate family status, which meant that unregistered status changes were no longer legally recognized *(todokede shugi).* As a result, the colonial state reached deeper into the private space of families in the colony.[8] In 1922 and 1923 a major reform of the Civil Ordinances drastically reduced the application of Korean customs and applied the Japanese Civil Code in its stead. As a result, the Japanese Civil Code was extended to family matters such as parental rights, divorce, and the legal age of marriage. These reforms in family matters stirred up great anxiety in colonial society. Although additional major reform of the Civil Ordinances did not happen until 1939, the two intervening decades were replete with discourses of reform.

Expanding women's rights emerged in this period as the new rallying cry for many different parties dedicated to reforming Korean family customs. The Government General tried to tap this energy and steer it toward support of their project of assimilation. In 1924 the Government General proposed to import son-in-law adoption as the next step in legal assimilation in civil matters, promoting the measure as a way to expand women's inheritance rights. In the process something as quintessentially Japanese as son-in-law adoption took on the meaning of "progress," while some Korean customs with potentially progressive impact, such as widow rights, were marked with the stigma of backwardness. Other avenues to expand women's rights were closed as well.

Korean reform demands were not uniform, nor were they united against the colonial state. While some Koreans welcomed the expansion of women's rights and even demanded more, other Koreans, the conservative elite in particular, strongly resisted such reforms, arguing that they would prompt chaos and resentment among the colonized population. Thus, it was not only the Japanese but also conservative Koreans who sought to produce and maintain colonial difference in the name of Korean distinction. Japanese and Korean customs were not static entities clearly distinguished from each other; distinctions and commonalities between Japanese and Korean customs were constantly constructed and renegotiated throughout the colonial period as assimilatory reforms proceeded. In other words, the reform discourses of the 1920s and the 1930s developed through a three-way competition among the colonial state with its assimilatory objectives, reform-minded Koreans and their demand for change, and conservative Koreans trying to protect lineage prerogatives. In the convergence of interests of the reform-minded Koreans and the Japanese colonial state, assimilation, for some, became congruent with progress. Yet Korean conservatives, or those Koreans who resisted such changes, exercised significant power to modify the reforms of the colonial state through the Korean Central Council (Chūsūin), the Korean advisory committee to the Government General; they were successful in delaying reforms in Civil Ordinances and deterring implementation of daughters' inheritance rights in Korea. The colonial state also seems to have tried to appease the conservative elite, conceding to their demands when introducing reforms on family matters.

Considering the high tension over matters of family-law reform in the Japanese metropole at the time, it is understandable that the Japanese were willing to heed conservative demands in Korea. While assimilatory reforms were unfolding in Korea, the Japanese metropole was being engulfed in its own set of reform demands. Japanese conservatives were unhappy that the customs of olden times were being lost in Japan's rapid socioeconomic transformations. Progressives, on the other hand, were frustrated that the Civil Code, which was designed to preserve traditional family customs, was growing increasingly out of sync with the realities of Japanese peoples' lives. Female activists' demands for more equal family laws also were growing stronger. The Temporary Committee to Deliberate on the Legal System on Personnel Affairs (Rinji Hōsei Shin'gikai) was installed in 1919, and the final compromise was announced as a resolution in 1927.[9] The resolution took many steps in the direction of constraining the rights of the household head and making divorce laws less discriminatory against women, but these were too minor to satisfy the growing demands of feminists of the time. This is understandable if one considers that the original reason the committee was convened was to strengthen the traditional family system rather than reform it toward progressive goals. Even with these limited endeavors, Civil-Code reforms failed to reach fruition, owing to the outbreak of hostilities between Japan and China in the Manchurian Incident of 1931 and the continuing war for fifteen years thereafter. Instead of Civil-Code reforms, a Personnel Affairs Reconciliation Law was promulgated in 1939 to facilitate resolution of family conflicts before they reached the point of formal trial in the courts. This law was devised to protect the traditional family structure and to deter further dissolution of families in a time of national exigencies. It also was devised to deal with the increasing number of family conflicts, as many families of those who died in the war became engaged in disputes over compensation and pension benefits.[10] On both the home front and the colonial frontier, then, the Japanese state was trying to deal with increasing demands that threatened the family-state ideology that it had established just a few decades before (or, in the colonies, was about to establish). The legal reforms that eventually transpired should be understood in terms of the state's attempt to control reform demands that were spreading rapidly in the empire at large.

In the end, the widespread reform discourse did not lead to much gain in terms of expanding women's inheritance rights in Korea. The 1939 reform failed to achieve full assimilation of inheritance laws and left Korean women's inheritance rights inferior to those enjoyed by women in the Japanese metropole. Only daughters' inheritance rights emerged as a viable route to expanding women's rights, although even those were compromised in the eventual Civil-Ordinances Reform of 1939.

The discourse on daughters' rights that emerged did so in conjunction with discourses (both academic and public) about phasing out widow rights and ancestral rites inheritance. While reform-minded Koreans were co-opted by the colonial state, having bought into its assimilatory reform regime, conservative Koreans were successful in pushing the colonial state to compromise with lineage principles that marginalized daughters in matters of inheritance. Widow rights eventually lost out entirely, abandoned by all three parties.

THE PROBLEM OF WIDOWS

Even though the Kabo Reforms had lifted the ban on widow remarriage in 1894, the practice continued to be stigmatized under colonial rule. If anything, cultural restrictions against widow remarriage may have become even more widespread in the colonial period because what had been an elite yangban class ideal seems to have spread to commoners. In 1924 a *Tonga Ilbo* editorial titled "The Problem of Widow Remarriage" demanded that widows in Korea be allowed to remarry without stigma. The author lamented that among fifty thousand households in the capital of Keijō (Seoul), one thousand were widow households. The article asserted that "it is already very much behind the times to talk about widow remarriage." The core of the problem, according to the author, was the discrepancy between the ideal of widow chastity and the reality: under the surface of stringent calls for morality, many illicit relationships were conducted, and efforts to hide them led to various ills. With the spread of new ideas about gender equality, the writer warned, women would no longer endure the unfair demands of chastity for women. There was only one country in the East that was worse in its treatment of widows and that was India, with its custom of sati: "Banning sati was the most benevolent policy of the British," the writer noted. The same kind of progress, he seemed to suggest, could be achieved in Korea under the civilizing force of Japanese rule. Other writers argued that it was inhumane to force widows to remain chaste when widowers remarried with impunity.[11]

Such sympathetic pronouncements were advanced in the face of a public suspicion about widows' chastity that had led to a shift, since the 1920s, away from earlier images of widows as victims of evil custom. Newspapers inundated readers with reports of widows "crushing to death" *(apsa)* babies whom they had had with secret lovers.[12] An article from 1935, for example, reported that about fifty cases of infanticide were committed by widows each year.[13] Association between widows and infanticide was so prominent in the public image of widows that when a dead infant's body was found, it was customary for the police to interrogate local widows.[14] Indeed one author in 1935 argued for widow remarriage not in the interest of the women but on the grounds that it would be a solution to the increasing crimes of infanticide.[15]

Despite such deleterious trends in popular thought, there continued to be authors arguing for a change in public attitudes toward widow remarriage. In 1935, for example, an article appeared with the imperative title, "Konggyu e urbujinnǔn kwabu e salgil ul chura [Rescue widows crying in seclusion]," that argued, citing unverified statistics, that young widows under the age of forty who were keeping chaste numbered upwards of three hundred thousand in Korea. Many of these widows were still bound by the old custom that banned widow remarriage, the writer noted.[16] In response to a petition from someone from the Kangwǒn Province to the governor general demanding the "liberation of widows," the Government General issued a notice confirming that there was no ban on widow remarriage, and young widows should be encouraged to remarry. Some argued that the problem was with men who favored only unmarried young women. "Even young widows would have to settle for widowers in their fifties," one writer pointed out, when "even old widowers looked only for young virgins."[17] There was no place for a young widow to go even if she did not wish to remain single.

Despite such efforts, it seems that many Koreans, even widows themselves, still appeared to be beholden to the ancient stigma of widow remarriage. One widow committed suicide in 1936 reportedly to avoid being married off to a new husband. This young widow of twenty-seven years of age, upon hearing her mother's urge to remarry, left her young son with her mother-in-law and strangled herself to death at her husband's grave site.[18] In 1936 a man burned the house of his sister-in-law in protest against her arranging a remarriage for her daughter-in-law. The man claimed that such a deed was an insult to the whole family.[19]

The frequent reports on widows' lawsuits over estates, though, suggest that there was a reason behind the growing concern over widows other than people's backward adherence to chaste widowhood. The real source of anxiety was that widows' inheritance rights had gained official backing in the colonial legal system. Many articles reported on lawsuits between widows and family members, also known as "lawsuits between bone and flesh" *(koryuksong)*. The articles were generally reprimanding in tone: one was not supposed to take a family member to court for personal profit. So Hyǒn-suk points to the many lawsuits that widows were involved in as evidence that they were subject to unstable and unequal legal standing under the colonial legal system.[20] Indeed, informal pressures on widows from their marital kinsmen must have significantly undermined widow's rights and legal capacity in practice. Yet it is more plausible to think that it was the increasing legal standing of widows (rather than the opposite) that led to the increasing number of lawsuits over widows' property.

Evidence of the increased anxiety over widows' rights can be found in newspapers' legal advice columns, which featured many inquiries sent in by both widows and their family members regarding the prerogatives of widows. In 1929 a man submitted an inquiry about how to stop his widowed sister-in-law from selling the property she inherited from his brother.[21] In 1930 a mother-in-law asked if she could retrieve her son's property from her widowed daughter-in-law. The answer was no.[22] In 1931 a young widow of twenty-two years of age asked if she would be able to keep the property she inherited from her husband, even if she remarried.[23]

Indeed, widows' rights over property were now more secure under the colonial legal system, not equal to male counterparts but enough to alarm family members. Perhaps family politics and cultural taboos continued to push widows to the social margins, but legally they had gained much standing and protection. From these inquiries we learn that although widows were subject to jealous legal maneuvers, kin members now had to take formal steps to restrict a widow's property rights. The mother-in-law mentioned earlier learned that there was no way that she could take away property that her widowed daughter-in-law had already inherited. The young widow learned that she would be able to keep her property even if she did not keep chaste.

THE JAPANESE PROPOSAL FOR SON-IN-LAW ADOPTION

As widows emerged as a source of social problems in the public media, daughters emerged as the alternative to widows as potential heirs. When the Government General began to expand legal assimilation, it chose daughters' inheritance rights as a useful channel through which to enlist Korean support for the project. There eventually emerged a growing consensus that widows' rights were the evil custom of old, and daughters' inheritance rights were the new trend of modern times.

In 1924 Matsudera Takeo, the chief of the Legal Division of the Government General, proposed, to the Korean Central Council, a plan to introduce the adopted son-in-law (*muko yōshi*) custom to Korea. Son-in-law adoption, where a son-in-law was adopted into the family as a son to be heir to the household, was a well-established custom in Japan. For Korea, however, this was not an easy proposal. The adoption of sons-in-law violated long-held adoption customs in Korea, which prescribed that only agnatic kin of the paternal lineage could be adopted as heirs. To make the reform measure palatable, Matsudera presented the adopted son-in-law system as a way of granting daughters inheritance rights. Current Korean customs, which forced families to bypass their own daughters and adopt a stranger, "violated human feelings [*ninjō*]," he pointed out. If Koreans were allowed to adopt sons-in-law as heirs, such a problem would be resolved. Matsudera further argued that allowing son-in-law adoption was "adapting to the trend of the times" and also promoting "the beautiful custom *[biten]* of the East" of "mutual love and respect between parents and child." Since love and respect does not discriminate between a daughter and a son, he continued, a daughter also should be allowed to inherit the household from her parents. In Matsudera's hands, son-in-law adoption was remade into a progressive measure to expand women's inheritance rights as well as promote happiness in the conjugal family.[24]

Matsudera's strategy proved successful in eliciting support from certain strata of Koreans ready for equal inheritance rights for sons and daughters. An article in the Pu'in (Women) column in the *Tonga Ilbo* a few days later chimed in with its approval of the reform. Titled "Chosŏn esŏdo ddal ege sangsokkwŏn ŭl chunda [Daughters will be given inheritance rights in Korea too]," the article also depicted son-in-law adoption as inheritance rights for daughters and criticized the Korean custom that denied daughters such rights. The *muko yōshi* system, as such, was presented by the writer as a step of progress toward gender equality rather than a policy of assimilation to Japanese customs.[25] Unfortunately for the Government General, the Korean response was not unanimously positive. While strong opposition to the reform measure from the Korean elite forced the Japanese to postpone the reform until 1939, demands for an extension of inheritance rights to daughters did not go away in the meantime.

Matsudera's strategy was to cast the two inheritance customs in terms of a temporal trajectory of evolution.[26] The argument had little factual basis: accurately speaking, neither the Korean nor Japanese family system practiced equal inheritance between sons and daughters. Son-in-law adoption fell significantly short of granting daughters equal inheritance rights. Not only did a daughter have less priority than her brothers to inherit the household, but even if she became the household head she had to yield the status to her husband when she married (*nyūfu kon'in*). If a daughter was already married at the time of inheritance, the son-in-law would be adopted as heir, and the daughter had only indirect inheritance rights through her husband. In both the Korean and the Japanese family systems, a female household head was merely a placeholder for a lacking male heir, to be replaced once the daughter married (in the case of Japan) or when the widow adopted an agnatic kin member (in the case of Korea).[27]

Rather than expanding women's inheritance rights, a goal for the colonial government in son-in-law adoption was to strengthen the household system. By enabling son-in-law adoption, a son-in-law could replace an agnatic kin member as a stand-in for a son, thus limiting potential heirs to household property to household members only. This meant a major redrawing of the boundary of inheritance from the boundary of the lineage to that of the household. An adopted son-in-law would help maintain household property within the household, in contrast to traditional Korean adoption customs, which merely kept the property within the wider boundary of the lineage. Son-in-law adoption also would advance

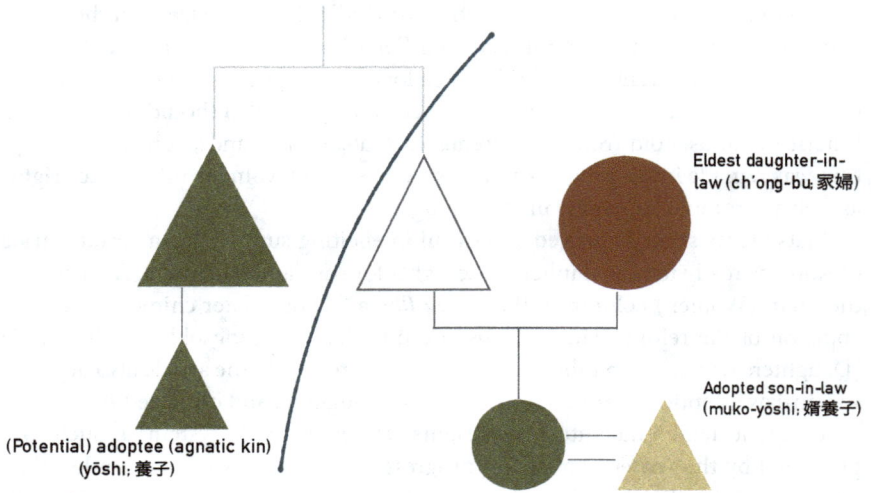

Eldest daughter-in-law (ch'ong-bu; 冢婦)

Adopted son-in-law (muko-yōshi; 婿養子)

(Potential) adoptee (agnatic kin) (yōshi; 養子)

FIGURE 6. A diagram of son-in-law adoption.

the stability and integrity of the household, as daughters married to the adopted son-in-law could not marry out, while widow household heads could. The objective of the reform proposal to implement son-in-law adoption, therefore, was to promote not gender equality but rather the disintegration of the lineage system, thereby eliminating the need for agnatic adoption and widow household heads.

Under the colonial household system and the civil-law regime, widows' customary rights posed several problems. One problem with widow rights was the vagueness that provided a continuing source of legal conflict. As women, widows were not eligible to inherit ancestral rites, which meant that their inheritance was not complete; the heir to property, according to Korean customs as defined by the Japanese colonial state, had to be the heir to ancestral rites.[28] As such, a household headed by a widow was in an inheritance limbo until a proper adoption was completed. Widow household headship, therefore, was a temporary role with not only an ill-defined length of tenure but also obscurely defined legal rights. In "posthumous adoption" *(sahu yangja),* when widows arranged an adoption for a deceased household head, there was no legal code that dictated precisely when this posthumous adoption had to occur. A widow naturally tried her best to make the most of her rights to arrange an adoption on her terms and secure heirs that she could trust, but when she could not find a suitable heir, she could and would indefinitely postpone the adoption, providing a source of tension with her in-laws. Dispute over heir selection was common between widows and agnatic kin who either disapproved of the widow's selection of an adoptee or objected to the widow's neglect in arranging an adoption.

On the other hand, widow household heads were a necessary provision for the seamless succession of the household head. Administratively, under the colonial legal system the household-head position could not be left empty, and somebody had to fill the post immediately. For those families without a "presumed heir" *(suitei katoku sōzokunin)*, that is, a son, and under Korean customary laws, where daughters lacked inheritance rights, widows were a necessary alternative. Yet widow inheritance had serious drawbacks; since the future heir eventually had to be chosen from agnatic kin outside of the household, adoption by widows potentially violated the integrity of the household boundary. The intricate lineage rules of *somok*, which an adopting family had to follow in choosing an adoptee, also continually reenacted and confirmed lineage ties that the colonial administration only equivocally acknowledged. The inherent ties that widow rights had with the traditional lineage system meant that they were incompatible in the long run with the colonial household system, which is why son-in-law adoption was an attractive alternative for the Government General. In contrast, a daughter's inheritance right depended solely on her membership in the household. The debate over daughters' inheritance rights, therefore, inevitably involved redefining the boundary of family and eventually involved breaking up the traditional lineage system into colonial households.

Korean newspapers in the 1930s show divergent attitudes among Koreans about the assimilation of civil laws in colonial Korea, but a sector of Korean society clearly supported legal assimilation as a way to expand women's rights. Although implementation of the son-in-law adoption proposal was delayed, reports about the pending Civil-Ordinances Reform continually adorned Korean newspapers. Especially following the announcement of the "Outline of Reforms in the Family Chapter of the Civil Code" (1927) in Japan, numerous articles reported on the pending major revision of the Civil Ordinances in Korea, including son-in-law adoption, lifting of the ban on intralineage marriage *(tongsŏng tongbon kyŏrhon)*, retirement of household heads, and so forth. On one end of the spectrum of opinions was a clear voice of caution; articles expressing this opinion tried to warn readers of the catastrophic effects of drastic reforms that might shake the Korean family system to the core. In one such article in *Tonga Ilbo*, titled "Tongsŏng tongbon kyŏrhon do inhŏ! [Even intralineage marriage will be allowed!]", the reporter relayed the news of a meeting within the Government General over the issue of the Civil-Ordinances Reform. With a title phrased clearly to sensationalize the reform, the article highlighted what it thought were the most shocking parts of the reform: the lifting of the ban on intralineage marriage and son-in-law adoption.[29]

On the other side of the spectrum were articles that called for a further reform of family customs in the colony to achieve a definitive expansion of women's rights. In contrast to the reservations and anxieties betrayed in the previously mentioned articles, one article in *Tonga Ilbo* a few months later called for an immediate extension of the reformed Japanese Civil Code to the Korean colony. The new Japanese Civil Code (actually the outlines for the Civil-Code reform), it claimed, gave property rights to women and abolished the "bastard" marker from the household-registration system, both strikingly progressive achievements that were desperately needed in Korea as well. Although the "revision of the Civil Code for Japan is a bit late, even compared to the backward country of China," Korea had it much worse in still being under the old Japanese Civil Code. It was critical, the author argued, for Japan to immediately extend the new Civil Code to Korea. "There is no reason why this [i.e., the issue of women's rights] should be an exception," the author added cynically, "when [Japan] is citing 'extensionism' [enchō-shugi] for everything else."³⁰

A few years later, on December 10, 1933, another article, titled "Yŏkwŏn ŭl sin-jang hara [Expand women's rights]," introduced a High Court decision that gave equal inheritance rights to a daughter as to a son, to a mother's estate. The column writer used this decision as an opportunity to call for equal inheritance rights to all estates. Citing numerous discriminative measures in the Civil Ordinances—adultery law, which was repealed in the Japanese Civil Code in 1930; paren-tal rights; lack of inheritance rights for daughters—the writer lamented, "How discriminatory is the legal treatment of women [in this country]! Expansion of women's rights! This is only a rational demand from women as humans."³¹

Despite such demands and anticipations, Civil-Ordinances reforms continued to be out of reach for Koreans. In 1932 *Tonga Ilbo* reported that it was uncertain when Civil-Ordinances reforms would be enacted in Korea. The article laid out in detail seven specific reform measures in the works for family and inheritance laws. Son-in-law adoption was definitely part of the picture. "[These reforms] were meant to correct the contradictions of the Civil Ordinances [that is, Korean cus-toms], such as [legal] disputes arising out of posthumous adoptions or marrying out one's own [children, that is, daughters] and passing on the house headship to an adopted kin." The article noted that although there was wide consensus among legalists in these matters, the Korean class of elders (*chosŏnin koro-kyegŭp*) and the majority of the Korean Central Council members were against it. Their opinion was that these reforms to the family laws were "destroying the beautiful customs" and that "to appear as if [Japan] was forcing Japanese customs on Koreans would disrupt the popular sentiment." The Legal Division therefore was hesitant to act on the reforms, the article reported.³² And it was thus that the reform was to be delayed until 1939.

DAUGHTERS AS ALTERNATIVE HEIRS

The expectation that widows' rights were a thing of the past and were giving way to daughters' rights inspired lawsuits between daughters and widowed mothers. In one case that traveled as far as the High Court in 1931, a daughter was suing her mother for her father's estate. The mother claimed that she had inherited the prop-erty following Korean family custom that gave inheritance rights to widows. The daughter argued that the Korean custom that gave inheritance rights to widows over daughters was an old custom that had become defunct under Japanese colo-nial rule. The daughter, moreover, accused her mother of having been involved with several men since she was widowed and of now living with one of them, with whom she had had a child. Even if such a Korean custom of widow inheritance rights was still valid in Korea, she argued, her mother should lose the rights because of her "immoral behavior." The daughter demanded that her father's estate be returned to her. The daughter lost the first suit, won the second suit, and lost this final suit. In the 1931 decision of the Chōsen High Court, the judges denied the daughter such rights and reaffirmed the widow's inheritance based on rights that had been recognized since the early 1910s. "Immoral behavior" could not be a reason for disinheritance.[33]

The daughter in this case seems to have believed that as colonial law progressed, daughters' rights were expanding. In this framework of legal progress, daughters' rights represented progress and widows' rights backwardness. Indeed, the 1922 Civil-Ordinances Reform had abolished a significant portion of Korean family customs and implemented the Japanese Civil Code in its stead. But, as the daughter discovered, the Korean inheritance custom of excluding daughters from household headship had not changed with it.

The expectation that eventually the Civil-Ordinances Reform would expand women's rights continued to spread and, to some, came to seem imminent. In 1934 a woman from the South Chŏlla Province sent an inquiry to a legal-consultation column about her chances for inheriting her father's estate in place of her widowed mother. In his answer the lawyer–column writer noted that a recent High Court decision gave daughters equal inheritance rights as sons (probably the same case cited in the December 10, 1933, column—misquoted, in fact, because in the High Court decision the estate was held by a mother and not a father), yet he was not sure it applied to a daughter who had already married out. The lawyer explained that he could not say for sure "[because] these things [the precedent] are not codified but [depend on] whatever the High Court decides is Korean custom."[34]

The anticipation that daughters' inheritance rights would be expanded alarmed those Koreans who were protective of lineage interests. The following case aptly illustrates that the conservative Koreans who represented the interests of the Korean lineage system were concerned not just about widows' rights but also about the inheritance rights of all women, including daughters. Yi In-gu was a widow who had the misfortune of losing both her husband and son in the same year just a month apart in 1931. Having lost her only son, she became the household head. The deceased husband's older brother, Choe Tuk-ryong, became anxious to arrange a posthumous adoption for his brother and claimed (falsely, as it was revealed later) that his brother had arranged to adopt a nephew back in 1922. He sued the widow Yi for not acting on the adoption. After having lost all three rounds of his suit, Choe then put together a family council and (re) arranged the adoption for Yi. The 1933 lawsuit was Yi's, accusing the family council of usurping her right as the widow to arrange the posthumous adoption. The family council accused the widow of refusing to adopt, and the widow denied the accusation. The High Court's decision was that the family council was presumptive in accusing the widow of not having an intention to adopt, and the widow won the case.[35]

What is notable about this case is in the details exposed in the arguments put forth by the family council in trying to defend their suspicions about the widow's intentions regarding the family property. The family council argued that the real reason behind the widow's neglect in arranging the adoption was her intention to pass the property on to her daughter, now her only remaining child. According to the family council's claim, the widow had already registered some of the property under her daughter's name, and her neglect to arrange an adoption, they argued, was her scheme to hand over the entirety of the estate to her daughter. They were suspicious that it was the daughter's fiancé who was persuading the widow not to adopt an heir; the fiancé had already moved in with the daughter and the widow.

The widow does not reveal much about her intentions, but it is possible that she indeed was making an effort to practice daughter inheritance on her own, while resisting adopting an agnatic nephew as heir. While the lineage suspected a plan for the family property to flow into the hands of the daughter and her fiancé, what they presented as their source of concern was something entirely different. After having entered these accusations of the widow handing over property to her daughter, the plaintiffs, in a revealing turn of argument, said that it was natural for them to worry about the widow's intentions, because the widow could remarry any time and take the property with her: "The spirit of the laws of the family system of our country prizes most the continuation of the family. If a person of great wealth dies without a son and leaves behind a young wife, and she is given the rights to inheritance and the rights to arrange posthumous adoption, *anyone would be suspicious about the wife's future intentions.* Human instincts are such that eight or nine out of ten such widows would just take the husband's property and remarry. In such cases, the house would lose the entire family property and have its family line discontinued." Because of the new freedom for widows to remarry, the plaintiffs argued, it was more dangerous for families to trust widows to arrange posthumous adoptions. The solution was to get rid of the widow as a "middle-heir" *(chūkan sōzokunin)* and have the lineage *(munhoe)* or family council arrange a posthumous adoption.

Instead of attacking the widow's choice to secretly squirrel away property for her daughter, which seems to have been at the heart of the conflict, the plaintiffs instead chose to attack what they alleged was the unstable commitment to the chastity of the widow and argued that this was what threatened the "continuation of the family" *(ikkei iji)* that was central to the spirit of the "family system of our country."[36] Their assumption was that the family council and the Japanese state shared an interest in the maintenance and continuation of the "family." The ironic fact here is that the family whose interest that the family council was defending was not at all the same as the family that the Japanese colonial state was trying to protect in colonial Korea. The solution that the plaintiffs presented, to replace widows with family councils to represent lineage interests, was laughable given the consistent effort of the colonial state in the opposite direction. It is likely that the family council knew that the colonial state's reform policies threatened the integrity of the lineage system and that they were trying their best to protect the lineage by appealing to what the Korean and Japanese family system shared in common: patrilineal succession.

It was not just widows' rights but all women's inheritance rights that Korean lineage interests resisted. As the Japanese colonial state continued with its reform measures to replace widows' inheritance rights with daughters' inheritance rights, the conservative sector of Korean society continued its resistance. Even after 1940, when the Japanese colonial state all but legally dismantled the lineage system through the Name-Change Policy (Sōshi Kaimei) and son-in-law adoption, it still had a difficult time implementing daughter household headship.

STATE DISCOURSES ON FAMILY-LAW REFORM IN THE 1930S

The family-law reform project was picked up again by the colonial government in 1932 with the establishment in the Chōsen High Court of the Committee for Surveying Family and Inheritance Laws and Regulations (Shinzoku Sōzoku ni Kansuru Hōki Chōsakai). The Outline of Reforms in the Family Chapter of the Civil Code (Minpō shinzokuhen chū kaisei no yōkō) in the Japanese metropole in 1927 motivated the colonial government to again push forward with a codification process through reform of the Civil Ordinances. The committee sent out questionnaires around Korea to heads of each local and appellate court asking for their opinions about the reform. The questions, forty-two in all, asked whether the direct application of the Japanese Civil Code was possible in certain cases, or if separate provisions for Korean exceptions still were necessary. The format of the questionnaire showed that the policy of extending the Japanese Civil Code to Korea was now firm, and the colonial government was going to make little provision for those cases that needed exceptional treatment in Korea. Opinions from the heads of the courts varied, but many of them argued for the complete elimination of Korean customary laws and the adoption of the Japanese Civil Code. Some of them supported the use of Korean customary laws but stressed that these exceptional laws should be codified.[37] They were unanimous in their discontent with the state of customary laws as it stood.

Although only indirectly mentioned, the questionnaire's focus was on whether the recognition of ancestral rites inheritance, together with all the idiosyncratic rules of inheritance and succession in lineage laws, should be continued. With the new discourse of family-law reform in the 1930s, the main objective of the initial efforts to import son-in-law adoption became clearer: to dissolve the lineage system into households. Increased advocacy for reform regarding the legal status of ancestral rites was an indication of the intention to weaken (phase out) the lineage system at large. As widow inheritance rights depended on ancestral rites, undermining that practice would be detrimental to widow rights as well.

From early on many Japanese legalists had recognized the problem of acknowledging customs of ancestral rites inheritance and utilizing them as a legal basis for inheritance between Koreans. Hozumi Nobushige argued that the origin of Japanese family law was in ancestor-veneration, and the basic unit of the Japanese society evolved from the clan to the house, and then to the individual. According to Hozumi's framework, the fact that Koreans still practiced ancestral rites inheritance was proof that Korea remained in the state of ancient society, where the religious power of the patriarch overruled individual rights over property.[38] Asami Rintarō (1869–1943), a Japanese judge who worked in Korea between 1906 and 1918, interpreted the customs of ancestral rites inheritance as an indication that Koreans lacked a modern concept of inheritance and, in fact, as proof that Korean society remained in the evolutionary phase of communal lineage society, which, according to Asami, was equivalent to the hunter-gatherer stage. Among all customs of inheritance, it was the ban on nonagnatic adoption that really troubled Asami. This was evidence that Korea remained in the stage of communal ownership; inheritance in Korea, therefore, was a "faux-inheritance" that functioned only to continue communal ownership by kin. Koreans merely "received" (keishō) property and "occupied" (senyū) it until handing it on to the next generation.[39]

Nomura Chōtarō (1881–?), a judge in colonial courts and the mastermind behind family-law reforms in Korea in the 1930s, critiqued the ban on nonagnatic adoption as an indication of "familism" (shuzoku shugi) that evidenced the primitive religiosity of Korean ancestral rites, which believed "that the spirit of the ancestor will not smell [i.e., consume] the sacrifice offered by a nonblood relative." Nomura therefore argued that ancestral rites should be eliminated entirely from the colonial civil laws as a basis for inheritance and that it was outside the realm of legal matters.[40] The right to become the purveyor of ancestral rites was and should be beyond the realm of civil courts to adjudicate. The Korean concept of ancestral rites inheritance was, in this sense, incommensurable with the Japanese concept of inheritance, which was more focused on passing on the status and the property ownership of the household head.[41]

Yet Nomura also argued that such a difference in ancestor-veneration customs need not hinder the legal assimilation of colonial Korea to the metropole. Nomura's argument was that the peculiarity of the Korean custom of ancestor-worship inheritance could be treated outside the legal realm. Conflict over the rightful heir to ancestral rites was, in fact, conflict over property inheritance or the status of the household head. Therefore, there was no need to treat ancestral rites inheritance as a separate legal matter from other matters of inheritance.[42] A number of years later, in 1937, when the Government General collected opinions on revising the Ordinances on Civil Matters, Nomura more explicitly expressed his opinion: "The basic concept of inheritance in Korea should be divided into two categories— inheritance of household headship and inheritance of property—just as in the [Japanese] Civil Code."[43] By writing out ancestor-veneration customs as irrelevant, Nomura eliminated the single major exception in Korean inheritance customs that hindered the full assimilation of Korean family laws to the Japanese Civil Code.

Nomura's strategy, the seemingly benign distillation of legal matters from sociocultural matters, was to ignore and therefore mute the peculiarities of Korean inheritance customs. In Nomura's formulation Korean inheritance customs under-went a major and significant modification that eliminated the role of the lineage and replaced it with that of the household. This was most apparent in Nomura's treatment of the Korean custom on grave-site ownership, which also involved extremely obscure customary laws concerning concepts of traditional statuses and communal ownership. Nomura declared that grave-site ownership was with the household of the lineage heir *(chong'ga),* and the heir to the ancestral rites suc-ceeded to its ownership as part of the privileges attached to the heirship.[44] This was a direct transplantation of household-head inheritance from the Japanese Civil Code. In item 987 the Japanese Civil Code stated, "In inheriting the ownership of the lineage register, the tools of ancestral rites and grave site are included in the privileges of inheriting the household-head status." This, in turn, meant that the grave site was now separated from the influence of the lineage and was subject to sole ownership of the lineage heir. The same applied for the ownership of the grave mountains *(myosan)* or *wit'o,* the ritual estates set aside to fund ancestral rites. Although cultural norms required that the heir consult the lineage representatives before selling such lineage property, it was not a legal requirement. In the legal sense the ownership of such property as lineage burial land resided solely with the individual heir. The fact that ownership of the grave site and ritual estate resided in the individual heir denied the influence of the lineage over that property; on the other hand, it gave the heir full power and greatly strengthened the freedom of action over that property. It specifically meant that the heir was free to sell or mortgage the property, thereby making the lineage property a liquid asset.

In 1934 the Government General promulgated Girei Junsoku (Guidelines for rituals), which aimed to reform family rituals, thus bringing the ancestral rites reforms into the realm of social reform. Girei Junsoku put forth regulations on Korean family rituals, including weddings, funerals, and ancestral rites. In an official note circulated to provincial governors around Korea *(dō-chiji)* on November 10, 1934, the minister of education *(gakubu kyokuchō)* laid out some rules for implementing the guidelines.[45] The governors were to make examples of themselves by following the guidelines; they were to open roundtables and lectures *(junkai kōgen, idō-zadankai)* to explain the objectives of the guidelines to the local

FIGURE 7. An example of a properly moderate wedding ceremony following Girei Junsoku (Guidelines for rituals) and organized by a financial union in Sunchŏn. Abe Kaoru, ed., *Chōsen kōrōsha meikan* [Who's who among (*kōrōsha*) in Korea] (Keijō [Seoul]: Minshū Jironsha, 1935), 175.

people; and they should encourage communities to buy ritual tools as a group and share them. Although the guidelines did not have legal authority, those local variations of rituals that harmed the simplifying objectives of the guidelines were to be strictly forbidden.

The guidelines advised simplification of all rituals. Nomura stated that Korean rituals were too elaborate and wasteful and that they sustained the classic problem of Korean "familism." In the guidelines Nomura proposed to simplify family rituals by scaling them down from lineage-wide celebrations to the parameters of the household. Ceremonial foods were to be simple. Lest anyone be nervous about slighting the ancestors with simple ceremonial food, the Korean translator kindly quoted the "sage" *(sŏnhyŏn)*, Confucius, who exhorted that sincerity *(cheng)* is the most important part of ancestral rites preparation. More important was the shrinking of the boundary of kinsmen with whom these rituals should be celebrated. The ancestral rites ritual should be carried out for only two generations: one's father and grandfather. Rituals for generations at further remove were discouraged. Ancestor-veneration for two generations had been advised for commoners in the Chosŏn dynasty. The higher one's status, however, the more generations for which one was required and privileged to carry out rituals. Rituals for earlier generations meant that one was capable of gathering larger reaches of one's relatives for the occasion.[46] Curtailing the ritual regulations beyond two generations, therefore, meant that the guidelines effectively shrank the reaches of the lineage to the limits of the household.[47] Scaling down elaborate ancestor-veneration rituals was, in some sense, returning to the basics of the Confucian guidelines for rituals proposed in the *Zhu Xi jiali*.[48] The guidelines also tried to suppress communal bonds of the rural community that were buttressed by communal rituals. It discouraged (or banned) the distribution of ceremonial foods and the invitation of nonfamily members to the ritual.

Members of the Korean Central Council supported the new regulations. In 1938 the governor general asked opinions of the Chūsūin members on measures to improve rural society. The majority of the members proposed that family rituals should be simplified.[49] Some even proposed that Korean rituals should be further assimilated to Japanese rituals and customs. The simplification of rituals proposed in the Girei Junsoku reinstated Confucian rationalism, which appealed to rural yangban elites who wanted to dominate social-reform efforts in rural society. In alliance with these rural elites, the state also found a space in the rural community to insert itself.[50]

Such modification of ancestral rites in colonial Korea was reflective of how ancestral rites had been modified by family-state ideology in the metropole. In the Meiji period Japanese ancestor worship went through a similar reformulation. Hozumi Yatsuka (1860–1912), the prominent legal scholar and one of the writers of the Meiji Civil Code, also had emphasized the household level of ancestral rites while deemphasizing communal and social rituals dedicated to ancestors and spirits. This meant a move away from emphasizing the universal world of "spirits" *(seishin)* in Confucianism to instead emphasizing the "spirit of the ancestors" *(sorei)* in ancestor-veneration, which in turn reinforced the family over the community in ancestor-veneration practice. In other words, the framework of Hozumi's theory on ancestor worship was to theoretically thread three different kinds of veneration rites—ancestral rites of the family, communal veneration rites, and the national veneration rites—into a single system of ancestral rites in the household.[51] With the new guidelines, the ancestor-veneration custom condoned and preserved in the 1920s was once more transformed to better fit the agenda of the colonial state: to shrink the boundary of worshippers from that of the lineage to the nuclear household.

The ties of lineage were weakened further in the 1940 Civil-Ordinances Reform, which lifted the ban on nonagnatic adoption, as well as by the implementation of the Name-Change Policy. This significance of the 1940 Civil Ordinances was not lost on contemporaries. The transition from a large-family to a small-family system was the main implication that Kim Tu-hŏn, a Korean family-law specialist, distilled from the 1940 Civil Ordinances. In the essay "Chosŏn kajok chedo ŭi chaegŏmt'o t'ŭkhi hyŏndae ŭi saenghwal kwa kwanryŏn haesŏ [Re-examination of the Korean family system: Especially regarding modern life]" (January 29–February 3, 1939), which he serialized in the Korean daily Tonga Ilbo, around the time when the new Civil Ordinances were promulgated, Kim asserted that the Civil Ordinances were a necessary adjustment to the inevitable trend of the times. In his framework existing Western family culture was the nemesis rather than the Japanese family system. Assimilation to Japanese family laws, Kim argued, facilitated Korea's progress toward an improved version of the Western family system. Kim emphasized that the Korean family system was part of the East Asian (tong'yang) tradition of communal family (chŏnch'e kajok), as opposed to the Western family tradition of individual nuclear family (kaebyŏl kajok); in the former the vertical relationship between father and son was much more important than the marital ties of the couple. Despite some serious shortcomings (p'yedan) in Korean family customs, namely the discrimination against sons of concubines and the ban on widow remarriage, Kim reminded readers that the Korean public should know better than to abandon the communal family system and blindly follow Western family culture. Rather than emulate the Western system of a nuclear family, Kim warned, Koreans should be aware of the shortcomings of Western family culture and be mindful of the principle of the communal family system.

In a similarly titled essay published the following year in the Japanese-language journal Chōsa Geppō (Research monthly), Kim tried to weave his concern for the loss of communalism in Korean society into his analysis of the new Civil-Ordinances Reform. He noted how the reform was the colonial government's effort to adjust to the changing trend of the times: the emergence of the individual and small families over large families and lineages. Kim contended that "the national polity [kokutai] of Japan and the spirit of the civil code and the national morals [kokumin dōtoku] consider the large-family system [dai-kazoku-sei] essential and try to maintain the good and beautiful customs based on these ideals." Yet, he continued, it was the declining communal consciousness among Koreans that led to the growing number of conflicts between families over property and thus necessitated the remedy of the Personnel Affairs Conciliation Law (Jinji Chōserei), which facilitated private reconciliation and compromises to cut down on the number of civil lawsuits (especially during wartime, when the colonial govern-ment was trying to cut down on administrative costs). The new policy on house-hold names, that is, the Name-Change Policy, was another response to the trend of the times, in which "the spirit of communal ownership of families was diminish-ing and the trend of individualistic [consciousness] that emphasizes individual ownership [was emerging.]"⁵²

Kim Tu-hŏn had a negative opinion about the Name-Change Policy, but not because he wanted to defend the Korean lineage system, much less the Korean national identity that postcolonial Koreans associated with Korean surnames. It was, rather, that he was nostalgic about the disappearing communal family tradi-tion, which he believed was the good and common ground of society that Japan and Korea shared. Even though he understood small families to be the origin of ethical and cultural problems, he nonetheless understood it to be part of an inevi-table progress, and the Name-Change Policy was a necessary adjustment to deal with these changes. As such, the emergence of small families, in the form of the household, was a natural and inevitable trend in Kim's analysis.

THE 1940 CIVIL-ORDINANCES REFORM

The 1940 Civil-Ordinances Reform, which was promulgated in 1939 and imple-mented in 1940, comprised two measures. The first measure was the Name-Change Policy, which compelled all Koreans to take Japanese-style surnames *(shi)*. The second part of the revision, son-in-law adoption, was implemented through revis-ing the ban on adopting from outside of the lineage, which had been acknowl-edged as a Korean custom since the beginning of colonial rule.

Beyond increasing the ease of intermarriage between Japanese and Koreans, the 1940 Civil Ordinances, it was expected, would expand women's rights in Korea through the extension of daughters' inheritance rights. Yet the eventual 1940 Civil Ordinances failed to deliver in this regard. Owing to strong resistance from conservative Koreans, son-in-law adoption was implemented, but daugh-ters were not given the right to become household heads on their own and thus gained only half of the daughters' inheritance rights provided for in the Japanese Civil Code. Although these measures largely assimilated Korean inheritance laws into those of the Japanese, there was a critical difference in that daughters could not become heirs on their own. In Japan there were two routes through which a daughter could inherit the household; one was son-in-law adoption, and the other was as a daughter household head. In the latter case the daughter would become the household head and then, when she married, have her husband register as a married-in husband. In other words, Japanese inheritance law was not imported in its entirety in 1939. In the Korean adaptation daughters' direct access to heir-ship was bypassed. In this sense son-in-law adoptions in Korea and in Japan were significantly different, the Korean one allowing daughters many fewer rights. Why this was so is evident in the following Chūsūin meeting minutes, which show that the Government General's continued effort to further assimilate civil laws in Korea was thwarted in part by the strong resistance from some sectors of Korean society, in particular to daughter inheritance rights.

The 1941 inquiry from the Government General to the Chūsūin members ran as follows: "When there is no presumptive heir *[hōtei suitei katoku sōzokunin]* to the household headship, should a daughter *[joshi]* be allowed to inherit the household head [position]?" Opinions varied. Some Chūsūin members were in favor of female heirship, saying that Korea was advanced enough to embrace the idea. They argued that the Korean custom of banning daughters from becoming heirs was backward, growing out of the Confucian way of "revering the men and despising the women *[danson johi;* K: *namjon yŏbi]*" and the thought that women were not capable enough. But now, when women received education, they gained the capacity to take care of a household.[53]

Kanemitsu Soeomi (Kim Kwan-hyŏn) agreed with this evolutionist framework, opining that since women's status in Korea had advanced, it was now suitable for Korea to incorporate matrilineality.[54] Kinoshita Toei (Pak Tu-yŏng) pointed out that Korean family conflicts originated from despising daughters and adopting from other families.[55] Some answered that granting daughters the heirship would be beneficial to preserving the bloodline of the family, or more suitable in terms of "human sentiments *[ninjō]*."

Others disagreed on the grounds that suddenly importing such a custom would be too violent for Korean sentiments. While Japan had a tradition of having daughters as heirs, Korea did not have such a tradition. One critic argued that this was even more drastic than the *muko yōshi* custom, for which Koreans had at least a comparable custom, *teril sawi,* whereby a son-in-law was brought into the daughter's family but, unlike the Japanese counterpart, did not change his surname to his wife's surname and could not inherit the wife's household.[56] There were others even stronger in their opposition. Jokawa Sōkun (Sŏ Sang-kŭn), who apparently had not quite grasped the concept of son-in-law adoption, argued that giving daughters rights to household-head inheritances would be impossible, considering Korean customs. If daughters became heirs, the household would be "discontinued," which would mean a "cruel conclusion" *(chanhokhan kyŏlgwa)* for the family.[57] He meant that if a daughter married a man from another family, the descendants would be of the son-in-law's descent, thereby discontinuing the family line. Many years of effort to convince Koreans to think in terms of household names before patrilineal succession of the lineage does not seem to have succeeded with these Chūsūin members after all.

Yet other Chūsūin members were concerned that daughters' rights could be conflated with widows' rights and that the new measure would strengthen widows' rights. They thought this would endanger the purity of patrilineal lines. Nanjō Chigyō (Hong Chi-ŏp) argued that heirship and son-in-law adoption marriage *(nyūfu kon'in)* should be granted only to the daughter of the household and not the widowed household head, because this would totally change the family relations of the household. Nachiyama Heitoku (Min Pyŏng-dŏk) echoed the wariness about widow household heads. Even when daughters were not given the heirship, if the widow, who was also the mother, became the household head and first passed on part of the household property to her daughter before she arranged adoption of an heir, the adoptee's property inheritance was in name only. Therefore, some measure to limit such treachery on the part of widows should first be implemented.[58]

Another argued that since a woman household head could hide the household property and then remarry, any important legal transaction by her regarding household property should be done with the approval of the court and the supervision of the family council.[59] In short, the long tradition of patrilineal succession painted women as forever outsiders despite the continuing legal reforms that tried to convince Koreans otherwise. In this sense the 1939 reform was not entirely successful in dismantling the lineage system in Korea. While the colonial state was able to legally dismantle the lineage system, it fell short of dismantling the lineage system in the minds of Koreans.

CONCLUSION

As widow household heads once were useful in delineating the boundary between lineage and household, daughter inheritance was the last frontier in the transfer of property ownership from the lineage to the household. Yet this was a line that many Koreans were loath to cross. Even as Koreans were forced to let go of their traditional surnames, which were the markers of their lineage membership, they balked at the idea of letting their daughters inherit family property.

At the very end of colonial rule, daughters did gain a small victory over their mothers. In August 1944 the High Court delivered a decision based on new priority standings that gave daughters precedence over widows in inheriting a man's estate.[60] This decision directly contradicted the mother-versus-daughter case from 1931 mentioned earlier. Even if it was not a granting of full equal inheritance rights to daughters, it did signal a new era of expanded daughter access to household property. Yet, as history would have it, exactly one year later Japanese colonial rule ended with Japan's defeat in the Pacific War, and the Korean legal system saw another round of tumultuous transformations under a newly independent Korean government.

4

Conjugal Love and Conjugal Family on Trial

In 1938 the Chōsen High Court delivered a decision on a divorce case. The wife had sued her husband for a divorce, claiming that he had "gravely insulted" her by keeping a concubine. "Grave insult" *(jūdaina bujoku)* was one of the legitimate grounds for divorce, according to the Japanese Civil Code. The High Court granted the wife divorce and alimony. To the husband's objection that concubinage was a legitimate custom among Koreans, the judge replied, "Just because some sectors of Korean society commonly practice the evil custom of concubinage does not mean that the above criminal activity of the husband should be condoned."[1] The decision overturned a decades-long precedent and was celebrated by the Korean newspaper *Tonga Ilbo* as a significant expansion of women's rights.[2] In another divorce case in 1943, the High Court again granted a divorce on the grounds of concubinage and explained that the decision was a response to how "the way of marriage" *(kon'in no dōgi)* was slowly spreading among Koreans.[3]

These High Court statements reflect the vision of legal assimilation then being applied throughout the Japanese Empire during its wartime period. Although the Japanese maintained separate legal spheres in their colonial territories with different degrees of integration with the Japanese home islands, marriage and divorce matters increasingly were subject to assimilation reforms. The status of concubines changed accordingly. Concubines had been allowed to register as such in the household registers *(minseki)* established in 1909. But in 1915 concubines no longer were allowed to register. When a major reform in the Household-Registration Law (Kosekihō) in 1922 redefined the registry as having a legal effect on all aspects of personal status, including marriage, all unregistered marriages became concubinage. A major reform in the Civil Ordinances in 1922 expanded the categories of family matters to be adjudicated under the umbrella of the Japanese Civil Code rather than Korean customs, with marriage and divorce being critical components.[4] With the 1922 reform, divorce by lawsuit was made possible among Koreans.

Yet the reality of legal assimilation on the ground was further complicated by the fact that even with the expanded application of Japanese laws in Korea, the colonial territory remained a separate legal sphere and the High Court of Korea still had the power to choose when to apply Japanese precedents to Korean cases. If the new Civil Ordinances had been fully implemented in 1922, divorce on the grounds of concubinage would have been possible in Korea, according to the Japanese precedent established in 1918. Instead, citing the prevalence and wide acceptance of concubinage among Koreans, the High Court of Korea declined to grant Korean wives divorce on the grounds of concubinage until the 1938 decision. The shift came only after a transition occurred in the colonial policy in Korea for "forced assimilation" *(kōminka)* by the colonial state, that is, the Government General, following the outbreak of the Second Sino-Japanese War in 1937. The extension of Japanese laws on son-in-law adoption and the Name-Change Policy (Sōshi Kaimei) with the 1939 Civil-Ordinances Reform were further steps toward assimilating the family laws in the colony to those of the Japanese metropole.[5]

The selective application of Japanese divorce laws between 1922 and 1938 created a legal limbo that influenced the meaning of the conjugal relationship, whether as legal marriage or concubinage, in colonial Korea. Affection and companionship emerged in this period as critical components of the conjugal relationship for Koreans.[6] This process, which I call the "affectivization" of the female spouse, coincided with a penchant for romantic love in public media and popular novels. The continuing condonement of concubinage in Korea, ironically, accelerated the affectivization of the female spouse. It was through the debates over concubinage, expressed mainly in newspaper articles and in the civil courts, that ideas about monogamy and conjugal love were most intricately articulated. Also notable was the shifting role of male spouses in this period, with the new legal obligation of male household heads to support their dependents economically. This strengthening of household-head rights through exclusive economic obligations went hand in hand with the affectivization of the female spouse. Yet the new obligation of husbands did not clash with Korean customs in the way monogamy did, and thus discourses about male spouses were nowhere near as close to the center of public attention as were issues concerning concubinage and wives.

The new ideal of conjugal love worked in conjunction with—rather than being antithetical to—the family-state ideology of the Japanese Empire and the family system that the colonial state sought to implement in Korea. Evidence suggests that ideas about conjugal love were sometimes used by both the colonial courts and the Korean litigants to frame nominally illicit relationships as, in fact, monogamous relationships compatible with the colonial family system. The colonial court, over time, moved from the strict enforcement of marriage registration to a looser acknowledgement of common-law marriage, which also assumed affective companionship as its critical component. The qualitative transformation of the conjugal relationship predated the 1938 full assimilation of Korean marriage and divorce law to that of the Japanese metropole, and in this sense "the way of marriage" seems to have spread earlier, at least among some segments of the educated, urban population.

THE PROBLEM OF CONCUBINAGE

There are ten cases of divorce in the *Chōsen kōtō hōin hanketsuroku* (Verdicts from the High Court of colonial Korea).[7] Among the ten, three were direct appeals to have concubinage acknowledged as suitable grounds for divorce. These numbers reflect only those cases that reached the High Court; judging from newspaper reports, the number of cases in the local and appellate courts were much higher. High-profile cases concerning divorce and concubinage frequently appeared in Korean-language newspapers, some of which I analyze here, and are evidence of the great interest among the literate public in the issues of concubinage and monogamy.

Monogamy had become normative in the Japanese metropole only a few decades prior. Concubinage had been rare in Tokugawa Japan, but considered an acceptable way to obtain an heir necessary to continue the family line.[8] After the Meiji Restoration, and after Western culture became the standard against which a culture's level was judged, monogamy became the marker of civilization and concubinage that of backwardness, as early as the 1870s.[9] With the 1872 Penal Code, concubinage in Japan lost legal recognition, although legal recognition of children born out of wedlock *(ninchi)* provided legal protection for concubines and their children.[10]

Monogamy emerged as one of the key topics of discussion, along with equal rights and women's education in the discussion of women's rights in the People's Rights Movement.[11] The norm of companionate marriage, recently established in the West, quickly traveled to Japan in the uneven political terrain of the mid-nineteenth to early twentieth centuries.[12] Ellen Key's *Love and Marriage* (English edition, 1911) was translated by the famous Japanese feminist, Hiratsuka Raichō, in 1913 and influenced many subsequent writings that promoted marriage based on love.[13]

That concubinage during the colonial period in Korea was not merely a stagnant remnant from the past has been pointed out by a number of recent studies. The Korean historian Chŏng Chi-yŏng (Jung Ji Young) has suggested that concubinage practiced by New Women in colonial Korea conformed to the modern liberal ideal of conjugal marriage.[14] In colonial Korea, according to Chŏng, concubinage was an appealing if not ideal option for educated young people as a way to realize the newly circulating ideal of companionate marriage, especially for men

who were already in arranged marriages.[15] So Hyŏn-suk has argued that the prevalence of concubinage in the colonial period was in fact a product of social and
legal changes during the colonial period that had diminished the stigma attached
to concubines and their offspring.[16] Both studies resist the simple characterization
of concubinage as a backward custom suffocating the marriage system in Korea,
instead analyzing it as an institution changing under Japanese colonial rule. I seek
to highlight the particular changes to concubinage that ensued from a dynamic
engagement between cultural discourse and the colonial legal system. Placing the
debate over concubinage at the center of my discussion furthermore enables me
to disrupt the dichotomy between the wife and the concubine, modern and traditional, and examine the legal transformation of the conjugal relationship at large,
which was moving in the direction of the affective conjugal ideal.

The ways in which the affective conjugal ideal in colonial Korea was spread in
part through the extension of the Japanese Civil Code challenges us to rethink
the political, social, and cultural role of the Japanese family system in the Korean
colony. In previous studies on Japan, the affective conjugal ideal was understood to
be an antithesis to the Japanese family system *(ie-seido)*, created by the Meiji state
by drawing on the Tokugawa family customs of the elite samurai class and codifying them in the form of the Meiji Civil Code (1898). The Japanese state utilized the
system to enforce familial hierarchy and to cultivate loyalty and the subordina-
tion of individual desires to family and state prerogatives.[17] Conjugal love, with its
assumption of equality in relationships and free choice of partners, thus stood in
opposition to this state-decreed concept of the family. In literature such tension
often was expressed in the narrative of family drama, where the young protagonist
is forced to choose between love (to his or her partner) and obligation (to his or
her respective parents).[18]

What I show in this chapter, in contrast, is how the conjugal-family ideal itself
was a critical component of the family system that the colonial state was implementing in the Korean colony. The contention over legitimate conjugal relationships that unfolded in the 1920s and the 1930s reveals that a significant part of
the legal assimilation of Japanese colonial rule involved mobilizing the emotions
and desires of the colonized Koreans. The consequence of Japanese family policy
delineated here shows us that the "affective grid of colonial politics" applied not
only to the colonizers but also to the recipients of the colonial policy.[19] The colonial power, in other words, not only shaped the colonized people's sentiments but
also informed their attitudes toward colonial policy. This is not to claim that the
impact of colonial legal policy on Koreans was uniform across all sectors of society. Some scholars have pointed out that, for example, the influence of Japanese
colonial legal policy on Korean family practices was minimal, especially in rural
areas.[20] Even so, I argue that previous scholarship has been too limited in considering the culture of love and romantic relationships that emerged in the 1920s as
something confined to literary and cultural phenomena alienated from the actual

experience of colonized Koreans.[21] New ideas about conjugal love in the urban, literate circles of Korea had an inherent relationship with colonial policy at large, and their impact on Korean society was not confined to literary discourses alone. In the legal debates—and novels—of the time we can see that love and the conjugal ideal were critical to the Japanese colonial project of assimilation as mediums through which the Japanese family system was implemented in colonial Korea. In other words, such emotions and desires were often produced and expressed through particular power relations dictated by the colonial state. Neither was the hegemonic language of love and affection limited to use by the New Women and Men—as evidence shows, such ideals were disseminated through the colonial legal system to a wider sector of Korean society, to the extent that common concubines previously considered passive victims of tradition were among the first to actively embrace the ideal of conjugal love.

CONCUBINAGE IN THE CHOSŎN PERIOD

The distinction between wife and concubine in Korea involved multiple layers of cultural meaning that originated as far back as the Koryŏ-Chosŏn transition period at the turn of the fifteenth century. As part of adopting neo-Confucianism as the official political ideology, the Chosŏn court reformed the polygamous practices of the Koryŏ dynasty along the lines of Confucian family prescriptions and allowed men of its ruling elite yangban class only one wife and one concubine.[22] Other legislation followed that discriminated between a husband's wife and his concubine and, further, between their respective offspring. Only wives could obtain official honorary titles and have a place in the lineage shrine of the husband's family, and only a wife's children could sit for civil-service examinations. Heightened competition between yangban elite families in the late Chosŏn dynasty led to the consolidation of the patrilineal kin group, which involved further stratification between the offspring of wives and concubines within lineage practices. Children of concubines could not be appointed as jural heirs, that is, heirs to ancestral rites, even when the family did not have other sons. Resentment by the children of concubines against such legal discrimination became a mounting social problem by the late Chosŏn dynasty (the late seventeenth to late nineteenth century) and functioned to continually put the problem of concubinage at the center of public demands for social reform.[23]

The definition of concubines in the Chosŏn dynasty depended more on the status of the women's birth families and the process of relationship formation than on the marital status of the male partner. Concubines of men from the elite yangban class were chosen from the commoner or the slave classes, and the relationships lacked the proper rituals required of formal marriages.[24] Because the definition and status of a concubine depended on her lower social origins, a concubine could never become her partner's wife even if his wife died. Records from the Chosŏn dynasty suggest that a relationship with a concubine could be managed in a variety of ways, from a fleeting affair lasting only for a few years to a lifelong connection.[25] A concubine could share dwellings with the main wife or live in a separate dwelling; in the latter case she might reside near the main home or in a remote region where the husband regularly visited, such as his government post or his hometown. Single men might acquire a concubine without also having a wife. A widower had the choice to keep a concubine or marry a new wife.

After the onset of Japanese colonial rule, the definition and status of concubinage shifted from a ritual to a legal basis. Instead of a definition based on family status and rituals, the colonial definition of concubinage was based on a lack of registration in the household registers. Therefore, even a common-law wife acquired through proper rituals could legally be considered a concubine if unregistered.[26] On the other hand, a concubine could always be made a wife by registering her as such, a path that had been denied to concubines in the Chosŏn dynasty.[27] Furthermore, since the Kabo Reforms in 1894 abolished the customary ban on making the offspring of a concubine a jural heir, a concubine in the colonial period possessed increased power in the relationship, as her son had the potential to become the future head of her partner's household.[28]

However, older definitions of concubinage, together with the lower-class stigma attached to the nomenclature, lingered on into the colonial period. Traces of the old ideas about concubinage can be seen in the legal records. Families would call a wife of a widower who remarried a "concubine," even if she was the legally registered wife, if she fit the typical mold of the traditional kind of concubine: a woman much younger than the husband or from a humble background.[29] The social shock about New Women becoming concubines comes as much from the stigma of low class attached to the nomenclature as the adulterous nature of the relationship.

CONCUBINAGE AS MARITAL OFFENSE

The normative form of the conjugal relationship is difficult to ascertain in the context of colonial Korea, because there was a discrepancy between legal codes and social practices. First of all, there was the chronic problem of unregistered marriages. After the first implementation of household registers in 1909, the governor general repeatedly declared the principle that registration was the only means through which personal status was officially recognized (*todokede shugi*), yet many Koreans put off registering a personal change of status, such as birth and marriage. Therefore, many conjugal relationships that Koreans considered legitimate were illegitimate in the eyes of the law. A government inquiry from the 1920s shows the discrepancy between the official vision and the local understanding of legitimate marriage: the local official referred to an unregistered spouse as a "wife," while the bureaucrat from the Office of the Governor General consistently referred to her as a "concubine," emphasizing her unregistered status.[30] One *Tonga Ilbo* article as late as 1934 surmised that all Korean couples delayed registering their marriages and, therefore, experienced a common-law stage at some point.[31]

Another problem was the ambivalent stance of the governor general on the issue of concubinage. While the colonial state officially backed the principle of monogamy, the colonial courts protected concubinage in legal decisions. Although excluded from household registration since 1915, concubines received de facto protection of their status in the civil courts. Until 1922 a concubine, rather than her partner's legal wife, had parental rights over her own children. Often concubines were treated just like wives, especially if there were no living wife with the partner.[32] If she was registered as a concubine before the 1915 ban, she was burdened with the same legal constraints as a wife, such as spousal cohabitation.[33] Even after the 1922 revision of the Civil Ordinances subjected marriage and divorce matters in Korea to the Japanese Civil Code, concubinage still was protected as a legitimate Korean custom in the colonial civil courts.[34] Citing the prevalence of concubinage among Koreans, the colonial court denied Korean wives the right to divorce on the grounds of concubinage. Such decisions blatantly ignored legal precedents established in the Japanese metropole. Japan had made concubinage a legitimate ground for divorce in 1918, with the Japanese Supreme Court (Daishin'in) ruling that concubinage amounted to a "grave insult" to the wife.[35] In other words, even after the official assimilation of divorce laws in 1922, Korean wives were not fully granted the same divorce rights as their Japanese counterparts. Such decisions illustrated for the Korean wives the legal consequences of living in the colony, where the country's supposed cultural backwardness was in fact arbitrated by the colonial state.[36]

Indeed, concubinage in the 1920s seemed to be far from declining. One writer claimed that "more than half of middle-class Korean families keep concubines" and that "some even keep three or four [concubines]," arguing for a national movement to abolish the custom.[37] Reports of concubinage gone awry frequently appeared in the newspapers: women committed suicide to escape the fate of becoming concubines; men killed themselves from the economic pressures of keeping many concubines. In an opinion piece, one writer suggested that Koreans could solve the school-shortage issue by persuading the rich to spend money on building schools instead of on luxury items and concubines.[38] Reports on possible taxation for keeping concubines also adorned the papers.[39] Scandalous accounts that emerged in the mid-1920s about the New Women, those paragons of globalized modernity who had chosen the status of concubines, seemed to further darken the prospect for Koreans overcoming this backward custom.

Despite being condemned as backward, concubinage seems to have been bolstered by the growing importance of love emerging in discourses at that time.[40] In opposition to the criticism that concubinage was an old, backward custom, others began to redefine it as a new and modern relationship based on love. Even in the writings that condemned concubinage as a serious social problem, the authenticity and inherent goodness of the romantic relationship undergirding such relationships were seldom questioned. Many of the newspaper articles that were critical of romantic relationships nonetheless implied that they were based not only on sexual attraction but also emotional and intellectual compatibility by mentioning the comparable levels of education of the two parties. While "moral depravity" in relationships with concubines was still condemned, so were the old customs that confined young people in loveless marriages. While men surely should be condemned for deserting their wives, they also were to be pitied for being trapped in marriages that had been arranged by parents when they were barely teenagers.[41] And while New Women were criticized for luring married men, blame also was assigned to the wives who failed to educate themselves to become suitable companions to their husbands.[42] Both concubines and their partners portrayed themselves not as perpetrators but as victims of old evil customs. Some intellectuals even asserted that concubines should be identified with a new name, the "second wife" *(chei pu'in),* rather than the stigmatized word "concubine" *(chŏp).*[43] Regardless of the morality of their status, they were victims, these intellectuals claimed, of the backward custom of early marriage, which tied men to unwanted marriages before they had a chance to meet companionate mates.

In other words, in a family culture where arranged marriages still prevailed, concubinage was embraced as an alternative institution that enabled young people to realize the new conjugal ideal in a romantic relationship.[44] Chŏng Chi-yŏng posits that perhaps the reason why some New Women became concubines was because concubinage offered them the unique (and rare) path to the affective conjugal-family ideal of the "simple home" *(tanch'ol'han kajŏng).*[45] Far from being ill-informed victims, they entered the extramarital relationship with their eyes wide open; it might have been a better option than what awaited them in a regular marriage: domineering in-laws, absent husbands, burdens of housework and child rearing. Chŏng suggests that, given the common Korean family structure of the stem family, where the married couple cohabited with the parents-in-law, concubinage perhaps provided a respite from the conventional arrangement of marriage.[46] For these women, then, a companionate relationship trumped the legal securities of marriage as the guiding principle in charting their lives.

Yet the hegemonic language of love also increasingly was used to support the monogamous relationship in legal marriages. In the 1920s women in the colonial civil courts began using the language of conjugal love to argue that Korean wives should be allowed to divorce when the marriage lacked an exclusive loving relationship, namely, when their husbands kept concubines. Records of civil litigations show us how colonized Koreans maneuvered within the colonial legal system to articulate or legitimize competing visions of conjugal relationships.

Contemporary newspaper reports about wives who alleged concubinage as grounds for divorce would have served as sources of information for literate women considering their legal options. Divorce cases were the stock of sensational journalism at the time and newspaper readers were treated to all kinds of details of the failed marriages. All too often, the failed marriage involved concubines. Divorce cases mentioning concubinage as the major source of marital discord appear as early as 1921, although the newspapers did not always report the verdicts.[47] In 1928 alone the newspaper *Tonga Ilbo* reported two cases of wives suing over their husbands' concubinage. In the first case, the wife sued for a divorce because, even after she married her husband, he continued to live with his concubine and refused to cohabit with or support her. The article reporting the complaint was titled "Ch'ukchŏp namp'yŏn silso: Sinyŏja ŭi ihon sosong [Doesn't want husband who keeps a concubine: A New Woman's divorce suit]." In the second article the wife implemented the unique strategy of suing her millionaire husband, Kim Yŏn-yŏng, for cohabitation and the expulsion of two concubines instead of divorce. She won the case. The judges in the Keijō Local Court affirmed that "concubinage is not only humanely unreasonable but also the main cause destroying the peace of homes, which should be the foundation of the state." While the title of the article—"Pŏmnyul sang ŭrodo ch'ukchŏp ŭn pulga [Concubinage is even legally impossible]"—clearly overstated the decision rendered by the court, a legal advice column in 1932 nonetheless recommended that a wife should sue for divorce on account of a husband's relationship with a concubine.[48]

In 1928, the same year in which *Tonga Ilbo* reported on two lawsuits over concubinage in the lower courts, Yi Myŏng-rye appealed the lower-court ruling in her divorce suit on the grounds of her husband's concubinage. Although she eventually failed, the case shows how the affective relationship as a primary foundation of legitimate conjugal ties began to emerge as a strong rhetorical tool in legal disputes. This case had all the common trappings of a 1920s divorce case: mother and daughter-in-law conflict; husband's battery of the wife; wife's escape to her natal home; and, in addition, the keeping of a concubine by the husband. The details of the case probably took cues from what was stipulated as grounds for divorce in the Japanese Civil Code, article 813, which had been partially extended to Korea in 1922.[49] Yi argued that the fact that her husband, Pak, kept a concubine and forbade Yi to return to the house amounted to "malicious abandonment" and a "grave insult," both stipulated as legitimate grounds for divorce in article 813. Pak claimed that it was his wife who provided reasons for the marital discord, and, when Yi ran away from the house, he had no other recourse than to take in a concubine to care for his mother and look after household tasks, such as cooking and cleaning. The local and appellate courts (*fukushin hōin*) sided with the husband and denied Yi the divorce. "If this is why the defendant is cohabiting with the concubine," the appellate court's statement concluded, "this does not amount to malicious abandonment or grave insult."[50]

The appellate court did not break any new ground here; it was merely following the precedents in the colonial Korean courts. At that point no Korean woman had had any success in obtaining divorce on grounds of concubinage. Nonetheless,

Yi ventured to appeal to the High Court probably because she, or her lawyer, thought that, with the 1922 reform in Civil Ordinances, the 1918 Japanese Supreme Court decision that declared concubinage a marital offense in Japan should also be extended to Korea.[51] She indeed cited the 1918 Japanese decision that had ruled that malicious abandonment and grievous insult are not affected by whether or not the other party provided a cause or if concubinage resulted from necessity.[52]

To demonstrate that she was due the protection of monogamy, Yi Myŏng-rye seems to have believed that she needed to demonstrate her faith in exclusive emotional ties as the legitimizing grounds for a marital relationship. In her appeal to the High Court, to emphasize that the principle of monogamy also applied to marriages in Korea, Yi declared, "Marriage can be sustained only with love *[ai]* between opposite sexes." She continued, "The love that is necessary for the sustenance of marriage is a holy one and must be singular and exclusive." She went on to criticize the appellate court decision for being discriminatory to women in the colony. To the court's reasoning that the husband's battery and concubinage did not amount to grievous insult because she, the wife, had provided the basis for the marital discord, Yi responded, "[Such a decision] would lead to producing a malicious custom even worse than the current malicious custom of concubinage. . . . Neither the [Japanese] Civil Code nor Korean custom today discriminate between men and women to such a degree. Rather, they condemn concubinage regardless of the reason."[53]

Despite all her efforts, Yi was unsuccessful and the High Court again turned down her appeal for divorce. The judge's reasoning, in short, was that Korea was different from Japan: concubinage was still too common in Korea; therefore, Korean wives should not feel so insulted as to impede the normal continuation of the marriage in such circumstances. The exact wording of the High Court decision decreed the following:

> The evil custom *[heifū]* of concubinage is still prevalent in certain strata of Korean society, and the general public has an accepting attitude toward the practice and does not consider it a grave wrongdoing. If such is the circumstance among Koreans, it is difficult to say that just concubinage alone constitutes a grave enough insult to impede cohabitation with the wife, in other words, grounds for divorce from the wife.[54]

To assert concubinage as grounds for divorce, Korean wives first would have to refute what the colonial court perceived as a prevalent Korean custom and then appeal to the established precedent in the Japanese metropole. How to wage such a struggle successfully was a tricky question, as the High Court's perception was not necessarily based on a quantifiable observation.[55] Legitimizing a separation of legal spheres between Korea and Japan on the basis of different customs seems barely supportable when we realize how closely and quickly some Koreans, such as Yi, were embracing the legal developments in the Japanese metropole. It also shows how the maintenance of such separate legal spheres may have motivated women from the colony, like Yi, to support expedient assimilation of civil laws in Korea. Yi Myŏng-rye expressed her belief not only in her rights as a wife to a monogamous relationship with her spouse but also in her rights to legal treatment equal to her metropolitan counterparts.

What is notable in this case is Yi Myŏng-rye's choice to foreground the language of love and affection in her argument despite the absence of any legal precedent for the effectiveness of such a strategy. The most common and successful reason for divorce was battery, either of the wife or the wife's parents.[56] Another frequent reason was "malicious abandonment" of one spouse of the other.[57] Yi's strategy may well have been based on her perception of the larger trends occurring in the legal arena at the time, but her argument was possibly inspired also by the popular discourse about conjugal love, which often called for exclusive love in marriage.[58] In August 14, 1928, *Tonga Ilbo* printed an opinion piece, "Ihon su ŭi kyŏkchŭng, sinjunghi koryŏ hal munje [Explosion of divorce rate, a problem of careful consideration]." The article noted that divorce itself was not new in Korea, but "what is notable is the divorce that derives from the transformation of thoughts *[sasang pyŏnchŏn]*, that is, the man abandoning a wife after he gained [modern] knowledge, and the wife abandoning a husband after she became progressive." The article also noted that many divorces resulted from a "free love-relationship" *(chayu yŏne)*. The writer then went on to argue that "the true meaning of married life is for the husband and wife to love each other and to pursue the happiness of home," and therefore people should distinguish this true domestic happiness from the "simplistic hedonism" *(tansunhan k'waerak ju'ŭi)* and "fleeting feelings" that are the source of a "temporary love-relationship."

In 1933 *Tonga Ilbo* ran a serialized article, "Segye kakkuk ŭi rihon pŏpche wa chosŏn rihonpŏp ŭi kwagŏ hyŏnjae kŭp changrae [Divorce laws in the world and the past, present, and future of the divorce law in Korea]," that argued for reforms to make it easier for Koreans to divorce. The writer argued that the difficulty of securing a divorce accounted for the increased instances of familial disputes and also the particular problem of female crimes in Korea that involved high rates of husband homicide and infanticide. In the eighteenth installment, the writer cried, "Why should a wife have the obligation to endure when her husband seeks the pleasure of concubinage! Those women who become concubines while fully knowing that the man has a legal wife! Know that you lead the men to concubinage and that you worsen the social system!" The last installment noted that "marriage without love is a constant rape."[59] In 1935 the author of another opinion piece questioned whether "a marriage should be maintained if the couple lacks affection *[aejŏng]*."[60]

These newspaper articles show how the growing discourse about conjugal love was not only transforming the understanding of marriage but also aggressively undermining the legitimacy of concubinage. Even articles that excused particular extramarital relations when the marriage was loveless still believed that the goal was to move toward companionate marriages that would make concubinage unnecessary. Such statements directly challenged the notion, expressed by the High Court judges in Yi's divorce lawsuit in 1928, that Koreans widely accepted concubinage as a legitimate custom. With the emerging popularity of love and the love relationship throughout the 1920s and the 1930s, the dominant discourse at least among the literate urban population seems to have privileged the alignment of love and marriage. Ironically, the demand for expanded divorce rights was one of the consequences of increased expectations of love and affection in marriage. By 1938, the year in which the High Court first granted a divorce to a Korean wife on the grounds of her husband's concubinage, very detailed legal knowledge about divorce and the unique challenges Korean women faced was made available through a popular novel serialized in a Korean newspaper. In this novel, *Millim* (The jungle), by Kim Mal-bong, the wife, Cha-kyŏng, decides to sue her husband for a divorce after she finds out about his concubine and their son. Her lawyer recommends, however, that she pursue divorce through agreement rather than a lawsuit, saying, "Since concubinage is acknowledged to a certain extent in Korea, victory would not easily come to the plaintiff." To this reasoning, Cha-kyŏng retorts, "When the husband gravely insults the wife, isn't this the biggest ground for a divorce?"[61] Cha-kyŏng's statement is very telling, revealing as it does what the contemporary author imagined was possible for an educated woman to know at that time about divorce lawsuits, particularly about the charge of concubinage as a marital offense.

COMPANIONSHIP AND COMMON-LAW MARRIAGE

Newspaper reports and popular fiction reveal that the emerging discourse of love increasingly came to define legitimate conjugal relationships among the urban middle class in the 1920s and the 1930s in Korea. Moreover, some Korean women marshaled the discourse of conjugal love in their attempts to expand divorce rights during the legal limbo of colonial rule regarding concubinage between 1922 and 1938. In this section I analyze a case where the discourse of conjugal companionship was mobilized conversely to legitimize a relationship that was itself on the margin of legality. This case highlights how the emotional component of a conjugal relationship emerged as a central and defining element in this period, to the extent that it overshadowed other elements that had thus far defined legitimate marital relations. In this particular case in 1933, a concubine claimed the status of a wife, and the High Court concurred, stating that her kind of concubinage could be acknowledged as a common-law marriage. The judgment rested on her provision of emotional companionship.

In the case the concubine Yi Sun-gyŏng went to court to claim a piece of property promised to her by her late partner. In a letter (written in 1932) appended to the land title, the man had promised to give her full rights to the land and building "if she continued living with him until 1937." As fortune would have it, he died soon after he wrote that letter and well before the agreed time of cohabitation was up. His son and heir refused to relinquish the property to Yi, claiming that she was not eligible to receive the land because she did not fulfill her contract. In addition, the son argued, the contract involved maintaining a concubinage relationship, which was against "public order and good customs."

The outcome of the litigation hinged on the definition of the concubine's relationship to her partner. Was it an illicit and fleeting relationship or was it a lasting relationship, more akin to that of marriage? The success of the concubine's case hinged on her ability to prove that the relationship was a familial one. Her argument reveals the subtle but important shift that had occurred in the definition of familial relationship, from legal and ritualistic to affective. The concubine Yi proceeded to argue that the land was promised to her not as a wage but as a provision for her livelihood and for the child she was carrying in her womb. To regard such a stable and exclusive relationship as a simple liaison, she argued, would actually contradict "our moral convictions" *(ware no dōtokuteki na shinnen)*. She also pointed out that her late companion did not have a (living) proper wife, and thus her relationship was more like an "engagement" *(kon'in yoyaku)*, eligible for legal protection.

Engagement was protected as a kind of common-law marriage under the Japanese Civil Code, extended with great publicity to the Korean colony in 1923.[62] The measure was meant to protect unregistered marriages to ameliorate public reaction to the 1922 Civil-Ordinances Reform, in which the governor general had recognized only registered marriages as legal *(hōritsukon shugi)*. The provision also could be used by wives of unregistered marriages when their husbands tried to "divorce" them without due support. In such cases the wives could sue for compensation on the basis of the husband not completing the promise of marriage. Notably, "engagement" referred not to all instances of unregistered cohabitation but only to those in the process of becoming registered marriages.[63] Such engagements could be considered full-fledged marriages if they featured a public wedding ceremony, cohabitation, and public representation of the marriage: all that was lacking was the formality of a legal registration. According to a 1935 local court decision, for a cohabitation to be acknowledged as a "common-law marriage," one had to have undergone at least part of the traditional wedding rites of *nap'ye* (exchange of wedding gifts) and *chŏn'an* (wedding ceremony).[64]

Yi Sun-gyŏng seems to have lacked the wedding ritual prerequisite; in its place she listed myriad facets of her relationship to depict that she and her partner had had a lasting relationship, like a marriage. Yi pointed out several things that she thought proved that her relationship with the deceased had been an enduring one: she was formally introduced to him by a go-between, and, after entering his house, she prepared his clothing and food. But the central feature of this "marital relationship" that she emphasized was her affective companionship to her partner.

Considering the age of the late husband when he entered the relationship (sixty), she claimed, he did not enter into it simply to satiate his sex drive but to have a good "companion" *(hanryo)* in his lonely old age. Yi noted more than once that she was chosen to "provide companionship to [the husband] in old age" and also to "console [him] in old age." She also cited an old Korean saying that "one evil wife is better than ten filial sons."

Yi's choice to present herself as the pseudowife was successful. The decision of the judges to approve her claim stipulated the following:

> A husband-concubine relationship [like the one cited] is just like the husband-wife relationship in that they are tied for life. It is not the same as pursuing transient pleasure in invariably seeking concubines or courtesans. One cannot generally dismiss it as being harmful to public order and good customs.[65]

The High Court was in fact making a new distinction in Korean concubinage between a transient and fleeting relationship versus a more lasting one, where "one man and one woman openly live together, having promised to live together for all their lives *[shūsei no kyōdō seikatsu wo yaku shite kōzen dōkyo suru].* In light of the status of concubinage during the Chosŏn dynasty, this distinction is clearly artificial. The judges went on to make sure that their decision did not amount to a categorical sanction of concubinage. They noted that, while the relationship was definitely not marriage *(fūfu kankei),* it was still a legitimate one, akin to a common-law marriage *(jijitsujō no fūfu).*

The High Court acknowledged Yi Sun-gyŏng's familial status not by acknowledging her claim that her relationship was an "engagement" but by introducing a new concept of "common-law marriage" into case history. Nevertheless, the ground on which both Yi Sun-gyŏng claimed legitimacy and the High Court judges rescued the relationship from the category of concubinage is similar. The High Court seems to have been preparing the way for applying the common-law marriage recognition then prevailing in the Japanese Civil Code into Korea, which did occur the following year. The categorical treatment of all forms of unregistered cohabitation as concubinage was being modified, and, critically, the factor that most influenced this redefinition was emotional companionship.

The emergence of emotional companionship as the defining element of a legitimate conjugal relationship was a new phenomenon in the legal scene of this period. The conjugal love that previously had been argued by wives and concubines in their cases did not have the same quality of feeling as the companionship claimed in this case, which definitely lacked a tone of romantic love. Nonetheless, all invoked an emotional element in representing their relationships, which was unprecedented in the prior legal discourse defining legitimate conjugal relationships. What was manifest, especially in the 1933 case, was how an emotional element emerged as the defining factor to tip the scale for a relationship on the margin toward legitimacy. The outcome shows that the ideal of companionate marriage that had emerged in the cultural sphere had made its way into the legal discourse to redefine the conjugal relationship. Such cases show that culture and law were not separate but porous spheres that shaped and bled into each other.

Although companionate conjugal love vied with legality in legitimizing conjugality, it did not subvert the marriage system in any way. If anything, the ideal of conjugal love strengthened the husband's exclusive economic rights within the family (especially with regard to property). To gain ownership of the land promised to her, Yi emphatically redefined the promise of the land not as a wage but as a form of economic support. The concept presumed the wife a dependent of the husband, the sole economic provider of a family. Such a redefinition of familial relationships, according to the sociologist Viviana Rotman Zelizer, was also central to the Victorian ideal of the domestic sphere, which had been built on the assumption that economic transactions were antithetical to the definition of family.[66] Zelizer thus reveals how the belief in separate spheres itself, which claims contradictions and separation between the economic and the affective, hides and nullifies the economic value of service and labor conducted within domestic relationships. What we see in Yi Sun-gyŏng's case is how the equation can work in the opposite direction; by denying the economic value of her domestic and intimate work, the concubine earned recognition of her familial status.

This 1933 case over the familial (or spousal) status of the concubine is in striking contrast to a case from the 1910s, where the concubine claimed independent economic rights as customary and as a marker of concubine status.[67] As the concubine of the late Han Che-uk, Yi Pogwanghwa ran a successful bar-restaurant (chumak) and accumulated great wealth. The problem arose when, after forty years of cohabitation, her partner died. Upon his death, Han's son, Han Kyu-yong, claimed all of the couple's property. When Han sold off 400 majigi of the land, Yi sued to reclaim it. Yi argued that the land was her separate property. "Separate property" was a Japanese Civil Code term for property owned by a wife or an adopted son-in-law (muko yōshi). The term was used to protect a designated property from the household head. While the household head retained management rights over the property, the wife of the adoptee could reclaim the property in case of a divorce or the severance of adoption ties (p'ayang). Thus, the assumption was that a household head held exclusive ownership of a household's property unless it was specially designated as "separate."

Yi argued that, since it was her business, the money she earned from it was hers and so was the land that she had bought with that money. To support her case, she provided two witnesses who testified that they had indeed sold the land to her. The defendants did not deny that it was Yi who had bought the land, but they argued that she merely had been acting on behalf of her husband, who had been sick for many years. They had many witnesses testify that Han Che-uk had, indeed, been ill for many years and thus incapable of handling the legal transactions of business. From the local to the High Court, all the courts acknowledged the defendants' argument. The High Court stated that "it was rare for Korean women to have a separate property [tokuyū zaisan] between 1898 and 1902." Since it was assumed that "separate property" was a rare designation in Korea, the burden fell on Yi to prove otherwise. Ultimately, the fact that Han was sick and probably needed a proxy to carry out his legal transactions tipped the scale against her. Ironically, for the reason that her husband was too weak to carry out his own business, Yi Pogwanghwa was denied all ownership of the property.

A few years later Yi came back before the courts with another case. In the second set of lawsuits, which came to the High Court on February 16, 1917, Yi was once again entangled in a dispute over the ownership of a piece of land. The defendants, headed by Han Kyu-yong, had won a case at the appellate court by arguing that all of the couple's wealth was generated from the initial capital provided by Han Che-uk to Yi's business. Therefore, the land belonged solely to Han Che-uk, which, in turn, made Han Kyu-yong the sole legitimate heir. In an effort to tarnish Yi's reputation, Han Kyu-yong and the other defendants provided seedy details of Yi's life. Before meeting Han Che-uk, she had been married to three other men, and before coming to live with Han, she had been poor and working as a laborer in an oil factory.

In response, Yi argued that it was Korean custom for a concubine to keep the profits from her business as separate property. After examining the evidence, the High Court concluded that Yi's contribution to the business alone made her eligible to become the owner of the land.

The judge stated,

In Korea, when a wife or a concubine cohabits with the husband, any nondesignated [i.e., separate] property should be presumed to be the husband's. But this is only a presumption, [reserved] only [for cases] when the ownership is unclear. When a wife or concubine, while cohabiting with the husband, purchases a property with the profit earned from her own business, she should be given ownership of this property. The previous decision [of the High Court, referring to the case discussed earlier] states only that it is rare for women in Korea between 1898 and 1902 to have separate property; it does not deny [the possibility] for a wife or concubine to have separate property.[68]

The fact that Han Che-uk was sick and unable to contribute to the business now became the basis for legitimizing Yi's ownership of the property and wealth. The High Court also dismissed the appeals court's argument that cohabiting with her husband automatically gave the husband ownership of Yi's profits and wealth. That is, cohabitation did not automatically rule out the possibility of separate property.

In these two cases, Yi Pogwanghwa challenged the definition of concubine that the colonial state and the plaintiffs were trying to impose on her and proactively redefined her own status as a concubine. She resisted the plaintiffs' strategy of using her status as a concubine to slight her moral character. And even though the colonial court tried to suppress her identity as a concubine and treat her as a wife,

Yi reclaimed the meaning of concubinage and embraced her ambiguous position in the family. Although her claim over the property was not granted through validation of her claims to the special customary rights of a concubine, the High Court judges clearly seem to have acknowledged Yi's contribution to the accumulation of property. By ignoring, or bypassing, Yi's claim to the special customary rights of a concubine and treating her rather as a wife with separate property rights, the High Court ended up serving two objectives at once: it delivered justice (by acknowledging rights to what it saw as a rightful owner of the property), and it successfully ignored a backward custom that the colonial government was trying to phase out. Yet what eventually happened was a strengthening of household-head rights, since the concept of separate property could exist only in the context of the monopoly rights of the household head over household property.

In light of the 1933 case, the proactive voice for independent economic rights in the 1917 case is striking. The love and companionship cited in the former presumed economic dependence on the male partner (or husband), thus aligning with the colonial household system more than challenging it. A household system where economic rights were ideally concentrated in the hands of the household head required that other members of the household lack economic rights. One perverse consequence was that a wife's gainful employment (against the husband's will) could be used against her in divorce lawsuits. In a 1931 divorce case, the husband cited the wife's gainful employment outside of the home as evidence of her intention to abandon him. The wife, on the other hand, forcefully defended her employment as a necessary last resort, since her husband had evicted her from their home.[69] The wife eventually won the case and succeeded in obtaining alimony.

Exclusive economic rights did not always work in favor of the husband, however, as they also meant that the husband household head had the obligation to financially support family members. Wives could, and did, utilize this legal tenet to their advantage, citing their economic incompetence to sue their estranged or ex-husbands for economic support.[70] Behind the growing attraction of companionate marriage were the harsh socioeconomic conditions of colonial Korea. It was not only cultural expectations that kept women from employment; the Korean economy provided little opportunities for women to achieve economic independence through employment. Although there exists only limited data about the rate and conditions of Korean employment in this era, we can still deduce some conclusions about the prospects for economic independence for women in colonial Korea.

According to a *Tonga Ilbo* report describing how well the Keijō Job Agency (Kyŏngsŏng Chigŏp Sogaeso) did in the month of March 1929, the largest market for Korean female workers in Kyŏngsŏng (Japanese: Keijō, i.e., Seoul) was as domestic labor for Japanese households: *omani,* who worked as nannies or housekeepers.[71] Of successful female employment seekers, 119 out of 121 were employed in such a capacity. These were the fortunate few who found employment, as opposed to the 343 women who were not successful. The situation for male employment seekers was even more bleak: only 74 out of 298 were successful in finding work.[72] Some people criticized unemployed women as "lazy free-riders" *(nolgo mŏngnŭn saram)* and blamed the "family system" *(kajŏng chedo)* for this phenomenon.[73] Articles from the journal Sin Yŏsŏng also affirm that educated women as well had limited career options. A statistical chart from the journal shows that while some became teachers, the majority failed to move onto gainful employment.[74] Until 1925 Korea lacked tertiary-level schooling for women, and any woman who wanted to continue education after secondary school had to travel abroad to Japan or other foreign countries. An accompanying article in the journal lists letters from students who lamented their postgraduation prospects; many wanted to continue education but lacked adequate funds. Most students complained about the pressure to marry they were receiving from their parents. Another article listed messages of encouragement from school principals; however, their exhortations to young women to continue learning and lead an enlightened life rang hollow in light of the desperation expressed by some of the female students.[75]

With limited prospects for economic independence, the choices for most women were restricted to finding a suitable spouse. Yet even these limited aspirations hit an impasse in the socioeconomic conditions of colonial Korean society. Its underlying economic structure, in addition to the post–World War I economic downturn, allowed for few male white-collar workers who could function as breadwinners for the idealized home. Also, the old custom of early marriage meant that there were only minuscule numbers of eligible bachelors by the time educated women were looking for partners. In such predicaments concubinage may have emerged as a viable option for educated women to acquire a compatible male partner. Behind the prominent and tenacious practice of concubinage existed the intricate workings of the colonial legal system, where women were disciplined into the household system as emotional companions and economic dependents.

The trend toward emphasizing emotional companionship in a conjugal relationship easily transitioned into an expedient wartime emphasis on conjugal ties throughout the Japanese Empire. As war continued after 1931, the ideal of "good wife, wise mother" *(ryōsai kenbo)* took on added importance as the state tried to strengthen women's ideological role on the home front.[76] In addition, conjugal ties as expressed through closer sexual relationships also were emphasized to buttress the state's pronatalist policy.[77] One could argue that the affective conjugal ideal that captured the minds of the educated, urban Koreans during the late 1920s and early 1930s provided a convenient tool for mobilizing these Koreans to support the wartime family ideal of the 1940s.[78] The conjugal-family ideal functioned as a convenient mode of familial relationship that encompassed both Korean desires for family-customs reform and the colonial state's desire for family-law assimilation. The "age of love" was in fact a palatable facade of the age of assimilation.

CONCLUSION

Through the lens of the legal discourse surrounding concubinage and monogamy, I have examined how the language of companionate love influenced a redefinition of legitimate conjugal relationships in the 1920s and 1930s. The hegemonic power of affective discourse in legal and cultural definitions of conjugal relationships, I argue, was a crucial component in the implementation of the colonial household system and played an important role in mobilizing the colonized population toward the successful implementation of legal assimilation and social reform. The ways in which the ideal of conjugal love facilitated legal assimilation in colonial Korea thus challenges the existing understanding of the conjugal-family ideal in colonial Korea, as well as in the Japanese Empire as a whole. While many have understood the conjugal family, or home *(katei),* to be antithetical to the Japanese family system, I argue, rather, that in the context of colonial Korea, the desire to realize the conjugal-family ideal was readily mobilized to support the transplantation of the family system then current in the Japanese metropole to the Korean colony through assimilation of its family laws. Some Koreans, particularly those in urban areas, accepted the expansion of the Japanese Civil Code to Korea as a useful means to reform family customs that they themselves had come to believe were backward and undesirable, such as early marriage and concubinage. Legal assimilation in family matters was one of the few means possible for Koreans to break out of the discriminatory separate legal spheres during colonial rule. The increasing aspiration among some Koreans to enjoy the conjugal ideal appears to have generated colonial consent for assimilationist measures promoted by the Japanese authorities.

In the process of the assimilation of family laws in colonial Korea, another significant process was taking place, namely, the "affectivization" of the female spouse. The more the ideal of the conjugal family gained ground in the cultural discourse, the more emphasized was the role of the affective companionship of the female spouse in the legal discourse. This had a somewhat perverse effect, as we have seen, for as concubines became more like wives and thus part of this affectivization process, they lost independent economic rights.

5

Consolidating the Household across the 1945 Divide

In 1952 a draft of the Family and Inheritance Law section of the new Civil Code of the Republic of Korea was unveiled. The new Civil Code was to replace the Borrowed Civil Code (Ŭiyong Minpŏp), the colonial civil laws from the Japanese colonial era, the use of which had been prolonged because of the Korean War (1950–53), which had broken out before a new Civil Code was fully prepared. The 1952 draft prompted an acute debate between those who wanted to reclaim what they considered Korean traditions from alleged "Japanese distortion" and those who saw an opportunity to push Koreans toward progress and gender equality. Chang Hwa-sun was one of those who were disappointed with the lack of a provision for daughter's inheritance in the draft Civil Code. She argued, "When a household head dies, leaving behind inheritance, no matter how smart and fine a daughter he has, just because she is a daughter . . . the widow has forced on her a distant nephew [as adopted heir] just because he is of the same lineage *[tongsŏng tongbon]*, and he inherits the family's household headship and property; this leads to contradictions in the love between parent and child, and strife and competition between kin."[1]

The resonance of Chang's statement with colonial-period rhetoric is striking: in fact, it repeats the colonial-era logic that criticized the Korean custom of agnatic adoption, which we examined in chapter 3, almost to the letter. This is not surprising, considering that Chang was a public intellectual active during wartime. Having been educated in Japan in the early 1930s, she frequently appeared in newspapers and on the radio, lecturing on various family matters such as how to best manage a simple and frugal household during wartime.[2] Repeating the colonial-period rhetoric about a daughter's inheritance, feminists like Chang argued that the new Civil Code of

South Korea should install son-in-law adoption *(sŏyangja ibyang)* as a way to give daughters inheritance rights. Many other commentators, however, considered son-in-law adoption one of the most egregious examples of the "Japanese distortion" of Korean family customs. After much debate, and albeit with significant compromises, son-in-law adoption was installed in the final draft of the Korean Civil Code.

As this example illustrates, there was a striking continuity between wartime and postcolonial reform discourses. Even though there was a strong public renunciation of "Japanese color" *(woesaek)* in the immediate postcolonial years in South Korea, the influence of colonial rhetoric nonetheless cast a long shadow in the Korean reform discourses of the postcolonial era. The legacy was strongest in the particular reform direction toward creating small families and replacing agnatic kin with daughters as backup heirs, both steps pretty much in line with the family system that the Japanese had been trying to institute in Korea. In other words, postcolonial reforms, while assuming the facade of "anticolonial cleanup," very much continued to be framed in the colonial rhetoric of reform; it can also be said that the family-reform program that began in the colonial period continued its course in the postcolonial period. What is different in the postcolonial years is that the proponents of lineage interests found a stronger voice as the representatives of "tradition" and thus were able to modify key features of the colonial household system. The result was a hybrid of the two family systems, in which Korean families had to comply with the doubly constrictive demands of small families and lineage interests. To understand this trajectory of reform discourses, we need to reexamine the 1940s, which in most previous scholarship has simply been set aside as a "period of darkness *[amhŭkki],*" a time of forced assimilation and national annihilation. How did the reform discourses of the 1920s and 1930s develop through the 1940s and reemerge in 1950s South Korea? And how did this continuity influence Korea's postcolonial reforms?

THE 1940 CIVIL ORDINANCES

The 1940s opened with new Civil Ordinances for Korea, which took effect on February 11, 1940. The date was Foundation Day (Kigensetsu), celebrated to honor the enthronement of the first mythical emperor of Japan and thus chosen to symbolize a new beginning for Koreans as Japanese imperial subjects.[3] Gov. Gen. Minami Jiro, in the pamphlet *Shi seido no kaisetsu: Shi towa nanika, ikani shite sadameruka* [Explanation on the (Japanese-style) surname system: What is a surname; how does one choose it?], explained the significance of that particular new policy as the last step in realizing Japan-Korea unity *(naisen ittai).*[4] As I have noted before, the assimilation of family laws, and thus the facilitation of marriage and adoption among Koreans and Japanese, was considered a critical component in achieving empire-wide unity.[5]

The 1940 Civil-Ordinances Reform implemented two key measures: the Name-Change Policy and the lifting of the ban on nonagnatic adoption in Korea, which enabled son-in-law adoption *(muko yōshi).* Of these two measures, the Name-Change

Policy has received more popular attention and been understood as the quintessential emblem of the forced assimilation policies designed to recreate Koreans as "(Japanese) imperial subjects" *(kōminka seisaku)*. Under the policy Koreans had six months to report their new household names. The response rate was very low at first, but by the end of the six months, about three million households, approximately 80 percent of the total number of households, had reported new names. Even if one did not report a new Japanese-style (i.e., two-character) surname, all Korean surnames became household names after the designated six-month term.[6]

Scholarly understanding of the 1940 reform has focused on cultural assimilation aimed at obliterating Korean national identity *(minjok malsal)*. Understanding the 1940 Civil Ordinances as an essential part of the forced assimilation policy that sought to make Koreans into imperial subjects, Miyata Setsuko interprets the Name-Change Policy as a policy to erase distinctions between the Koreans and the Japanese to facilitate their blending in with Japanese soldiers in the military.[7] With an increasing number of casualties since the war with China began in 1937, the Japanese faced an imminent need to conscript Koreans into the Japanese military. There were several roadblocks to such plans because of the status of colonial Korean subjects within the empire: one was that Koreans lacked representation in the Japanese diet, and another was that they were considered not integrated enough with the Japanese to function seamlessly in a single military unit. Suspect loyalty among colonial subjects was another glaring problem. The late 1930s, therefore, saw a series of legal reforms to incorporate Koreans into the fabric of the Japanese Empire that culminated in the 1940 Civil-Ordinances Reform.

Yet while the Name-Change Policy was part of the wartime assimilation policy to facilitate the mobilization of colonized Koreans, both literally and ideologically, the policy was not necessarily designed to achieve the erasure of distinctions between Koreans and Japanese, but rather to impose integration of the former to the latter. Historian Yang T'ae-ho has pointed out that surname politics had a tradition reaching into the ancient history of Japan, when surnames were important tools for incorporating new subjects into the imperial political structure. Conferring Japanese-style surnames on foreign immigrants was a practice from the era of the Yamato court to the Meiji period, when the emperor conferred new surnames on the Ainu and Okinawan peoples.[8] Many Koreans, therefore, perceived the new Civil Ordinances as a measure of drastic assimilation, but also one with the potential to promote inclusion of Koreans in the Japanese Empire and equality between Koreans and Japanese. Takashi Fujitani has emphasized the potentially powerful equalizing effects of a forceful assimilation policy, which only a desperate war situation could propel. Fujitani argues that the various wartime policies that Japanese deployed to assimilate Koreans into the Japanese nation were not aimed at making them indistinguishable from Japanese but rather at including them, albeit with distinctions along racial lines, into an "enlarged concept of the Japanese nation."[9]

The 1940 Civil-Ordinances Reform, therefore, was aimed at facilitating the integration of Koreans into the Japanese Empire, all the while maintaining the distinctions between Koreans and Japanese. Given a policy that, in effect, served to maintain Korean differences, family laws continued to function as the arena in which differences were articulated. Korean families were again placed in the forever "waiting room," where they were always on the path to progress, which was always equated with the family customs of Japan. The particular traits that were Japanese and promoted as universally progressive were the small family as realized in the household system structured by the household registry *(koseki)*.[10] This was increasingly so in wartime, when Japan was trying to break away from the Western norm and push its own path to "modernity." As a result of maintaining the difference between Korean and Japanese family customs, the 1940s was also the time when certain unique (or allegedly unique) traits of Korean family customs became fossilized and naturalized into "tradition." The postcolonial trajectory of family-law reform was shaped by these two discursive forces that emerged in the 1940s that naturalized the following aspects of the Korean family: nuclearization and the particular Korean custom of inheritance.

In the following section, I examine the reform discourses on the Korean family and family laws in the 1940s, which continued to produce Korea-specific reform plans that hovered around expanding daughters' inheritance rights and weakening widow rights. This direction of reforms was promoted not as particularly Japanese but as a natural trend toward universal progress, made better thanks to the Japanese modifications designed to protect the family community and to impede the harms of Western individualism. These reform discourses in colonial Korea, which shared great commonality with wartime Japanese discourses, ended up shaping postcolonial legal reforms in South Korea to a surprising degree. The conflation of specific reforms in the 1940 Civil Ordinances with the inevitable transition toward the small, modern family continued to shape postcolonial legal reforms. The result was that the reforms for expanding women's rights centered around the issue of son-in-law adoption even after 1945.

RESPONSE FROM THE MARGINS

The impact of the 1940 Civil-Ordinances Reform did not reach all Koreans in the same way, nor to the same degree. In other words, the experience of the 1940 reform cannot be neatly contained in one national or nationalist narrative. One case aptly illustrates how surname customs were not uniformly practiced by all Koreans and how the Name-Change Policy thus affected Koreans differently. The case, from 1942, concerned a eunuch family that tried to adopt an heir to continue the ancestral rites.[11] As eunuchs could not procreate, the long-standing practice was to adopt young boys from poor families to pass down their occupation as well as the responsibility of ancestral rites.[12] Since the Office of Eunuchs (Naesibu) was abolished during the Kabo Reforms, no new eunuchs were appointed to palatial positions, but existing eunuchs stayed in the palace and continued to serve the royal family.[13] But when this particular family decided to adopt an heir in 1923, the family learned to their surprise that the adoption would not be acknowledged. The reason was that, according to the Japanese-instituted Civil Ordinances, the eunuch family had to follow the Korean custom of adoption, which banned nonagnatic adoption. The colonial government allowed no provisions for exceptional cases such as eunuchs. Same-surname adoption, it was decided, was the only recognized norm for Koreans. The eunuch family could not register their adoption. Nonetheless, they took in the intended adoptee, Sun-bong, who was three years old at the time, and brought him up in the family.

When the Name-Change Policy lifted the ban on different-surname adoption, the eunuch family jumped at the opportunity. But just as the adoption arrangement was underway, Sun-bong's adoptive father to be, Hong Pong-gǔn, died unexpectedly, on March 29, 1940. Even with the 1940 reform, different-surname adoption was not allowed for posthumous adoption *(sahu yangja)*. Regardless, Oh Kǔng-hwa, Hong Pong-gǔn's adoptive great-grandfather and the household head, proceeded to register the adoption with the local office on October 30, 1940. Kǔng-hwa's daughter-in-law, Pok-dong, was not happy with this arrangement. If it were not for Sun-bong, now with the Japanese given name of Nagayoshi, she would have been next in line for household-head succession as the *ch'ongbu*, eldest daughter-in-law of the family. When Kǔng-hwa passed away soon after, and Nagayoshi succeeded to the household headship, Pok-dong sued Nagayoshi and his adoptive mother and daughter-in-law for arranging an illegitimate adoption. In her statement she argued, "the plaintiff has the obligation to protect the Harashiro family and continue the household name." Oddly, for a daughter-in-law of a eunuch family, Pok-dong seems to have fully embraced the custom of same-surname adoption. Nagayoshi and other defendants protested that it was nonsense to annul the adoption on the grounds of different surnames, when, in fact, all heirs of the family had been adoptees of different surnames for generations.

In the end, the Chōsen High Court ruled in favor of the adoptee, Nagayoshi. The court produced a convoluted explanation that since the Harashiros were an exception to the custom of adoption in Korea, legitimate adoption for them could be achieved by adopting from families that shared surnames with any of the adopted ancestors. Nagayoshi, by the original name of Yi Sun-bong, coincidentally shared the same surname and lineage seat (Chǒnju Yi-ssi) with his adoptive great-great-grandfather. One suspects that the judges at the courts worked out this far-fetched explanation to protect the adoptee from what they considered an arbitrary accusation on the part of the adoptive grandmother, Pok-dong.

The Name-Change Policy, it can be said, involved a redefinition and reeducation of what surnames meant in Korea. The policy was not simply about taking a Japanese-style surname with two Chinese characters instead of the more common Korean-style surname with one character. Numerous explanatory essays were published in Japanese and Korean at the time to explain the difference between Korean surnames (K: *sǒng;* J: *sei*) and Japanese household names *(shi)*. The writers explained that Korean surnames signified the name of a lineage, while the

Yi Ku-won

Lineage seat of Chŏnju

Oh Kŭng-hwa
(Harashiro
Kŭng-hwa)

Household head at the
time of adoption

Harashiro Pok-dong

Choe Ki-hyŏn

Brought Nagayoshi into the
house (according to Sun-
dong)

Harashiro (Han)
Sun-dong

Hong Pong-gŭn

Arranged adoption of
Sun-bong (according to
Pok-dong)

Harashiro Nagayoshi
(Yi Sun-bong)
(b. 1920)

Brought into the family in
1923; "posthumous
adoption" registered,
October 30, 1940

Lineage seat of Chŏnju

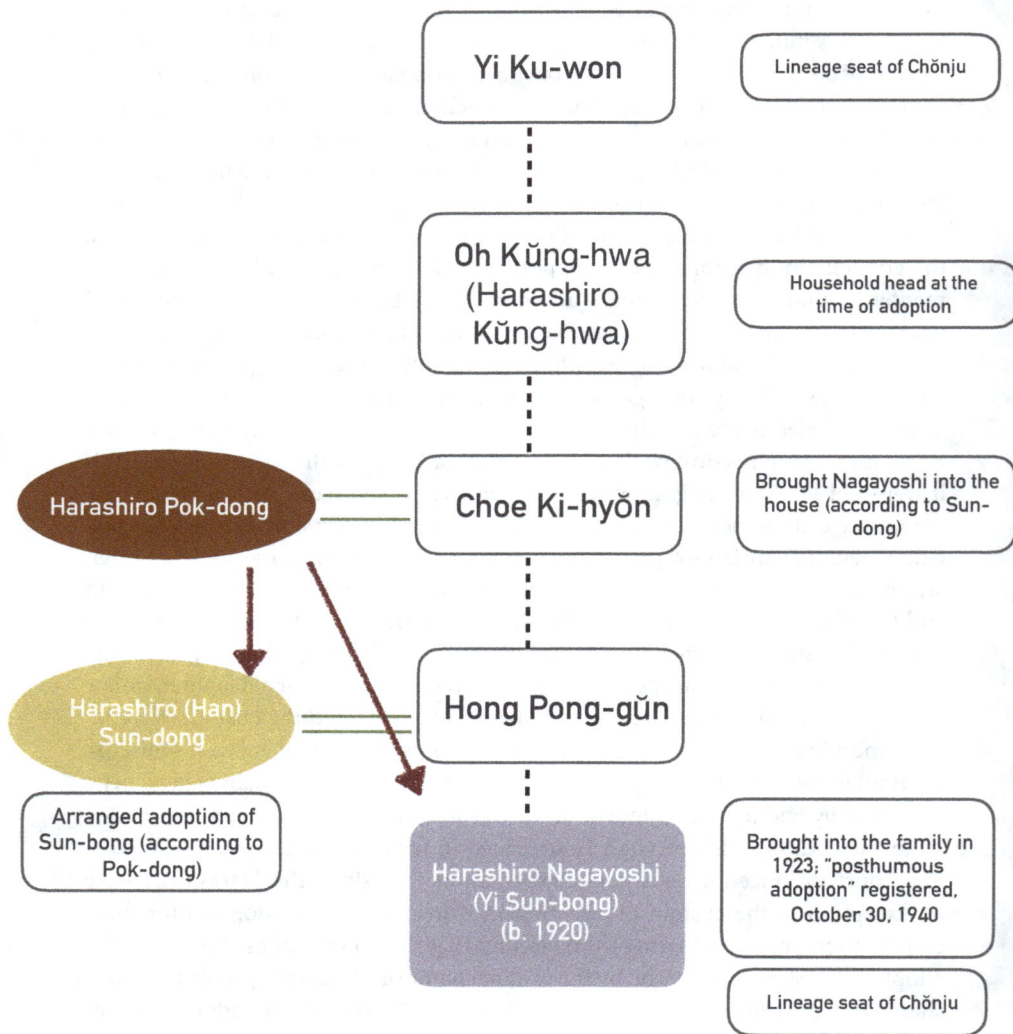

FIGURE 8. A diagram of the Yi Sun-bong case.

Japanese *shi* signified the name of a household. This was a distinction fabricated in 1940 because *sei* and *shi* had been used interchangeably until that point.[14] With the existing understanding that the lineage system was of the past, and the household system was of the future, the Name-Change Policy thus could be depicted as a policy of progress in the family system. In his pamphlet Gov. Gen. Minami Jirō, indeed, explained that, as times advanced, it was more fit for members of Korean

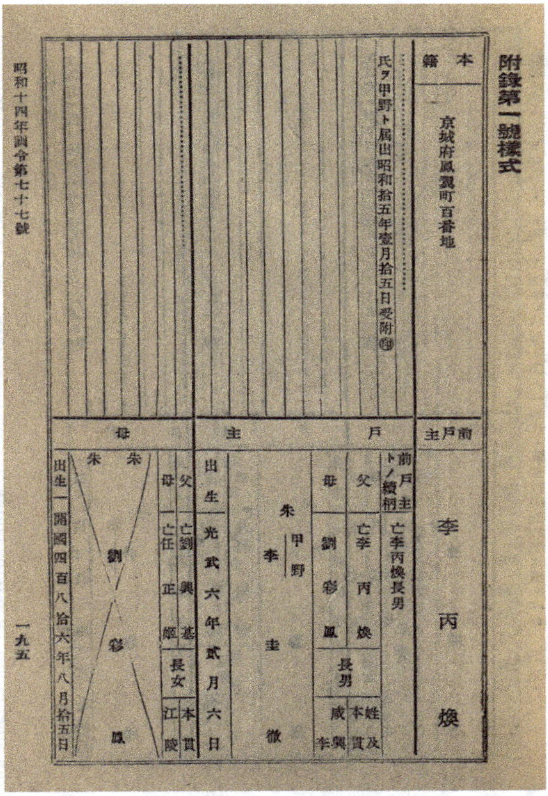
附錄第一號様式

本籍 京城府鳳翼町百番地

氏ヲ甲野ト屆出昭和拾五年壹月拾五日受附㊞

前戸主 李丙煥

前戸主トノ續柄 亡李丙煥長男

戸主 甲野 李圭徹

父 亡李丙煥

母 劉彩鳳

長男

姓及本貫 成興李

出生 光武六年貳月六日

母 劉彩鳳

父 亡劉興基

母 亡任正姫

長女

本貫 江陵

出生 開國四百八拾六年八月拾五日

昭和十四年訓令第七十七號

一九五

FIGURE 9. An example of name-change documentation. After a name change the original Korean surname would be crossed out but remain visible in the registry. Chōsen Sōtokufu Hōmukyoku, *Genkō chōsen koseki hōreishū* [Collection of current household registration laws in Korea] (Keijō [Seoul]: Chōsen Koseki Kyōkai, 1942), 195.

households to have names to designate their household.[15] Both the Japanese and Korean authorities explained the new policy as "adding a household name *[shi]* to the lineage name *[sei]*." In fact, Korean surnames were kept in the household registers, and the new household names (Japanese sounding or otherwise) were added to the existing surnames.[16] In a legal sense, then, it meant choosing a name for the household in addition to (not in place of) the Korean surname.

The Japanese household name also was meant to be shared by all members of the household, which had not been the custom for Koreans. Since all Koreans had to have a household name, regardless of whether or not they reported a "Japanese style surname," all household members ended up bearing the same household name after the Name-Change Policy. This had its most visible impact on married women who hitherto had customarily kept their maiden names. Regardless of whether or not the household chose a new surname, maiden names of married-in women were erased. Helen Kim (aka Kim Hwa-lan), the famous New Woman of Korea and the principal of the Ewha Womans School at the time, pointed to this

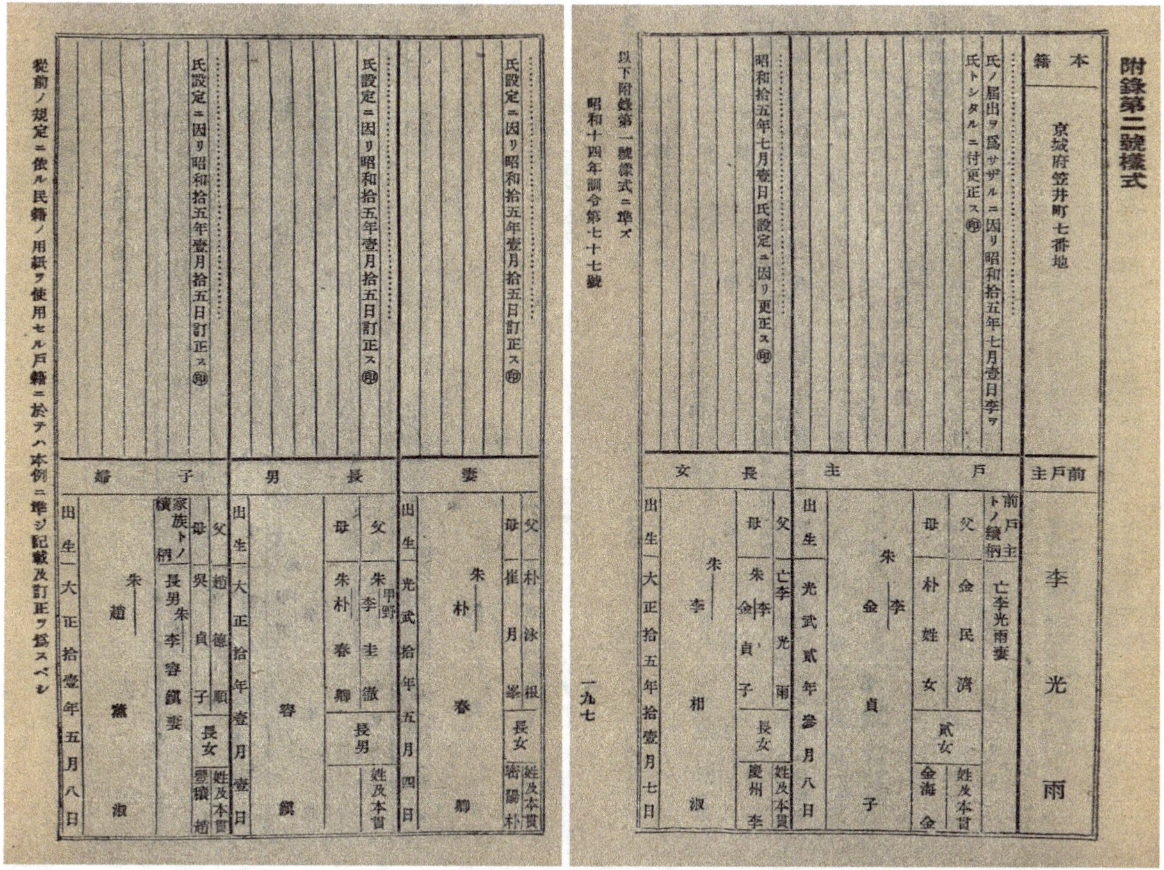

FIGURE 10. An example of name-change documentation. Even if the family chooses not to take a new (Japanese-style) surname, the maiden names of married-in women would be erased. Chōsen Sōtokufu Hōmukyoku, *Genkō chōsen koseki hōreishū*, 196–97.

change as a positive one that elevated the married woman's status from that of a child following her father's surname to an equal partner sharing her husband's surname: "One should appreciate this from the perspective of harmony of the home."[17]

Helen Kim herself took the Name-Change Policy as an opportunity to define her own identity through her choice of a new Japanese surname, "Amagi," instead of the name that members of her lineage decided to all take, "Kane'umi" (K: Kimhae), after the name of their lineage seat. Such collective selection of new household names by lineage groups was discouraged by the colonial state and regarded by Koreans as a way of resistance.[18] The name she chose, Amagi, was more appealing to her because the Chinese characters of the name meant "heaven," a meaningful representation of her Christian identity.[19] The 1940 Civil-Ordinances Reform allowing—even encouraging—each household head to choose a separate household name independent of the larger lineage enabled Helen Kim and her mother, who was a widowed household head, to choose a different name from the relatives of her father's lineage. Such a move was not one of the intended outcomes of the 1940 reform and, arguably, despite Kim's contention, a woman more commonly lost a piece of her identity when she was forced to replace her maiden name with her husband's name. The case of Helen Kim, nonetheless, shows that some women were able to use the Name-Change Policy to express their independence from the patriarchal family order. Kim's case also can be seen as an outgrowth or continuation of discursive trends from decades prior. Kim's feminist appropriation of the new Civil Ordinances was not merely a single anomaly but a product and reflection of the long strand of thoughts developing since the 1920s that framed changes in inheritance rights in the colonial household system as an expansion of women's rights.

Helen Kim's ability to turn the Name-Change Policy to her purposes, however, evidences the fact that, despite the apparently benign explanations of officials, the main objective of the Name-Change Policy was to starkly render the distinction of the household from the lineage rather than simply making Korean surnames similar to those of Japanese. In fact, Government General pamphlets recommended that Koreans not take existing Japanese names but instead invent their own based on the names of their hometown or lineage seat.[20] While the Japanese had to keep their main family's household name when they divided the house (bunke), that is, established a separate household, each household in Korea was encouraged to choose its own name, possibly and preferably different from that of the main branch of the family. It was emphasized that the new surname in Korea was a signifier for the household and not the lineage. Historian Yang T'ae-ho has pointed out that, although the fears of genealogy extinction felt by some Koreans about the 1940 Civil-Ordinances Reform—such as that a family's genealogy record would be abolished—were inaccurate about the policy itself, they were insightful about the potential harm the Name-Change Policy would have on the lineage.[21] The Name-Change Policy was therefore much larger than an issue of names; it was in fact an attempt at structural transformation of the Korean family system itself, a "Japanification of the family system *[kazoku seido no nihonka]*."[22]

REFORM DISCOURSES IN THE 1940S

Exceptional responses to the 1940 Civil-Ordinances Reform illustrate that the impact of the reform cannot be simplified to one result or another. Likewise, the variations among intentions, expectations, and consequences cannot be reduced to simple formulae. The potential for positive benefits of inclusion by way of assimilation was not lost on Koreans and led many cultural nationalists to turn to vociferous support for assimilation measures. Yi Kwang-su, one of the most famous of these cultural nationalists, explained his choice to take a Japanese name with the logic that Koreans would someday achieve equality of status within the Japanese Empire.[23] Yet efforts to maintain the distinction and differences between Koreans and Japanese continued after 1940. As noted, anxiety about diminishing differences between Koreans and Japanese led the Japanese colonial government to discourage Koreans from choosing existing Japanese names.[24] When Koreans, as encouraged, created new names from the names of their hometowns or their professions, the resulting names were easily distinguishable from Japanese names. Even without such easily distinguishable names, Koreans were kept separate legally from the Japanese through the separation of household registers. Continued demands (both from Koreans and from Japanese residing in colonial territories) to allow people to move their "original place of registry" *(honseki)* to different territories of the Japanese Empire were denied, thereby effectively making the distinction between the Japanese and the colonial populations permanent.[25]

Moreover, information about legal, cultural, and customary differences between Japanese and Koreans was continuously disseminated even after the Civil-Ordinances Reform supposedly boosted Korean assimilation. In the early 1940s legal journals in colonial Korea were inundated with articles offering an overview of the history of Korean legal reforms and the differences between the Korean and Japanese legal systems. These articles did more than merely address practical issues about how to treat specific legal matters. As a group, the articles also established narratives about the transformation of family laws in colonial Korea, the nature of the unique customs that remained, what these remaining unique customs said about the nature of Korean society, and how the Japanese colonial rulers—or the writers themselves, as legal authorities in the colony—were to manage this colonial difference. In other words, rather than erasing the differences between Korea and Japan, the so-called forced assimilation of 1940 perpetuated the differences that still remained and their legal significance. In these articles two major differences emerge in striking relief: the lack of daughters' inheritance rights and the continuing inheritance rights of widows in Korea. The bias against daughter's inheritance rights was written into the lineage laws, and partial reforms in the inheritance custom were not enough to change that. But, more significant, we see in the 1940s that legal specialists in colonial Korea clearly were approaching this problem of difference (failure of assimilation) less as a temporal problem, that is, a problem owing to Korea's place in the singular trajectory of progress, but more as a matter of local variances that the colonial legal authorities must manage. Through these discourses that highlighted Korean differences, in other words, the Korean customs based on the lineage system became further fossilized as unique Korean traits, and their longevity ironically was strengthened.

Utilizing his extended expertise in family matters, Nomura Chōtarō continued to publish on the characteristics of the Korean lineage system and explained for his readers the continuing differences in Korean family customs that needed to be attended to in adjudicating family cases in Korea. In several articles published after 1940, Nomura expounded on the differences between Korean family law and the Japanese Civil Code, focusing on matters of family laws such as adoption, lineage property, and inheritance. In a 1941 article Nomura focused on Korean inheritance customs, explaining how the Korean concept of inheritance required lineage membership and followed the laws of ancestral rites inheritance (K: *chesa sangsok*; J: *saishi sōzoku*). Emphasizing to readers that these differences remained after the 1940 reform, Nomura slightly shifted his previous position from the 1920s and the 1930s on reforming ancestor-veneration inheritance. He maintained the position that there should be only two kinds of inheritance in Korea—household-head and property inheritance, just as in the Japanese Civil Code—but now argued that Korea should use the laws of ancestral rites inheritance from the traditional Korean laws of lineage *(chongpŏp)* as the substantial laws for household-head inheritance among Koreans. At the end of the article, Nomura explained his reasoning: he noted that the division between household-head inheritance and ancestral rites inheritance, which was utilized only when widows became household heads, had created much confusion over the rights of the widowed household heads and had led to much conflict among kin. Nomura noted that even though after the 1940 reform the women of the family (i.e., married-in women) came to also use the same family name, lineage laws that excluded widows from full inheritance still stood. To diminish the confusion and conflicts, Nomura suggested that widow inheritance be given a different term than "inheritance."[26] In this new age after 1940, Nomura seems to have approached the enterprise of family-law reform as a reform not toward progress but as a practical adjustment to diminish conflict and simplify adjudication processes.[27] In his view established customs such as lineage laws were to be respected and maintained, and customs less central, such as widow rights, were to be disposed.[28]

Not everyone thought that Korean widow rights were necessarily a backward custom. In "Chōsen ni okeru kafu no sōzokuken [Widows' inheritance rights in Korea]," Judge Yama'uchi Toshihiko compared the difference between widows' rights in Korea and Japan and tried to explain them in terms of the different degrees of belief in communal property rights in the two countries.[29] Unlike many other writers, such as Asami Rintarō, discussed in chapter 3, Yamaʼuchi argued that strong widow rights and the power of testimony in deciding the heir or heir-adoptee in Korean customs proved that Korea had a more individualistic take on property ownership. In contrast, weak widow rights in the Japanese Civil Code showed that Japanese property ownership had a stronger foundation in communal ownership. Of course, by the height of wartime in 1940, individualism was no longer a prized marker of progress but a marker of Western modernity that was to be overcome by the traditional virtue of Japanese communalism.

The son-in-law adoptions that became possible in Korea in 1940 also were the focus of detailed analyses of Korean and Japanese differences. In a serialized essay titled "Chōsen minjirei ni okeru muko-yōshi ni tsuite [On son-in-law adoption according to Korean Civil Ordinances]," the head of the Civil Affairs Section in the Legal Division, Iwajima Hajime, gave an overview of son-in-law adoption in colonial Korea and laid out the differences between son-in-law adoption in Korea and Japan.[30] He noted that, unlike in Japan, an adopted son-in-law in Korea was the presumed heir of the house. In Japan the adopted son-in-lawʼs access to inheritance was determined by his wifeʼs inheritance status. Therefore, if a natural son is born to the parents after the adoption, in Japan the adopted son-in-law lost his heir status, whereas in Korea the adopted son-in-law still had top priority to become the heir. This, the author explained, was owing to the difference in adoption customs between Korea and Japan: adoption in Korea was limited only to adopting an heir, and therefore the adopted son-in-law was "adopted as heir." In contradiction to all the talk at the time about son-in-law adoption expanding a daughterʼs inheritance rights, he added that the Japanese custom of equating the adopted son-in-lawʼs status to heirship with the daughterʼs did not make sense in Korea, where daughters did not have the right to inherit the household headship. The authorʼs purpose in citing the difference was less about casting Korean customs in a negative light than about emphasizing the benefits of such customs. The author, for example, noted that Korean son-in-law adoption solved the Japanese problem of the insecure status of adopted sons-in-law. But the author made clear that the lack of daughtersʼ inheritance rights in Korea was a problem that needed to be reformed. Other differences as well, such as the ban on intralineage marriage, he presented in a negative light and in immediate need of reform.

Other unique customs that persisted in Korea also were topics of scholarly attention. In "Dōsei dōhon fukon [The ban on intralineage marriage]," Korean ethnologist Chang Sǔng-du examined the history of the Korean ban on marrying within the same lineage seat and same lineage. After recounting a long list of examples of such a ban from historical texts dating back to the *History of the Wei Dynasty (Weizhi)* and the Three Kingdoms period (first century BCE to sixth century CE), Chang concluded with the observation that, despite the long ban, there were cases where Koreans had married within the lineage. Citing one survey,

Chang compared numbers from urban and rural areas, showing that the number of marriages within the lineage was higher in urban areas. This, Chang argued, showed that rural areas were more beholden to the old customs. The underlying assumption, of course, was that the old custom of banning marriage within the lineage was backward and irrational and that more enlightened urban residents had managed to free themselves of it.[31]

The works published in the short period between the 1940 Civil-Ordinances Reform and the end of colonial rule in 1945 continued to produce knowledge about Japanese and Korean differences. These pieces of knowledge, as they were not necessarily marked as "Japanese" per se, continued to be disseminated without much alarm in the postcolonial years. The fact that the same Korean scholars, as the few experts on family law in the postwar years, continued to produce similar works did not help to create a clean slate for debates on family customs. Indeed, the long legacy of their works directly influenced the writing of the 1960 Civil Code in South Korea.

THE WRITING OF THE NEW CIVIL CODE

When Japan, after its surrender, relinquished all of its former colonies, the United States and the Soviet Union separated the Korean Peninsula along the thirty-eighth parallel and began the demilitarization process. On the northern side the Soviet Union immediately annulled all Japanese colonial laws. On the southern side, in contrast, the United States annulled only a portion of the Japanese laws. On October 23, 1946, the 1940 Civil-Ordinances Reform was repealed by U.S. military government's Ordinance 122. Japanese-style names that came into effect through the Name-Change Policy were nullified, and all Korean names were changed back to their original forms.[32] Those who wanted to retain their Japanese names needed to make a special request to the authorities within sixteen days. As one of the first reform measures undertaken by the U.S. military government, the repeal of the Japanese-surname policy was supposed to signify a symbolic ending of the Japanese colonial distortion of Korean family customs and the beginning of decolonization in Korea.

Not all Koreans agreed that repealing the colonial Civil Ordinances in Korea was a good idea. Kim Tu-hŏn, in his *Han'guk kajok chedo yŏngu* (Research in the Korean family system), criticized the U.S. policy of repealing the 1940 Civil Ordinances. Kim argued that the repeal, while it abolished the colonial legacy, also did away with the positive features of the law: "The Name-Change Policy was not just implementing Japanese-style names; it also had an aspect of modernizing the Korean family system itself. But the [U.S. policy to repeal the law] did not consider this aspect at all."[33] In an earlier edition of the book, Kim noted that even though the Name-Change Policy was inspired by the political goal of assimilation, the Korean surname would eventually change from being a marker of kinsmen *(hyŏljok ch'ingho)* to a marker of family *(kajok ch'ingho),* following the inevitable trend of lineage reduction.[34] Repeating verbatim his wartime argument (see chapter 3), Kim asserted throughout the book that Korean families had modernized during the colonial period through a process of lineage divisions into smaller nuclear families. A spike in divorce rates and the expansion of women's rights (which also propelled the divorce rate upward) were major and important factors that sped up the process. The 1940 Civil-Ordinances Reform and its policy of household names, Kim pointed out, was another factor that divided the lineage into small families and strengthened the nuclear household.

Apart from the reversal of Japanese surnames, however, all of the colonial civil laws initially were kept intact by the U.S. military government. Ordinance 21, issued November 2, 1945, ordered all Japanese laws to be retained for the practical purpose of sustaining stability for a temporary period, but their use was unexpectedly prolonged because of the Korean War (1950–53). The compilation of the new Civil Code was delayed until 1958 and then came into effect only in 1960. Since Japan replaced its own prewar Civil Code with a new Civil Code in 1948, the prewar Japanese Civil Code had a longer life in Korea. Until the new Civil Code was promulgated, the Borrowed Civil Code *(ŭiyong minpŏp),* that is, the colonial law of Civil Ordinances, was used, which meant that family matters still were decided according to Korean customs as defined by the Japanese colonial courts. Thus, the end of Japanese colonial rule brought about little change in the civil-law regime in the immediate postwar period.[35]

With the delayed preparation of the new Civil Code, the effects of the Borrowed Civil Code continued to run long and deep. Thus, civil lawsuits over widows' rights, for example, manifested striking continuity across the 1945 divide. In a case from 1959, a widow's right to designate an adoptee was challenged.[36] The narrative of the litigation is now familiar to us: a male relative of the widow, backed by the family council *(ch'injokhoe),* forced an adoption agreement, arguing that the widow had refused to choose an heir for her deceased husband and thereby neglected her obligation. In this case the widow had registered some of the household property under the name of her son from a previous marriage. The widow refused the adoption agreement and argued that only she had the customary right to choose an heir. The Supreme Court confirmed that the widow indeed had the right to choose an heir and just because she did not exercise her right was not sufficient proof that she did not have the intention to choose an heir indefinitely. The family council, therefore, could not designate an adoptee and force the choice on her. This case, even to the very details of the litigants' arguments, was strikingly similar to cases from the colonial period described in chapter 3. What is also notable is the similarity of the format and argument of the decision made by the postliberation Supreme Court to that of the colonial High Court. The Borrowed Civil Code in fact continued to influence civil cases even after the promulgation of the new Civil Code, leading one legal scholar to argue for its abolition as late as 2008.[37]

During the time of the new Civil Code's preparation, public anticipation (and anxiety) for a major reform ran high. The so-called Japanese color was to be abolished, it was said, and the tool was to be the newly codified civil law. The family laws in particular were considered a crucial area of decolonization. The problem was that despite the popular perception that postliberation South Korean society had a uniformly negative position against the wartime colonial civil laws, Korea in the immediate postliberation period was quite diversely divided over the direction of the new Civil Code. There was not a consensus over what elements had been Japanese impositions to begin with nor what to do with such a colonial legacy.

Preparation for the new Civil Code began immediately after the new constitution was promulgated in July 1948. The new constitution was based on democratic principles—declaring equal rights for all, including equality of the sexes—with which the civil laws from Japanese colonial rule were deemed incompatible. On September 15, 1948, the Codification Committee (Pŏpchŏn P'yŏnch'an Wiwŏnhoe) was formed to prepare civil, penal, and commercial laws. Legal specialists from all areas were sought to staff the committee.

The process of writing the laws was not smooth. Family law turned out to be especially divisive. Chang Kyŏng-gŭn, one of the committee members, highlighted the special challenges when he published the basic principles of family- and inheritance-law preparation in 1948: "Preparing family and inheritance laws is the most difficult enterprise of all law preparation, as we cannot rely on foreign laws, and there is no consensus among scholars and the public on whether to focus on custom and tradition or progress and reform. . . . I have drafted the following principles focusing on maintaining the good and beautiful customs but effecting gradual progress by discarding those feudal evil customs that are uncivilized, illegal, and unfit for present times and that impede our nation from developing in step with the world."[38]

The "gradual progress" that seemed to be a calm and rational approach to what could be a caustic and divisive matter in a still-volatile postwar environment was in fact a veneer over a conservative position to keep most of the laws from the colonial period. This was not surprising, as Chang himself was a legal specialist from the colonial era, a former judge at the Keijō (K: Kyŏngsŏng, i.e., Seoul) local and appellate courts. His understanding of the effects of the laws and their reformative effects on customs was quite similar to the positions of judges' during the colonial period that we have seen in previous chapters. The following statements sound almost the same as those by colonial-era judges and show how many of the ways of thinking from colonial times continued into the postliberation era. Chang writes in the same essay,

> Our current family and inheritance law . . . has its basis in the unique East Asian family system, which is centered on not the actual communal unit of living but the larger family *[kwangbŏmwi ŭi ka]* under the strong authority of the household head [and maintained by] the desire to contain the community that shares common ancestral rites among the male agnatic kin (eldest son or grandson) and therewith continue

the family [*ka*, that is, *ie* in Japanese] without break. This is true to the Confucian rituals and teachings [*yugyo ŭi yegyo sasang*] and is a beautiful custom from the old [*kore ŭi sunp'ung misok*] but also is behind the times when the familial communal unit is transitioning from a large organization that is a production and management unit to the small organization of a consumption unit; from submission of the individual to enlightenment of the individual: the strong control and management of the family system therefore has turned into an evil custom that impedes the growth of the individual [*kae'in sinjang*].[39]

Chang's observation that the transition from large to smaller families is natural and inevitable was exactly the same as that made by scholars in the colonial period, in particular Kim Tu-hŏn and Chŏng Kwang-hyŏn. The perception led those two to interpret the 1940 Civil-Ordinances Reform, especially the Name-Change Policy, as an impetus toward a modern family system and a corrective to Korea's lineage-oriented family system. Common perceptions and characterizations of the Korean family system on the eve of the liberation carried on into the post-1945 moment and deeply influenced the direction of the postcolonial reforms of the family laws.

Multiple attempts at a consensus on a new Civil Code all went for naught with the outbreak of the Korean War, which led to the death or abduction of many of the committee members as well as the loss of the Chang draft. In the aftermath of the Korean War, the chair of the Codification Committee, Kim Pyŏng-ro, took on the task of writing new family and inheritance laws. Kim had quite a different position from Chang's view of "gradual progress," which essentially meant the maintenance of colonial laws and sharply conflicted with Kim's focus on entirely restoring the good and beautiful customs, that is, returning to the old and traditional ways. Kim himself was a traditionalist and nationalist. Even though he was a Japan-educated former judge and lawyer during the colonial period, he was famous for his work defending Korean nationalists indicted for their activities in pursuit of Korean independence. Many of Kim's statements expose his strong anti-Japanese and nationalist sentiments. His adherence to nationalism meant that he considered restoration of what he saw as Korean tradition more important than realizing the constitutional principles of gender equality. In the revised Civil Code, Kim's position translated into restoring strong patriarchal rights of the household head, maintaining the principle of primogeniture in household-head succession, and abolishing son-in-law adoption.

The draft completed in 1952 drew much criticism from legal scholars as well as the public. Chŏng Kwang-hyŏn criticized the new draft for disregarding the original principles laid out in 1948. Yi T'ae-yŏng, the first female lawyer in Korea, criticized the draft for blatantly violating gender equality, and she began a social movement to repeal the proposed draft. Yi and women's groups presented a formal proposal demanding various reforms, including the abolition of the household-head system itself. They also demanded the repeal of the ban on intralineage marriage. Against such demands from women's groups, the Association of Confucian

Scholars (Yurim) also organized a strong movement. They fiercely defended the household-head system as the foundation of social order and morality. They also considered intralineage marriages as "barbaric acts, unthinkable for humans."[40] Yi recounted that when she and the leaders of nine women's organizations met with Kim Pyŏng-ro, he severely reprimanded them and declared that he would not change one dot in the draft before he was dead.

Legal experts from the colonial era who had been educated in Japan and worked within the legal system, such as Chang Kyŏng-gŭn and Kim Tu-hŏn, pushed for reforms—or to maintain the direction of reforms underway during the colonial period—that would ensure more equality between the sexes. Those who came of age after liberation, students of Chŏng Kwang-hyŏn, were more open to abolishing the colonial family system altogether for more radically progressive laws. But it was the ardent nationalists like Kim Pyŏng-ro who were so strongly against the colonial legal system that they, quite ironically, left the more feminist reforms to be driven by the lingering rhetoric of colonial reform discourses.

When a public hearing was held for the draft Civil Code, an acute debate broke out between those who wanted to continue the modernizing efforts that the Korean legal system had been undergoing during Japanese colonial rule and those who sought to seize the postcolonial moment to rescind the changes that they considered damaging to Korean cultural identity and to return Korea to a precolonial (and pure) past. Some of the hotly debated issues were "lifting the ban on intralineage marriage," "lifting the ban on nonagnatic adoption," "giving daughters rights to household-head inheritance," and "allowing girls to be adopted (as heirs)."[41] The Confucian Association castigated such moves and accused those who advocated them of "trying to damage the beautiful customs of our country."[42]

Chŏng Kwang-hyŏn argued that the whole purpose of writing the new Civil Code was to have a set of civil laws that followed the principles of the new constitution. Therefore, any part of the Civil-Code draft that violated the constitution should be abolished. He noted, "We have already implemented land reform in 1949 to liberate tenant farmers. I cannot find any rational reason why we are not yet implementing laws to liberate women to ensure equality between the sexes and men and wives." Lawyer Yi T'ae-yŏng argued that Koreans needed to abolish any family customs that violated the spirit of the constitution. During the public hearing she declared, "[some family customs] might appear to men as good and beautiful customs but from women's perspective these customs and system could be [a source of] resentment bitter to the bones" [ppyŏ'e samuch'inŭn wŏnhan]; then this good and beautiful custom is not objectively good or beautiful."[43] The audience applauded her statement.

A record of National Assembly Committee hearings relays the high-tension debate over the new Civil Code. On April 8, 1957, the first public hearing for the official draft of the new Civil Code was held. The head of the preparation committee was traditionalist Kim Pyŏng-ro, head of the Supreme Court of Korea

(Tae'pŏpwon'jang), continuing his push for a restoration of Korean family traditions. In the introductory speech that he gave to the committee, Kim emphasized the need for the new Civil Code to restore Korean traditions, the essence of which was patrilineal descent groups and patriarchal hierarchy. Kim believed the tradition of the patrilineal descent group to be the marker of Korean superiority compared to the Japanese. He denounced the demand for gender equality in family laws, arguing that gender equality should be sought in the society, not in the family.[44] Kim further denounced the influence of Japanese laws during the colonial period that tainted the great Korean family tradition. With strong words he denounced the "barbaric family culture of the Japanese" that had no regard for patrilineal descent groups. Kim argued that patrilineal descent was not only moral but scientific. He also stated, "if you sought equality between parents and children, and husband and wife, within the family, nothing could be done. Its ill effects would lead to corrosion of morals and ethics and chaos in society."[45] Not all agreed. The strongest and most vociferous opponent to Kim was Representative Pak Yong-jong, a Japan-educated former newspaper reporter, who pointed out that the Civil-Code draft violated the gender-equality clause of the Korean Constitution and, in that regard, was inferior even to the new postwar Japanese Civil Code. He even claimed that gender inequality was one of the reasons why Korea was colonized by the Japanese in the first place.[46]

The new Civil Code was promulgated in 1959 and implemented in 1960. It ended, ostensibly, the use of the colonial civil laws that had continued after Korea's liberation from Japanese colonial rule in 1945. While the 1960 Civil Code declared that it implemented the principle of equality of the sexes, many of its codes fell short of this promise. The new Civil Code, according to some evaluations, was "a conciliatory law modeled on the basic principles of the old-fashioned lineage law system [i.e., household-head system] but with an effort to eliminate as much as possible those undemocratic aspects of family life that hampered individual freedoms and the development of individuality."[47] The 1960 Civil Code did advance women's rights on some fronts. Wives now had separate and independent property rights from their husbands, they could sue for divorce on grounds of infidelity (just as their husbands could), and they had full legal capacity in household affairs.[48] Inheritance rights for widows were strengthened: widows now had full inheritance rights if there was no one else eligible for inheritance (thus, the temporary provision was eliminated), and their share of inheritance was increased from half to equal to the amount of inheritance direct descendants were due. Yet other stipulations preserved the conservative slant that customary laws had in the colonial period. Wives could be divorced for disharmony with parents-in-law (article 840). Although wives had separate-property rights, any property for which ownership was unclear was assumed to be the husband's (article 830, no. 2). Wives were required to live in the husband's household after marriage (article 826, no. 2), and husbands still had the right of guardianship over wives and children (article

934). A husband did not need to obtain his wife's permission to register a child born out of wedlock in their household register (article 782), while the wife did need such permission. Wives were further disadvantaged in divorce under the 1960 Civil Code. Upon divorce, husbands had precedence over wives for parental rights over children (article 909). Wives did not have the right to ask for a division of household property, nor were they guaranteed alimony.[49] These stipulations were codifications of the patriarchal aspects of the previous customary laws that strengthened household-head rights and fell well short of the principles of equality between individuals and sexes.

A number of these new codes in Korea were even more conservative than the new Japanese Civil Code. For example, while the Japanese Civil Code assumed common ownership by a married couple of any property that had unclear ownership, the 1960 Korean Civil Code attributed such property to the husband's ownership. Also, while the Japanese Civil Code stipulated that the husband and the wife had shared responsibility to provide for the marital economy, the new Korean Civil Code assumed that the husband provided living expenses for the married couple.

Other parts of the law stipulated even fewer rights for women than during the colonial period. The 1960 Civil Code did not merely inherit the household system of the colonial period but modified it by incorporating the stronger male centricity of the Korean lineage laws, where all male members of the lineage were considered equally valuable in continuing the family line. Under the Japanese laws the main branch of the household and its heir, the eldest son, was privileged in inheritance. Therefore, the separate property of the non–household head was not protected as *kazan,* the family property, and was equally distributed among all children, daughters as well as sons. But in the Korean Civil Code, all property held by male members of the household was considered family property, and sons were privileged over daughters in all property inheritance. While during the colonial period daughters had equal share with their brothers, in the case with the non–household head's inheritance, under the 1960 Civil Code daughters were due at most half the share of the inheritance received by their brothers. A daughter's share would be one-third that of her eldest brother, the heir to the household headship. If she already had married out of the household, her share shrank to one-fourth of her brothers' shares. In some sense the 1960 Civil Code in Korea expanded the family-property concept, while the colonial court had contained it by privileging the main line of a household over branch families. As a result, the inequality between the sexes was strengthened in the postcolonial household-head system in Korea compared to the colonial household system.

SON-IN-LAW ADOPTION REINSTATED

Among the very few laws that did change in the immediate aftermath of Japan's defeat, the most dramatic shift occurred in son-in-law adoption. Unlike

Japanese-style family names that were unmistakably recognizable as Japanese and were immediately abolished, the custom of son-in-law adoption was less easily defined as such and had a motley career in the postcolonial Korean civil-law regime. It was first categorically repealed as a Japanese-imposed custom, then reinstated in the new Civil Code of 1960.

Initially, son-in-law adoption was considered one of the quintessential examples of the Japanese distortion and violation of Korean customs, on par with "Japanese-style surnames." A newspaper article in 1949 reported on a Supreme Court (Taebŏbwŏn) decision that nullified son-in-law adoption in South Korea. The article, titled "Sŏyangja nŭn sangsokkwŏn ŏpta, chŏnt'ong sallin taebŏpwŏn sinp'an'gyŏllye [Sons-in-law have no inheritance rights, new decision by the Supreme Court that revived tradition]," described a civil case in which a wife had sued her husband for a divorce and nullification of his son-in-law adoption. In the local court, she had won the divorce case but failed to nullify the son-in-law adoption. The Supreme Court overturned this decision and nullified the adoption. The press interpreted this decision as a denial of son-in-law adoption: "The Japanese colonial state, when it was invading [our land], had imported Japanese law in its entirety, ignoring our customs, but the Supreme Court decided to invalidate the law, since it goes against our custom and the beautiful ways of life [mi'p'ung]."[50]

The Supreme Court reduced the rights of sons-in-law by establishing that (1) sons-in-law cannot become the head of the wife's household, (2) sons-in-law cannot become the adopted sons of the parents-in-law, and (3) sons-in-law do not have inheritance rights to a parent-in-law's property. The decision came long before the details of the new Civil Code were hammered out, but it illustrates how son-in-law adoption could be perceived as a cultural affront in the anticolonial ambience of the early liberation period. With this decision the Supreme Court redefined and overturned what during the 1930s was lauded and advertised as the harbinger of women's inheritance rights.

Son-in-law adoption did not go down in an easy death, as its proponents began pushing for its reinstatement in the new Civil Code. It again appeared as a prominent focus of debate in newspaper reports about the process of drafting a new Civil Code. In 1953, in one of the earliest articles about the new Civil Code, a newspaper reported that "son-in-law adoption at the least would be abolished," betraying some level of anxiety on the part of those who feared that it would not be abolished.[51] Yet another article a few years later reported that allowing son-in-law adoption was in line with the spirit of abolishing "feudal vestiges" (pong'gŏn chan'jae), by advancing equality between sons and daughters in inheritance.[52] Adoption laws were one among the few concessions that women's groups achieved, and son-in-law adoption was reinstated.[53]

In newspaper articles introducing and explaining the new Civil Code, married-in-husband and son-in-law adoption were considered "representative examples of how the new Civil Code confers equal legal rights to women as men."[54] In a newspaper column titled, "14-nyŏn kwa yŏsŏng haebang [Fourteen years (after liberation) and (finally) the liberation of women]," Yi T'ae-yŏng lauded the achievements of the new Civil Code just promulgated in Korea. In an overview Yi laid out the details of the revolutionary changes in family law and concluded that with these changes "women were finally freed from being merely child-bearers [for the husband's family]."[55] Everything was in fact propagated with the language of gender equality and the trend of the times (sidae ŭi pyŏnhwa), and the new adoption law was evaluated in those terms. What is striking here is the similarity between this rhetoric that associated the expansion of women's rights with son-in-law adoption and the rhetoric of the colonial government in the 1930s that was utilized to garner support for the 1940 Civil-Ordinances Reform.

Despite the high anticipation about its progressive effects, the hodgepodge nature of the various compromises made in the 1960 new Civil Code meant that son-in-law adoption was more of an idea than an actual new measure that could benefit daughters. A serious catch in the new adoption system was that if the adopted child was not from the agnatic kin group, he could not inherit the household. Therefore, son-in-law adoption was allowed, but with an awkward restraint: an adopted son-in-law could never become the heir to the household headship, and a son-in-law thus also could not become the heir to ancestral rites. This compromise to uphold the lineal laws by restricting inheritance of the household headship and ancestral rites to agnatic kin was probably to appease the traditionalists in Korea. In addition, the 1960 Civil Code also banned adopted sons-in-law from changing their surnames to the wife's surname. The compromise basically disabled the use of son-in-law adoption and daughter household headship and significantly restricted the inheritance rights of daughters.

Most important, the new laws could not resolve the need and desire of Korean families to designate heirs to ancestral rites and the household headship. Even though the newspapers emphasized that "times have changed," customs and beliefs did not change that much; many Koreans still believed in ancestral rites inheritance and saw adoption as usually a resort only for families that needed an heir to ancestral rites.[56] While the immediate imperative to abolish colonial influences meant that the most apparently Japanese-looking reforms were repudiated, reforms that seemed more neutral and were cloaked in the language of modernity remained intact and had a continuing influence on the direction of reforms into the new Civil Code of 1960. Still, although the discourse of progress toward daughters' inheritance rights that began during the colonial period had a lasting impact on the direction of the reform of family laws after liberation, the new Civil Code failed in many ways to fulfill the promise of modernity for Korean women because the forces of tradition remained strong in practice.

A newspaper legal inquiry section, "Wŏryo ŭngjŏpsil" (Monday salon), in 1958 published a letter from a man in his sixties who was wondering if there were a way he could adopt his son-in-law as his heir. He himself was an only son, as were his father and grandfather, and although he had tried with all his might to produce a natural son for an heir, he had failed. The lawyer explained to him that when the new Civil Code was promulgated, he could very well adopt his son-in-law but that this adopted son-in-law, as nonagnatic kin, would be ineligible to become the heir to the ancestral rites.[57]

Son-in-law adoption remained an unattractive option for Korean men for both cultural and practical reasons. The traditional form of adopted son-in-law, *teril sawi*, was looked down on because it was considered a sign of the man's incompetence and need to depend on his wife's family. An old Korean saying was that if one has only three bushels of coarse barley, one does not become a *teril sawi*. Although a grandchild from an adopted son-in-law could become the heir, for the grandson to become eligible as heir, the marriage had to have been registered as "married-in husband."

A newspaper article from November 19, 1965, titled, "Ddak'han munam dong'nyŏ" (Pathetic only daughter) relays a story about a mother of three who sent an appeal letter to the family court in Seoul about her predicament as an only child. Since her natal family was in danger of being "discontinued" *(chŏlga),* and her husband was unwilling to leave his house for her house, she was considering getting a divorce to marry another man willing to marry into her family *(ippu honin).* To this the judge who answered her query agreed that son-in-law adoption was practically unrealizable in Korea "because of a [culture that emphasizes] men's face," meaning it would be too demeaning for the husband to become an adopted son-in-law. He sympathized with the woman's situation and agreed that family law should be revised to implement "same surnames for married couples." Another article a few days later reintroduced this letter but emphasized the judge's advice that the woman's decision to get a divorce to continue her natal family was an "extremely dangerous thought" *(wihŏm chŏnmanhan saeng'gak).*[58] If the husband was unwilling to become an adopted son-in-law—and such a decision indeed was understandable, it was implied, as son-in-law adoption would scar the husband's pride—the judge advised that the woman had the option to arrange a posthumous adoption for her father. The article then provided information about the procedure in detail, probably to educate the readers challenged with the same issue.

CONCLUSION

Contrary to state propaganda, the 1940 Civil-Ordinances Reform neither abolished discrimination nor granted equal rights to colonized Koreans. Instead, it attempted to strengthen the household system by naturalizing it with the new name system and continuing the reform discourses to expand daughters' inheritance rights. From the perspective of women's and family issues, what is remarkable about the reform was not its conspicuous break from the past as a drastic assimilatory measure but its continued policy toward reform in the inheritance regime. Reform discourses that continued into the 1940s left a long and strong legacy in postcolonial Korea. Examination of civil cases after the 1945 independence and the 1960 new Civil Code shows that the legacy of the colonial customary laws lived on in Korea. Even though the postcolonial period brought a broad abolishment of Japanese legacies, the household system, with its strong patriarchal rights, was slow to be identified as one of those legacies. Although the purpose of strengthening the rights of the household head supposedly was to dismantle the Korean lineage system, rather ironically, household-head rights came to be accepted as a Korean tradition rather than a Japanese import.

Conclusion

It was not until the twenty-first century that the long legacy of the household system finally began its demise. Despite the consistent efforts of women's rights activists, the laws that upheld the small patriarchal family persisted throughout the postcolonial decades.[1] Incremental reforms since the 1970s expanded women's rights in a piecemeal manner, but the system itself was preserved.[2] The movement to abolish the household-head system took a decisive turn in the 2000s, when, in the recession after the International Monetary Fund takeover of Korean financial reform and with the wind of newly kindled anticolonial sentiment at their backs, the reform activists reframed the issue of household-head abolition as an anticolonial project rather than as a movement for gender equality.[3] The new anticolonial strategy proved to be very effective in rekindling public debate over the household-head system. Also helpful was the demographic transformation of Korean society that was underway. The continuing decrease in the birthrate and the shrinking family size meant that society could no longer sustain the demands of the household-head system, where sons were required to continue the family lineage.[4] Beginning in 2003 public hearing sessions over the legality of the household-head system were held at the National Assembly. In 2005 the National Assembly passed a new family law that did away with the household-registration system that had formed the basis of civil administration since the end of the colonial period. With it, the basis of the small patriarchal family too was drastically weakened.

In this book I have shown how it was that the small patriarchal family came to be the dominant unit of family organization in Korea in the colonial period. The process, essentially, was a contest between the strong agnatic principles of the existing lineage system in Korea and the household-based family system from

Japan. Women on the margin of the family emerged as critical agents in articulating the new family boundary established by Japanese colonial policy and abetted by a new legal framework, as it chipped away at the agnatic principles and the strong lineage ties that, in the Japanese view, were a barrier to the integration of Koreans into the larger empire.

The trajectory of household consolidation that I trace shows how this process affected different kinds of women in succession—first widows, then daughters, wives, and concubines. Women often were on the forefront of change, as they had been particularly affected in the course of lineage formation and the strengthening of agnatic principles in inheritance that marginalized their position in family-property relations. A widow's right to inherit the ancestral rites and family property was in an increasingly ambivalent position by the end of the nineteenth century, with some widows driven to the extreme margins of the family. As the various court cases examined here illustrate, widows found new support in protecting their rights in the colonial legal system. As the new colonial policy aimed to strengthen the boundary around the household against the reaches of the lineages, widowed household heads were protected against the claims of lineage elders.

The emergence of new reform discourses in the 1920s and the 1930s that targeted certain Korean customs gave the Government General further pretext for strengthening the household system. This is evident in the debate over a proposal to extend inheritance rights to daughters through allowing son-in-law adoption in Korea, presented as an opportunity for women to gain greater equality. The debate over concubinage, also framed as a modernizing reform, became, as we have seen, an avenue for introducing ideals of conjugal love. The language of conjugal love, used by Korean litigants at this time in lawsuits over divorce and inheritance, worked in the direction of consolidating the household. It proved, as well, to be one of the many instances where change did not necessarily mean equality, as it emphasized a woman's dependence on the household head, the male spouse. In a final effort to legally consolidate the household, in 1940 the Japanese colonial state launched the assimilatory Civil-Ordinances Reform, implementing the Name-Change Policy and son-in-law adoption. The latter, as shown, was compromised by the remnants of Korean agnatic principles. As a result, daughters were not allowed to become heirs to households in Korea. Thus, while the Japanese household system had gained legal predominance in many respects, compromises made along the way led to a severely constrained inheritance regime in the post-1945 era, where adoptees from outside of a lineage (adopted sons-in-law or non-kin) were denied full inheritance rights.

An important aspect of the process of implementing the household system, highlighted by the court cases examined here, is that it was not carried out unilaterally by the colonial state but involved the participation of many Koreans with competing desires. Those who took to heart the promise of equality and the potential of progress excitedly supported assimilatory measures such as son-in-law adoption to bring Korea closer to the goal of equal inheritance. Others criticized such assimilatory measures to defend the agnatic principles of the Korean lineage system. As we have seen, much of the conflict unfolded in the colonial court system, as women litigated against their own families, who were keen to protect the agnatic principles of the lineage system. In other words, the colonial household system was shaped through competing and at times conflicting desires of the Koreans as well as the colonial objectives of the Japanese state. In the end, the desire to maintain the agnatic principle won out, especially after Koreans regained independence in 1945.

How colonized Koreans' desire for a modern conjugal family was implicated in the colonial policy of assimilation sheds new light on the workings of the family system in the Japanese Empire at large. Colonized Koreans' desire for legal assimilation to realize what they perceived as a more progressive and modern conjugal family challenges us to rethink the nature of the Japanese wartime family system and its place in the Japanese Empire as a whole. So far, the dominant understanding has been that the Meiji family system of Japan was antithetical to the modern ideals of family, such as love marriage and conjugal love.[5] In the same vein the cultural ideal of "home" *(katei)* was conceptualized as a resistance point to the "lineal family" *(ie)*.[6] What my analysis of the Korean cases show, in contrast, is that in colonial Korea the modern ideals of family seem to have very much worked *through* the incremental entrenchment of the family system into everyday lives of the colonial subjects rather than in resistance to it. In other words, although the legal arrangement of the Japanese family system was not entirely progressive and modern, it was perceived as such, partly because it was different enough from existing family structures in Korea to propel change toward the direction of modernization. Also, the progressive and "civilizing" language in which it was couched led the colonial subjects to demand more reforms toward the ideals it purportedly espoused.[7] Colonial subjects in Korea, therefore, perceived the Japanese family ideology as potentially conducive to realizing modern family ideals and thus creatively engaged with the Japanese colonial state to further demand progressive measures that would push the colonial customary laws in that direction.[8] The collaborative relationship that emerged in the process challenges the previously dominant view in colonial history that emphasized the dichotomy of domination and resistance. Yet taking the perspective of women in the civil courts has enabled us to see the conflation of modern family ideals and the Japanese family system, with its long legacy in the postcolonial period in Korea, as the small patriarchal family continued to provide the framework of family organization for decades to come.

My goal has been to shift the previous focus of women's history in Korea in several ways. In emphasizing the continuity across the 1945 divide, I move the focus of the history of women's rights in South Korea away from the concerns of postcolonial feminism and place it in the larger historical context. I have also emphasized women litigants from various walks of life entering the colonial civil courts to wage private struggles for personal gains instead of educated women pushing for a more universal expansion of women's rights in the postcolonial period. Many of these women existed outside the small coterie of New Women, who have received the lion's share of attention in the history of women in colonial Korea. The female litigants who appear in this book were not feminists per se, but in their personal legal pursuits they expose for us the legal conundrums of the colonial legal system, where the contradictions and the gaps between the colonial household system and the Korean lineage system posed particular problems as well as new opportunities. Female litigants continue to expose for us the legal conundrum that remains in today's family law even after the 2005 abolition of the household-head system. A series of recent lawsuits over lineage property show that the 2005 abolition began a process larger than just the abolition of the household-head system. In the first decade of the 2000s, two groups of daughters sued their lineage organizations for an equal distribution of profits from the disposal of lineage property. These daughters accused the lineage system of perpetuating sex discrimination, which violated the Korean Constitution. Some lineages excluded daughters who had married; other lineages distributed more money to male members of the lineage.[9] As the title of a newspaper article ("Dasi pulpunnŭn 'ddaldŭl ŭi chŏnjaeng [Daughters' war reignited]") aptly captured, these cases signaled the fact that there was a new kind of attack on the lineage system. By asking for equal inheritance as their brothers, these women were challenging the very basis of lineage organization, namely, the principle of agnatic inheritance. Although both groups of women lost their cases, the mere fact that these cases went as far as they did in the legal system signals that the Korean lineage system may be finally nearing its end.[10]

CHRONOLOGY

Era Names and Events
Koryŏ, 918–1392
Chosŏn, 1392–1910

Legal Changes

Monogamy enforced, 1413
Chastity land (susinjŏn) rescinded, 1466
Widow remarriage banned, 1485

Imjin War, 1592–98

Kanghwa Treaty, 1876
Kapsin Coup, 1884
Sino-Japanese War, 1894–95

Kabo Reforms, 1894–96: Ban on widow
remarriage lifted; discrimination against
sons of concubines (sŏja) abolished

Russo-Japanese War, 1904–5
Korea becomes Japan's protectorate, 1905

Japanese assume control of legal matters 1909

Modern court system first established, 1909

Civil-Registration Law (Minsekihō, 民籍
法), 1909

Annexation of Korea, 1910

Civil Ordinances (Minjirei, 民事令), 1912
Concubines denied registration, 1915
Divorce by consent acknowledged, 1915
Common Law (共通法), 1918

March First Movement, 1919
Beginning of Cultural Rule, 1920

Civil-Ordinances Reform, 1921
(implemented 1922): Japanese Civil
Code extended to parental rights, legal
sponsorship, assistantship, and family
council for persons of legal incapacity

Civil-Ordinances Reform, 1922
(implemented 1923): Japanese Civil Code
extended to age of marriage, judicial divorce,
recognition of child, parental rights, legal
sponsorship, assistantship, family council,
acknowledgement of inheritance, and division of property.

Regulations on Korean household
registration (朝鮮戶籍令), 1922
(implemented 1923)

Manchurian Incident, 1931
Second Sino-Japanese War begins, 1937
Beginning of Korean volunteer corps, 1938

Civil-Ordinances Reform, 1939 (implemented 1940)

Japan's defeat and Korea's liberation, 1945
U.S. military government in (South) Korea
(USAMGIK, 1945–48)

Separate governments established in North
and South Koreas, 1948
(South Korea)

Constitution of the Republic of Korea, 1948

Korean War, 1950–53

New Civil Code (Sin-minpŏp), 1960

Pak Chung-hee presidency, 1960–79

Chun Du-hwan presidency, 1980–87
June Uprising, 1987
Roh T'ae-woo presidency, 1987–93

Kim Dae-jung presidency, 1997–2002
Roh Muhyun presidency, 2002–7

Household-head system *(hojuje)* declared unconstitutional, 2003

Abolition of the household-head system, 2005

Family-relations registry
(kajok kwan'gye tŭngnokpu), 2008

GLOSSARY

ai	愛
apsa	壓死
besseki yizai	別籍異財
biten	美点
Bunka Seiji	文化政治
bunke	分家
bunseki	分籍
chakushi	嫡子
chei pu'in	第二婦人
ch'injokhoe (J: *shinzokukai*)	親族会
ch'inyŏng	親迎
chŏn'an	奠雁
chŏn'ga	傳家
ch'ongbu	冢婦
chong'ga	宗家
chongpŏp	宗法
chŏngri	聽理
chŏp	妾
Chōsen kōtō hōin	朝鮮高等法院
Chōsen kōtō hōin hanketsuroku	朝鮮高等法院 判決録
chumin tŭngnok	住民登録
Chūsūin	中枢院
Daishin'in	大審院
dōka	同化
enchō-shugi	延長主義

fukushin hōin	副審法院
Girei Junsoku	儀礼準則
hanryo	伴侶
heifū	弊風
hojŏk (J: *koseki*)	戸籍
hojuje	戸主制
honseki (K: *pon'jŏk*)	本籍
hōritsukon shugi	法律婚主義
ie (K: *ka*)	家
ie-seido	家制度
ikkei iji	一系維持
inkyo	隠居
isshi dōjin	一視同仁
jo'i (*sosa*)	召史
kaitō (K: *hoedap*)	回答
kajang	家長
kajok kwan'gye tŭngnokpu	家族關係登錄簿
kanshū	慣習
kasan (J: *kazan*)	家産
katei	家庭
katoku sōzoku	家督相続
keishō	継承
ketsu'i	決意
kokumin dōtoku	国民道徳
kokutai	国体
kōminka (K: *hwangminhwa*)	皇民化
koryuksong	骨肉訟
Kosekihō	戸籍法
koshu (K: *hoju*)	戸主
Kyōtsūhō	共通法
mindo	民度
Minjirei	民事令
minjok malsal chŏng'ch'aek	民族抹殺政策
minseki	民籍
mi'p'ung (J: *bifū*)	美風
muko yōshi	婿養子
munhoe	門會
munjung (J: *monchū*)	門中
munki	文記
munkwŏn	文券
musong	無訟
naichika	内地化
naisen ittai	内鮮一体
namjon yŏbi (J: *danson johi*)	男尊女卑
nap'ye	納幣

ninchi	認知
ninjō	人情
nyūfu kon'in (K: *ippu honin*)	入夫婚姻
pan-ch'inyŏng	半親迎
pon'gwan	本貫
Pŏppu	法部
pun'ga pyŏl'jae	分家別財
ryōsai kenbo	良妻賢母
sahu yangja	死後養子
saishi sōzoku (K: *chesa sangsok*)	祭祀相続
sedaeju	世帯主
senyū	占有
shi (K: *ssi*)	氏
shōkei	承継
shuzoku shugi	種族主義
sŏja	庶子
sojong	小宗
somok	昭穆
sŏng (J: *sei*)	姓
Sōshi Kaimei	創氏改名
sŏyangja ibyang	婿養子入養
susinjŏn	守信田
Taebŏbwŏn	大法院
taejong	大宗
todokede shugi	届出主義
tokuyū zaisan	特有財産
tong'gŏ'in	同居人
tongsŏng tongbon kyŏrhon	同姓同本結婚
tsūchō	通牒
tsureko	連子
Ŭiyong Minpŏp	依用民法
ŭmsaji	淫祀地
wit'o	位土
woesaek	倭色
yangban	兩班
Yurim	儒林

NOTES

INTRODUCTION

1. Chōsen Kōtō Hōin Shokika, *Chōsen kōtō hōin hanketsuroku* [Legal decision of the High Court of Colonial Korea], 30 vols. (Keijō [Seoul]: Daesŏng, 1912), 1:440–442 (hereafter cited as *Hanketsuroku*).

2. Korea had a long history of the household-registration system. In chapter 2 I include a detailed discussion of the history of household registry in Korea.

3. Clark W. Sorensen, "The Korean Family in Colonial Space – Caught between Modernization and Assimilation" in Hong Yung Lee, Yong-Chool Ha, and Clark W. Sorensen, ed., *Colonial Rule and Social Change in Korea, 1910–1945* (Seattle: University of Washington Press, 2013), 314–315.

4. This response happened despite the fact that such debates had existed since the 1970s. Han'guk Minsapŏp Hakhoe, *Minsapŏp kaejŏng ŭigyŏnsŏ* [Opinions on the civil-laws reform] (Seoul: Pakyŏngsa, 1981), 109–10. Anti-Japanese sentiment was heightened under the Roh Mu-hyŏn government, as one of his key policy goals was to abolish colonial legacies.

5. Yang Chŏng-ja, "Siron," *Chosŏn Ilbo*, July 12, 2000.

6. Kim A-yŏng, "Ch'wi'jae p'a'il: Chaehon kajŏng dŭrŭi sogari, 'tong'gŏ'in chiuryŏ p'yŏnpŏp kamsu [Investigation file: Agonies of remarried families; Daring illegal methods to erase 'coresident (marker)']," *SBS News*, March 30, 2015, http://news.sbs.co.kr/news/end Page.do?news_id = N1002903175&plink = ORI&cooper = NAVER.

7. By using *lineage* to refer to the traditional Korean patrilineal descent group, I am following the usage of Roger L. and Dawnhee Yim Janelli and Kyung Moon Hwang. Janelli and Janelli, *Ancestor Worship and Korean Society* (Stanford: Stanford University Press, 1982), 2; Kyung Moon Hwang, *Beyond Birth: Social Status in the Emergence of Modern Korea* (Cambridge, MA: Harvard University Asia Center, 2004), 20.

8. Chŏng Kŭng-sik, *Kugyŏk kwansŭp chosa pogosŏ* [Korean translation of the Customs-survey report] (Seoul: Han'guk Pŏpche Yŏn'guwŏn, 1992); Marie Seong-hak Kim, *Law and*

Custom in Korea: Comparative Legal History (Cambridge: Cambridge University Press, 2012), 193–201.

9. Chulwoo Lee, "Modernity, Legality, and Power in Korea under Japanese Colonial Rule," in *Colonial Modernity in Korea*, ed. Gi-wook Shin and Michael Robinson (Cambridge, MA: Harvard University Asia Center, 1999), 28. Such policies had proved important in pacifying Taiwan, which likewise had a governor general with the significant prerogatives of a separate legal sphere. Separate legal spheres allowed colonial governments not only to appease local sentiments but also to exercise legislative power free from the diet of the Japanese homeland. Mark R. Peattie, "Japanese Attitudes toward Colonialism, 1895–1945," and Edward I-te Chen, "The Attempt to Integrate the Empire: Legal Perspectives," in *The Japanese Colonial Empire, 1895–1945*, ed. Ramon H. Myers and Mark R. Peattie (Princeton: Princeton University Press, 1984), 80–127, 240–74. For an example of how separate legal spheres were deployed to discriminate the colonial population in Korea, see Alexis Dudden, *Japan's Colonization of Korea: Discourse and Power* (Honolulu: University of Hawai'i Press, 2005).

10. Jaeeun Kim notes how regional categories became subgroups of the Japanese Empire by managing the "place of origin" or "original place of registry." "The Colonial State, Migration, and Diasporic Nationhood in Korea," *Comparative Studies in Society and History* 56, no. 1 (2014): 34–66, 40–42.

11. Michael Kim, "Sub-nationality in the Japanese Empire: A Social History of the *Koseki* in Colonial Korea, 1910–45," in *Japan's Household Registration System and Citizenship: Koseki, Identification and Documentation*, ed. David Chapman and Karl Jakob Krogness, 111–26 (London: Routledge, 2014).

12. Yi Sŭng-il [Lee Seung-il], *Chosŏn ch'ongdokpu pŏpche chŏngch'aek: Ilche ŭi singmin t'ongch'i wa chosŏn minsaryŏng* [Legal policy of Korean Government General: Japanese colonial rule and the Civil Ordinances of Korea] (Seoul: Yŏksa Pip'yŏngsa, 2008), 348–55.

13. Mark Caprio, *Japanese Assimilation Policies in Colonial Korea, 1910–1945* (Seattle: University of Washington Press, 2009); Jun Uchida, *Brokers of Empire: Japanese Settler Colonialism in Korea, 1876–1945* (Cambridge, MA: Harvard University Press, 2014).

14. Oda Mikijirō (b. 1875) was a judge from Japan who came to Korea in 1906 and served in the Government General as a legal investigator. He worked in customary law–related positions in the Central Council (Chūsūin) and the Government General until 1922. Chōsen Chūō Keizaikai, *Keijō shimin meikan* [Who's who among Keijō [Seoul] citizens] (Keijō [Seoul]: Chōsen Chūō Keizaikai, 1921), 88; Yi Yŏng-mi, *Han'guk sabŏp chedo wa Ume Kenjiro* [Korean judicial system and Ume Kenjiro], trans. Kim Hye-jŏng (Seoul: Iljogak, 2011), 297.

15. Yūhō Kyōkai, ed., *Chōsen ni okeru shihō seido kindaika no sokuseki: Chōsen shihōkai no ōji o kataru zadankai* [The footprints of modernization of judicial system in Korea: A roundtable on the past of the judicial association of (colonial) Korea] (Tokyo: Yūhō kyōkai, 1966), 83.

16. For example, Chŏng Kŭng-sik defines Japanese colonial policy as direct rule through assimilation, which in turn is equated with "national annihilation policy." *Han'guk kŭndaepŏpsa go* [Study of the modern legal history of Korea] (Seoul: Pakyŏngsa, 2001), 186–87. But elsewhere Chŏng himself also advances a more nuanced understanding of assimilation when he notes that rather than an intentional distortion, the colonial customary laws were produced through the Japanese reinterpretation of existing Korean customs within the framework of the Japanese Civil Code and Korean legal acts based on the new

perception of Korean customs. See "Singminjigi sangsok kwansŭppŏp ŭi t'adangsŏng e tae-han chaegŏmt'o: Kajogin chang'nam ŭi samang kwa sangsogin ŭi pŏmwi" [A reexamination of the legitimacy of inheritance customary law from the colonial period: The death of an eldest son who is a family member and the candidates to be heirs], *Sŏul Taehakkyo Pŏphak* 50, no. 1 (2009): 287–320.

17. Chŏng Kŭng-sik, "Singminjigi sangsok kwansŭppŏp ŭi t'adangsŏng e taehan chaegŏmt'o," 312.

18. T. Fujitani, *Race for Empire: Koreans as Japanese and Japanese as Americans during World War II* (Berkeley: University of California Press, 2013)

19. Janet Poole, *When the Future Disappears: The Modernist Imagination in Late Colonial Korea* (New York: Columbia University Press, 2014).

20. This is not to say that the Chosŏn court was not interested in inserting itself in defining the personal status of its subjects. As a state power, the Chosŏn court was interested in regulating its subjects in its own terms, yet these efforts were largely restricted to taxing operations, as manifested in the household registry in the Chosŏn dynasty. Regulations on personal status and family relations were focused mostly on the yangban elite class, but these regulations deferred much to lineage laws, which had claims to Confucian family prescriptions that the Chosŏn court could not ignore. I examine this matter further in chapter 1.

21. Yi Yŏng-mi, "Kankoku kindai koseki kanren hōkyu no seitei oyobi kaisei katei: 'Minsekihō wo chūshin ni" [The establishment and demise of the laws concerning household registers in modern Korea: Focusing on the Household-Registration Law] *Tōyō bunka kenkyū* 6 (March 2004): 1–30.

22. Hong Yang-hŭi [Hong Yang-hee], "Singminji sigi sangsok kwansŭppŏp kwa 'kwansŭp' ŭi ch'angch'ul [Customary law on inheritance during the colonial period and the invention of 'custom']," *Pŏpsahak Yŏngu* 34 (2006): 99–132.

23. Yi Sŭng-il [Lee Seung-il], "Chosŏn ch'ongdokpu ŭi pŏpche chŏngch'aek e taehan yŏngu: Chosŏn minsaryŏng che 11 cho "kwansŭp" ŭi sŏngmunpŏphwa rŭl chungsim ŭro [A study on the legislative policy of the Korean Government General; Focusing on codification of article 11 'customs' of Korean Civil Ordinances]" (PhD diss., Hanyang University, Seoul, 2003).

24. Marie Seong-hak Kim, "Law and Custom under the Chosŏn Dynasty and Colonial Korea: A Comparative Perspective," *Journal of Asian Studies* 66, no. 4 (2007): 1086, 1090.

25. This is where I differ from Kyung Moon Hwang, who has read this transitional period as a continual process of "rationalization" of state power. See *Rationalizing Korea: The Rise of the Modern State, 1894–1945* (Berkeley: University of California Press, 2015).

26. Chŏng Kŭng-sik, "Singminjigi sangsok kwansŭppŏp ŭi t'adangsŏng e taehan chaegŏmt'o"; Yang Hyun-ah, "Hanguk kajokpŏp ŭl t'onghae pon singminjijŏk kŭndaesŏng kwa yugyojŏk chŏnt'ong tamron [Colonial modernity and discourses of Confucian tradition examined through Korean family law]," *Hanguk Sahoehakhoe Hugi Sahoehak Taehoe Palp'yomun Yoyakjip,* December 1998, 345; Hong Yang-hŭi and Yang Hyun-ah, "Singminji sabŏp kwanryo ŭi kajok 'kwansŭp' insik kwa gendŏ chilsŏ: Kwansŭp chosa pogosŏ ŭi hojukwŏn e taehan insik ŭl chungsim ŭro [The colonial judicial officials' perception of family custom and gender hierarchy: On perception of household-head rights in the Customs-survey report]," *Sahoe wa yŏksa,* September 2008, 189.

27. Jisoo M. Kim, *The Emotions of Justice: Gender, Status, and Legal Performance in Chosŏn Korea* (Seattle: University of Washington Press, 2015), 151–52.

28. Martin Chanock, *Law, Custom, and Social Order: The Colonial Experience in Malawi and Zambia* (Portsmouth, NH: Heinemann, 1998).

29. Tamara Lynn Loos, *Subject Siam: Family, Law, and Colonial Modernity in Thailand* (Ithaca NY: Cornell University Press, 2006).

30. Mytheli Sreenivas, *Wives, Widows, and Concubines: The Conjugal Family Ideal in Colonial India* (Bloomington: Contemporary Indian Studies, Indiana University Press, 2008), 46–47.

31. Chen Chao-ju, "*Simpua* under the Colonial Gaze: Gender, 'Old Customs,' and the Law in Taiwan under Japanese Imperialism," in *Gender and Law in the Japanese Imperium*, ed. Susan L. Burns and Barbara J. Brooks (Honolulu: Hawai'i University Press, 2014), 189–218.

32. "New Women" were a group of women who emerged at the turn of the twentieth century in Korea and who received the new Western-style education. They considered themselves pioneers in social reforms concerning women and family and strived for independence and gender equality. For more information, see Kenneth M. Wells, "The Price of Legitimacy: Women and the Kŭnuhoe Movement, 1927–1931," and Kyeong-Hee Choi, "Neither Colonial nor National: The Making of the 'New Woman' in Pak Wansŏ's 'Mother's Stake 1,'" both in Gi-wook and Robinson, *Colonial Modernity in Korea*, 191–220, 221–47. See also Hyaeweol Choi, *Gender and Mission Encounters in Korea: New Women, Old Ways*, vol. 1. (Berkeley: University of California Press, 2009).

33. The image of women being victimized under the colonial laws is mostly owing to the "incapacity of wives *[tsuma no munōryoku]*" clause in the Japanese Civil Code, which was extended to Korea in 1922 and abolished in postcolonial Korea with great fanfare. The restrictions the clause put on married women's legal capacity in Korea was real but also led many to imagine its effects to an extremely exaggerated level. A similarly exaggerated perception about women's oppression during wartime was also seen in Japan under the Allied Occupation and utilized by the United States to legitimize its occupation and reforms in Japan. See Lisa Yoneyama, *Cold War Ruins: Transpacific Critique of American Justice and Japanese War Crimes* (Durham, NC: Duke University Press, 2016), 81–107.

34. Gayatri Spivak, "Can the Subaltern Speak?," in *Marxism and Interpretation of Culture*, ed. Cary Nelson and Lawrence Grossberg (Urbana: University of Illinois Press, 1988), 300.

35. Betty Joseph, *Reading the East India Company, 1720–1840: Colonial Currency of Gender* (Chicago: Chicago University Press, 2004), 19.

36. One exception would be Theodore Jun Yoo's *Politics of Gender in Colonial Korea: Education, Labor, and Health, 1910–1945* (Berkeley: University of California Press, 2008), which analyzes lives of prominent New Women on a par with the lives of working-class women, considering their lives as a product of the larger sociopolitical transformation of the Korean colony.

37. Chŏng Kŭng-sik, *Kugyŏk kwansŭp chosa pogosŏ*, 264.

38. Chŏn Pyŏng-mu, *Chosŏn ch'ongdokpu chosŏnin sabŏpkwan* [Korean judges in the Korean Government General] (Seoul: Yŏksa kong'gan, 2012), 98; Pak Ŭn-kyŏng, *Ilcheha chosŏn'in kwan'ryo yŏngu* [Research on Korean bureaucrats under the Japanese colonial rule] (Seoul: Hangminsa, 1999).

39. Official agreement of the Judicial Association was one of the ways customs became legally acknowledged *(hōnin)*. Chŏng Kŭng-sik, *Han'guk kŭndaepŏpsa go*, 275. See also

Chŏng Chong-hyu, *Kankoku minpōten no hikakuhōteki kenkyū* [Comparative research on the Korean Civil Code] (Tokyo: Sobunsha, 1989); and Marie Kim, *Law and Custom*, 175.

1. WIDOWS ON THE MARGINS OF THE FAMILY

1. *Pŏppu sojang* [Appeal letters to the Ministry of Legal Affairs] (Seoul: Sŏul Taehakkyo Kyujanggak, 2004), 1:403.

2. Kim Sŏnju and Chu Chin-o, *Han'guk yŏsŏngsa kip'i ilki: Yŏksasok mal ŏmnŭn yŏsŏngdŭl ege malgŏlgi* [Reading deep into Korean women's history: Speaking to the voiceless women in history] (Seoul: P'urŭn Yŏksa, 2013), 175. See also Martina Deuchler, *The Confucian Transformation of Korea: A Study of Society and Ideology* (Cambridge, MA: Council on East Asian Studies, Harvard University, 1992), 279.

3. Jungwon Kim, "'You Must Avenge on My Behalf': Widow Chastity and Honour in Nineteenth-Century Korea," *Gender and History* 26, no. 1 (2014): 131.

4. By the seventeenth century it became increasingly difficult to obtain official recognition for a chaste widow, and, as competitions became more heated, more widows committed suicide to obtain honor. Kim and Chu, *Han'guk yŏsŏngsa kip'i ilki*, 177.

5. Jungwon Kim, "You Must Avenge."

6. Kim Pyŏng-hwa, *Han'guk sabŏpsa* [Judicial history of Korea], 3 vols. (Seoul: Iljogak, 1979), 1:20–22.

7. Young Ick Lew, "Minister Inoue Kaoru and the Japanese Reform Attempts in Korea during the Sino-Japanese War, 1894–1895," *Journal of Asiatic Studies* 27, no. 2 (1984): 152–65.

8. Andre Schmid, *Korea between Empires, 1895–1919* (New York: Columbia University Press, 2002), 29.

9. Hwang, *Beyond Birth*, 59–61.

10. Dorothy Ko, *Cinderella Sisters: A Revisionist History of Footbinding* (Berkeley: University of California Press, 2005), 17.

11. Yi Suk-in describes the knowledge about family customs around the world, including of India, that was introduced to the Korean reading public in the late nineteenth century to criticize and promote reforms of the family customs of Korea. [Lee, Sook-in], "Kŭndae ch'ogi yŏgwŏn ŭi yuip kwa yugyo ŭi chaegusŏng [Influx of women's rights in the early modern period and the reconstruction of Confucianism]," *Kukhak Yŏngu* 24 (2014): 194. Later-period essays also repeat this knowledge. For example, in "Kaega munje," *Tonga Ilbo*, July 22, 1924, 1, the author discusses the need to promote remarriage of widows and cites how the British successfully abolished the practice of sati in India.

12. "Haesŏl [Explanation]," in *Pŏppu sojang*, 1:5.

13. Hanguk Kojŏn Kugyŏk Wiwŏnhoe, ed., *Kugyŏk taejŏn hoet'ong* (Seoul: Koryŏ Taehakkyo Ch'ulp'anbu, 1960), 600–601; Kim Pyŏng-hwa, *Han'guk sabŏpsa*, 1:202. This must have been common knowledge: one plaintiff mentions this in his appeal letter. *Pŏppu sojang*, 3:240.

14. *Pŏppu sojang*, 7:523.

15. Some cases were clearly civil in nature. In one case a widow accused her in-laws of taking away her land, house, and clothes. *Pŏppu sojang*, 5:94.

16. Spivak, "Can the Subaltern Speak?," in Nelson and Grossberg, *Marxism and Interpretation*.

17. Jungwon Kim, "You Must Avenge," 140.

18. Jungwon Kim notes that it was almost impossible for a widow to sue someone for slander. "You Must Avenge," 142. This is an interesting contrast to what Jisoo Kim has argued about the opportunities that existed for women during the Chosŏn dynasty for public legal appeals. But the cases that Jisoo Kim examines in *Emotions of Justice* do not concern the reputation of chastity of the female plaintiffs themselves.

19. Veena Talwar Oldenburg, *Dowry Murder: The Imperial Origins of a Cultural Crime* (Oxford University Press, 2002). I thank Mithi Mukherjee for this reference.

20. Cho Yun-sŏn states that many widows sued family members (both marital and natal families) to maintain property in the late Chosŏn dynasty, despite strong social chastisement of such lawsuits. Cho argues that this was because of the change in property inheritance customs that threatened widows' property rights. *Chosŏn hugi sosong yŏngu* [A study of lawsuits in the late Chosŏn dynasty] (Seoul: Kukhak Charyowŏn, 2002), 160–62.

21. Deuchler, *Confucian Transformation of Korea,* 273–74.

22. There is a debate over whether it was the elite society or the state that initiated this push toward more tightly ordering family life to conform to Confucian patrilineal norms. Against the dominant argument that Chosŏn society underwent a process of Confucianization led by the elite class through a long and slow dissemination of Confucian ideology, Chŏng Chi-yŏng argues that it was initiated by the Chosŏn court through the implementation of patrilineal principles in the *hojŏk* registration. *Chilsŏ ŭi kuch'uk kwa kyunyŏl: Chosŏn hugi hojŏk kwa yŏsŏngdŭl* [The construction of and fissures in order: Women and household registry in the late Chosŏn dynasty] (Seoul: Sŏgang Taehakkyo Chulp'anbu, 2015), 393–96.

23. Mun Suk-cha, *Chosŏn sidae chaesan sangsok kwa kajok* [Property inheritance and family in the Chosŏn dynasty] (Seoul: Kyŏng'in Munhwasa, 2004), 100–105.

24. Roger and Dawnhee Janelli shows how ancestral rites function to keep the community of agnatic kin together, through cooperative work and communal gatherings, as well as the flow of resources through such occasions. *Ancestor Worship,* 123–29.

25. Kim Mi-yŏng, *Kajok kwa ch'injok ŭi minsokhak* [Folk studies of family and kinship] (Seoul: Minsogwon, 2008), 114–15.

26. Chŏng Chi-yŏng [Jung Ji Young], "Chosŏn hugi ŭi yŏsŏng hoju yŏngu: Kyŏngsangdo tansŏnghyŏn hojŏk taejang ŭi punsŏk ŭl chungsimŭro [A study of female household heads in the late Chosŏn dynasty: Analysis of census registers from Tansŏng County, Kyŏngsang Province] (PhD diss., Sŏgang University, Seoul, 2001), 93.

27. Chŏng Chi-yŏng points out that loss of house headship did not necessarily mean a decline of status for mothers. In most cases, the mother still kept the rights to manage family property. *Chilsŏ ŭi kuch'uk kwa kyunyŏl,* 165–71.

28. The uxorilocal marriage custom supposedly was supportive of polygyny, which was an acceptable form of marriage among the aristocracy. Deuchler, *Confucian Transformation of Korea.* Whether polygyny was a normative practice during Koryo is in dispute. Chang Pyŏng-in argues that it was a nonnormative practice among a small number of aristocrats that was problematized in the Koryŏ courts. *Chosŏn chŏn'gi honinje wa sŏngch'abyŏl* [Marriage system in the early Chosŏn period and gender discrimination] (Seoul: Ilchisa, 1997), 50–53.

29. Deuchler, *Confucian Transformation of Korea,* 65–71.

30. Kim and Chu, *Han'guk yŏsŏngsa kip'i ilki,* 148.

31. Yi Hyojae, *Chosŏnjo sahoe wa kajok: Sinbun sangsŭng kwa kabujangje munhwa* [Society and family in Chosŏn dynasty: Elevation in status and patriarchal culture] (Seoul: Han'ul, 2003), 92.

32. Kim and Chu, *Han'guk yŏsŏngsa kip'i ilki*, 149–50.

33. Deuchler, *Confucian Transformation of Korea*, 66–69.

34. Yi Hyojae, *Chosŏnjo sahoe wa kajok*, 106.

35. Martina Deuchler, "Propagating Female Virtues in Chosŏn Korea," in *Women and Confucian Cultures in Premodern China, Korea, and Japan*, ed. Dorothy Ko, Jahyun Kim Haboush, and Joan R. Piggott (Berkeley: University of California Press, 2003), 153.

36. Mark Peterson, *Korean Adoption and Inheritance: Case Studies in the Creation of a Classic Confucian Society* (Ithaca, NY: Cornell University Press, 1996), 107.

37. Cho Ŭn's argument is that women's marginalization in property inheritance rights began before the Confucianization of the Korean family system. "Kabujangjŏk chilsŏhwa wa pu'in gwŏn ŭi yakhwa [Establishment of patriarchal order and the weakening of wife rights]," in *Chosŏn chŏn'gi kabujangje wa yŏsŏng* [Patriarchal domination and women in early Chosŏn], ed. Choe Hong-gi et al. (Seoul: Ak'anet, 2004), 255; see also Haejoang Cho, "Male Dominance and Mother Power: The Two Sides of Confucian Patriarchy in Korea," *Confucianism and the Family*, ed. Walter H. Slote and George A. De Vos (Albany: State University of New York Press, 1998).

38. Deuchler, *Confucian Transformation of Korea*, 66–69.

39. Mun Suk-cha, *Chosŏn sidae chaesan sangsok kwa kajok*, 105.

40. Mun Suk-cha, *Chosŏn sidae chaesan sangsok kwa kajok*, 100–101.

41. Hanguk Chŏngsinmunhwa Yŏnguwŏn Yŏksa Yŏngsil, *Yŏkchu kyŏngguk taejŏn: Pŏnyŏkp'yŏn* (Sŏngnam: Hanguk Chŏngsinmunhwa Yŏnguwŏn, 1985), 9, 442. A 1471 version of *Kyŏngkuk taejŏn* also is said to have carried provisions against sons of thrice-married women. Debates about banning widows from remarrying began as early as 1389, when heated debate erupted in 1468 over Kim Kae (1405–84), whose mother married three times and yet achieved a high-ranking status through royal favor. Deuchler, *Confucian Transformation of Korea*, 277–79.

42. Deuchler, *Confucian Transformation of Korea*, 161.

43. Widows in the Koryŏ dynasty also remarried without social taboo. Deuchler, *Confucian Transformation of Korea*, 72.

44. Deuchler, *Confucian Transformation of Korea*, 221, 265.

45. Anne Griffiths, "Doing Ethnography, Living Law: Life Histories and Narratives in Botswana," *Practicing Ethnography in Law: New Dialogues, Enduring Methods*, ed. June Starr and Mark Goodale (New York: Palgrave Macmillan, 2002), 160–81.

46. There is a debate over whether China possessed a civil-law tradition before the impact of Western legal tradition. Philip Huang has argued that China did have a civil-law tradition, although it was not codified or compiled as such. *Civil Justice in China: Representation and Practice in the Qing* (Stanford: Stanford University Press, 1996). Jérôme Bourgon denies that these were civil laws; instead, he states, they were merely examples of abnormalities or local eccentricities, without a noticeable trend toward norm building such as happened in Europe. Korea, having been under Chinese civilizational influence, thus had a similar lack of civil-law tradition. See "Rights, Freedoms, and Customs in the Making of Chinese Civil Law, 1900–1936," in *Realms of Freedom in Modern China*, ed. William C. Kirby (Stanford: Stanford University Press, 2002); and Bourgon, "Uncivil Dialogue: Law and Custom Did Not Merge into Civil Law under the Qing," *Late Imperial China* 23, no. 1 (2002): 50–90.

47. For more information on the late Chosŏn legal system, see Sun Joo Kim and Jungwon Kim, *Wrongful Deaths: Selected Inquest Records from Nineteenth-Century Korea* (Seattle: University of Washington Press, 2014).

48. Chŏng Chi-yŏng [Jung Ji Young], "Chosŏn sidae hon'in changryŏch'aek kwa tok-sin yŏsŏng [Single women and the policy of promoting marriage in the Chosŏn dynasty]," *Han'guk Yŏsŏnghak* 20, no. 3 (2004): 9.

49. Kim Pyŏng-hwa, *Han'guk sabŏpsa*, 2:212–16.

50. Cho Yun-sŏn, *Chosŏn hugi sosong yŏngu*, 18, 159, 202.

51. Cho Yun-sŏn, *Chosŏn hugi sosong yŏngu*, 160–61.

52. Later in the colonial period this concept of "separate family, separate property" became *besseki yizai* (separate register, separate property), a translation modified to fit the household-registration system.

53. Cho Ŭn, "Kabujangjŏk chilsŏhwa wa pu'in gwŏn ŭi yakhwa," in Choe, *Chosŏn chŏn'gi kabujangje wa yŏsŏng*, 238.

54. Asami Rintarō's idea of linear progress from collective to individual property, therefore, was erroneous. *Chōsen hōseishi kō* [A study of Korean legal history] (Tokyo: Ganshodo Shoten, 1922).

55. Deuchler, *Confucian Transformation of Korea*, 157–58.

56. *Susinjŏn* was abolished in 1466 as a result of reform in office land. See Deuchler, *Confucian Transformation of Korea*, 278. For a detailed list of court debates over widows' inheritance rights, see Cho Ŭn, "Kabujangjŏk chilsŏhwa wa pu'in gwŏn ŭi yakhwa," in Choe, *Chosŏn chŏn'gi kabujangje wa yŏsŏng*, 233–37.

57. Deuchler, *Confucian Transformation of Korea*, 161.

58. Son Kwang-hyŏn vs. Choe Tŭk-ch'ung, in Mun Suk-cha, *Chosŏn sidae chaesan sangsok kwa kajok*, 159–68.

59. Yi Ham vs. Kim Sa-won, in Mun Suk-cha, *Chosŏn sidae chaesan sangsok kwa kajok*, 169–74.

60. Mun Suk-cha, *Chosŏn sidae chaesan sangsok kwa kajok*, 175–76, 178.

61. Cho Yun-sŏn, *Chosŏn hugi sosong yŏngu*, 200.

62. Mun Suk-cha, *Chosŏn sidae chaesan sangsok kwa kajok*, 104–5, 168–70.

2. WIDOWED HOUSEHOLD HEADS AND THE NEW BOUNDARY OF THE FAMILY

1. Yi Sŭng-il, "Chosŏn ch'ongdokpu ŭi pŏpche chŏngch'aek e tehan yŏngu."

2. It is difficult to consider civil cases in the East Asian legal tradition since Civil Codes did not exist separate from penal codes, which dominated the judicial system. There is a debate over whether China possessed a civil-law tradition before the impact of Western legal tradition. In *Civil Justice in China*, Philip Huang has argued that China did have a civil-law tradition, although it was not codified or compiled as such. Jérôme Bourgon denies that these were civil laws; instead, he states, they were merely examples of abnormalities or local eccentricities, without a noticeable trend toward norm building such as happened in Europe. Korea, having been under Chinese civilizational influence, thus had a similar lack of civil-law tradition. See "Rights, Freedoms, and Customs," in Kirby, *Realms of Freedom;* and Bourgon, "Uncivil Dialogue." Recently, Marie Seong-hak Kim has added a Korean perspective to this debate, largely siding with Bourgon. Kim notes that both Japan and Korea follow the Chinese legal tradition centered on state law and argues that Korea also lacked a tradition of civil law. *Law and Custom*, 41, 73–78.

3. Marie Kim, *Law and Custom*, 41. See also Kim Pyŏng-hwa, *Han'guk Sabŏpsa*, 1:212. On this issue, Asami Rintarō (1869–1943) also notes that there was no process of customary law production in Korea, although he used this statement to emphasize Korea's backwardness and deny the validity of Korean customs in matters of property rights. Asami also overlooked the fact that Japan shared this lack with Korea. *Chōsen hōseishi kō* [A study of Korean legal history] (Tokyo: Ganshodo Shoten, 1922), 381.

4. According to Takushokukyoku, *Ōshū rekkoku shokuminchi hōsei gaiyō* [Outline of colonial legal systems of European empires] (1911), Japan modeled its colonial legal system mostly after Germany's, but also took notes from British policies in acknowledging local customs. Chŏng Kŭng-sik, *Han'guk kŭndaepŏpsa go* [A study of the Korean legal system] (Seoul: Pakyŏngsa, 2001), 350. For examples of legal policies in European colonies, see Chanock, *Social Order;* Alice L. Conklin, *A Mission to Civilize: The Republican Idea of Empire in France and West Africa, 1895–1930* (Stanford: Stanford University Press, 1997); and Richard Roberts and Kristin Mann, eds., *Law in Colonial Africa* (Portsmouth, NH: Heinemann Educational Books, 1991).

5. Yi Yŏng-mi, "Chōsen tōkanfu ni okeru hōmu hosakan seido to kanshū chōsa jigyō: Ume Kenjirō to Oda Mikijirō wo chūshin ni (4) [Judicial advisory system of the Resident-General Office and the customs-survey project: Focusing on Ume Kenjirō and Oda Mikijirō, no. 4]," *Hōgaku Shirin* 99, no. 3 (2002): 184.

6. Kim Pyŏng-hwa, *Han'guk sabŏpsa*, 1:20–25; Yumi Moon, *Populist Collaborators: The Ilchinhoe and the Japanese Colonization of Korea, 1896–1910* (Cornell University Press, 2013), 33–35.

7. More biographical information about Ume Kenjirō can be found in Yi Yŏng-mi, *Han'guk sabŏp*, 296.

8. Peter Duus, *The Abacus and the Sword: The Japanese Penetration of Korea, 1895–1910* (Berkeley: University of California Press, 1995), 235–41.

9. Yi Yŏng-mi, "Chōsen tōkanfu ni okeru hōmu hosakan seido to kanshū chōsa jigyō: Ume Kenjirō to Oda Mikijirō wo chūshin ni (3) [Judicial advisory system of the Resident-General Office and the customs-survey project: Focusing on Ume Kenjirō and Oda Mikijirō, no. 3]," *Hōgaku Shirin* 99, no. 2 (2001): 223, 239.

10. Yūhō Kyōkai, ed., *Chōsen ni okeru shihō seido kindaika no sokuseki*, 97–99.

11. There were more Korean lawyers than Japanese lawyers. Against 835 Korean lawyers (55 percent), there were 666 Japanese lawyers throughout the colonial period. Chŏng Kŭng-sik, *Han'guk pŏpchesa go*, 274.

12. So Hyŏn-suk [So Hyun Soog], "Singminji sigi kŭndaejŏk ihon chedo wa yŏsŏng ŭi tae'ŭng [A study on the modern divorce and women as historical actors during the Japanese colonial period in Korea]" (PhD diss., Hanyang University, Seoul, 2013), 83–84. An older figure from the Meiji period ("Minji soshō hiyōhō, Meiji 23-nen [1890]") is listed in Chōsen Sōtokufu Saibansho Kōtō Hōin, *Chōsen shihō teiyō* [Summary explanation of laws in Korea] (Keijō [Seoul]: Ganshōdō Keijōten, 1923), 547. One can see the variety of fees, according to this record, involved in bringing a case to the courts: scribes, drawings (land related), a translator (if needed), wages for witnesses, fiscal stamps *(inshi)*, and mailing fees, among other expenses, on top of lawyers, if applicable.

13. Kim Tong-in, "Yakan jaŭi sŭlp'ŭm," in *Yakan jaŭi sŭlp'ŭm oe* [Sadness of the weak and other works], ed. Kim Yun-sik (Seoul: Pŏm'u, 2004), 54–60. The novel was originally

published in *Kaebyŏk*'s inaugural issue in 1919. I thank Jun Yoo for informing me about this novel.

14. Chŏng Kwang-hyŏn, *Han'guk kajokpŏp yŏngu* [Research on the Korean family law] (Seoul: Sŏul Taehakkyo Ch'ulp'anbu, 1967). A more detailed overview of the position of "distortion" in earlier studies on the colonial civil laws can be found in Hong Yang-hŭi [Hong Yang-hee], "Singminji sigi ch'injok kwansŭp ŭi ch'angch'ul kwa ilbon minpŏp [Invention of family customs during the colonial period and the Japanese Civil Code]," *Chŏngsin Munhwa Yŏngu* 28, no. 3 (2005): 123–24. See also Yi Sŭng-il [Lee Seung-il], "1910, 20 nyŏndae Chosŏn ch'ongdokpu ŭi pŏpche chŏngch'aek: Chosŏn minsaryŏng che 11 -cho 'kwansŭp' ŭi sŏngmunhwa rŭl chungsim ŭro [Legal policy of the Korean Government General in the 1910s to 1920s: Centering on the codification of custom [shown in] Civil Ordinances in Korea article 11]," *Tongbang Hakpo* 126 (June 2004).

15. Marie Kim, *Law and Custom*, 175.

16. In "Singminji sigi ch'injok kwansŭp ŭi ch'angch'ul kwa ilbon minpŏp," Hong Yang-hŭi also states that the postcolonial scholars in Korea also assumed that a uniformed set of Korean customs existed in Korea before the onset of the colonial rule.

17. Hong and Yang, "Singminji sabŏp kwanryo ŭi kajok 'kwansŭp' insik kwa gendŏ chilsŏ," 176. For the process of customs surveys and how it combined field surveys and textual studies, please see Chōsen Sōtokufu Chūsūin, *Chōsen kyūkan seido chōsa jigyō gaiyō* [Outline of the customs-survey project in Korea] (Keijō [Seoul], 1938); Chŏng Kwang-hyŏn, *Han'guk kajokpŏp yŏngu*; Chŏng Kŭng-sik, *Kugyŏk kwansŭp chosa pogosŏ*; Yi Sŭng-il, *Chosŏn ch'ongdokpu pŏpche chŏngch'aek*, 117–37; and Yang Hyun-ah, *Han'guk kajokpŏp ilki* (Seoul: Ch'angbi, 2011), 114–15.

18. Concubinage was nonetheless acknowledged as part of the custom in divorce cases. Please see chapter 4 for a more detailed discussion.

19. With the Official Notice 240 (August 7, 1915), concubines could no longer be registered in household registers. Yi Chŏng-sŏn, "Han'guk kŭndae hojŏk chedo ŭi pyŏnchŏn: Minjŏkpŏp ŭi pŏpchejŏk t'ŭkching ŭl chungsim ŭro [Transformation of the modern Korean household registration system: Focusing on the legal characteristics of the Civil Registration Law]," *Han'guksaron* 55 (2009): 275–328; So, "Singminji sigi kŭndaejŏk ihon chedo wa yŏsŏng ŭi tae'ŭng," 220.

20. Terazawa Tokusaburo, "Kanshū chōsa: Kōkaido chihō [Customs survey: Hwanghaedo region]," manuscript, 1924; and Ariga Keitarō, "Kosekini kansuru jikō: Chūwa-gun [Cases concerning household registers: Chunghwa county]," manuscript, 1913, both in East Asian Rare Collection, C. V. Starr East Asian Library, University of California, Berkeley. Terazawa's report lists the occupation of the interviewees, while Ariga's report has the age of those interviewed. Terazawa's report was part of a series of investigations on customs commissioned by the Central Council in 1921. For more information, please see E. Taylor Atkins, *Primitive Selves: Koreana in the Japanese Colonial Gaze, 1910–1945* (Berkeley: University of California Press, 2010), 69–70.

21. Cho Pyŏng-jo, "Gogun no kyūkan chōsa hōkokusho [Report of old customs in five counties]," manuscript, 1919, East Asian Rare Collection, C. V. Starr East Asian Library. Chŏng Chi-yŏng notes that *kajang* in the Chosŏn dynasty was quite distinct from *hoju*: while *hoju* was the first name listed in the household register, *kajang* had the authority over family members. "Chosŏn sidae 'kajang' ŭi chiwi wa ch'aegim: Pŏpchŏn ŭi kyujŏng ŭl

chungsim ŭro [Family head in Chosŏn dynasty: Focusing on the rules in the law codes]," *Kajok Kwa Munhwa* 25, no. 1 (2013): 121–49.

22. Yi Yŏng-mi, "Kankoku kindai koseki kanren hōkyu no seitei oyobi kaisei katei," 13–14.

23. In principle the legal system in colonial Korea was not based on a common-law system bound by legal precedents, but in practice precedents had a strong influence on how later cases were decided. Marie S. Kim explains this as the following: "The Chosŏn High Court effectively engaged in creating law based on precedents. The colonial customary law regime amounted to a common-law system in Korea. The lower courts were strongly urged to follow the highest court's decisions, although there was no recognition of the principle of *stare decisis.*" Kim, *Law and Custom*, 207.

24. Chōsen Sōtokufu Hōmukyoku Hōmuka, *Chōsen no shihō seido* [Judicial system of Korea] (Keijō [Seoul], 1936), 33–34.

25. Similar dynamics have been examined in other colonial situations. See Roberts and Mann, *Law in Colonial Africa*, 22. Women in Egypt used the colonial courts as forums for affirming their legal rights. See May Ann Fay, "From Warrior-Grandees to Domesticated Bourgeoisie: The Transformation of the Elite Egyptian Household into a Western-Style Nuclear Family," in *Family History in the Middle East: Household, Property, and Gender,* ed. Beshara Doumani (Albany: State University of New York Press, 2003), 77–78.

26. Chōsen Kōtō Hōin Shokika, *Hanketsuroku,* 4:1–4, 5–10.

27. *Pŏppu sojang,* 7:593, 603, 609. There were three separate appeal letters on behalf of this widow.

28. Cho Yun-sŏn, *Chosŏn hugi sosong yŏngu,* 62–67.

29. This, of course, is only one case and does not represent the overall condition of women's legal status in the Chosŏn period. Jisoo Kim tells us that women's power for legal representation was quite strong during the Chosŏn dynasty. *Emotions of Justice.*

30. Chōsen Sōtokufu, *Kanshū chōsa hōkokusho* [Customs-survey report] (Keijō [Seoul], 1912), 16, 310.

31. Chōsen Sōtokufu, *Kanshū chōsa hōkokusho,* 352, 356; emphasis added.

32. Chōsen Sōtokufu, *Kanshū chōsa hōkokusho,* 297.

33. Official Notice 240; Yi Sŭng-il, "1910, 20 nyŏndae Chosŏn ch'ongdokpu ŭi pŏpche chŏngch'aek: Chosŏn minsaryŏng che 11 -cho 'kwansŭp' ŭi sŏngmunhwa rŭl chungsim ŭro; Yi Sŭng-il [Lee Seung-il], "Chosŏn hojŏngnyŏng chejŏng e kwanhan yŏngu [A study about the Household-Registration Law (of colonial Korea)]," *Pŏpsahak Yŏngu* 32 (October 2005): 37–68.

34. Son Pyŏng-gyu, *Hojŏk, 1606–1923: Hogu kirok ŭro pon Chosŏn ŭi munhwasa* [Household registry: Cultural history of the Chosŏn dynasty seen through census records, 1606–1923]" (Seoul: Hyumŏnisŭtŭ, 2007), 27–28, 34–35, 39–53.

35. Son Pyŏng-gyu argues that because the household registry was used to collect household tax, registries from the Chosŏn dynasty were manipulated to shrink the number of households. *Hojŏk,* 310–29. *Chuho* was a more common term for household heads during the Chosŏn dynasty, but *hoju* or *hosu* were also used (168–69).

36. Chŏng Chi-yŏng, *Chilsŏ ŭi kuch'uk kwa kyunyŏl,* 264–65.

37. Terazawa, "Kanshū chōsa: Kōkaido chihō."

38. Hwang, *Rationalizing Korea,* 201–2. Kyung Moon Hwang argues that from the perspective of the rationalization efforts of the state, there is a continuity between the Kwangmu Registry of 1896 and the Japanese-installed household registry. Yet this rationalization

attempt in the Kwangmu Registry was far from perfect, as there was not much time to realize its goals. Despite the goal of more accurately depicting existing households, the Kwangmu Registry captured only one third of the number of households recorded by the first household registers *(minseki)* under the Japanese. Son Pyŏng-gyu speculates that some of the features of the Kwangmu Registry might have originated in the 1871 Meiji household registry of Japan. For an overview of the Kwangmu Registry as well as a case study of particular examples from Tansŏng County, South Kyŏngsang Province, see Son, *Hojŏk,* 330–55.

39. Hwang, *Rationalizing Korea,* 202.

40. Son Pyŏng-gyu, *Hojŏk,* 366–70.

41. Yi Yŏng-mi. "Kankoku kindai koseki kanren hōkyu no seitei oyobi kaisei katei."

42. Ariga, "Kosekini kansuru jikō." For dates of legal reforms, see Yi Sŭng-il, "1910, 20 nyŏndae Chosŏn ch'ongdokpu ŭi pŏpche chŏngch'aek: Chosŏn minsaryŏng che 11-cho 'kwansŭp' ŭi sŏngmunhwa rŭl chungsim ŭro"; and Yi Sŭng-il, "Chosŏn hojŏngnyŏng chejŏng e kwanhan yŏngu."

43. Ariga, "Kosekini kansuru jikō."

44. Yi Yŏng-mi, "Kankoku kindai koseki kanren hōkyu no seitei oyobi kaisei katei," 10–12.

45. Chōsen Kōtō Hōin Shokika, *Hanketsuroku,* 4:8, 9.

46. Chōsen Kōtō Hōin Shokika, *Hanketsuroku,* 4:8; emphasis added.

47. Mun Suk-cha, "Koryŏ sidae ŭi sangsok chedo [Inheritance system in the Koryŏ dynasty]," *Kuksagwan Nonch'ong* 97 (2001): 30.

48. Chōsen Kōtō Hōin Shokika, *Hanketsuroku,* 1:402–404.

49. Chōsen Kōtō Hōin Shokika, *Hanketsuroku,* 3:132. *Jo'i,* or *sosa,* was an honorific term for a married commoner woman or a commoner widow.

50. Kim Tu-hŏn, *Han'guk kajok chedo yŏngu* [A study on the Korean family system] (Seoul: Sŏul Taehakkyo Ch'ulp'anbu, 1968), 597.

51. Chōsen Kōtō Hōin Shokika, *Hanketsuroku,* 1:44–46, 109–111, 132–135, 369–372.

52. Chōsen Kōtō Hōin Shokika, *Hanketsuroku,* 1:294–96.

53. Chōsen Kōtō Hōin Shokika, *Hanketsuroku,* 1:234–237.

54. Wagatsuma Sakae ed., *Meiji zenki Daishinin minji hanketsuroku* [Verdicts of the Supreme Court from the early Meiji period], 12 vols. (Kyoto: Sanwa Shobo, 1957–66), 1:193–94.

55. Chōsen Kōtō Hōin Shokika, *Hanketsuroku,* 1:475–477.

56. Chōsen Kōtō Hōin Shokika, *Hanketsuroku,* 1:426–430.

57. Chōsen Kōtō Hōin Shokika, *Hanketsuroku,* 20:396–402.

3. ARGUING FOR DAUGHTERS' INHERITANCE RIGHTS

1. "Yisipmanwŏn ŭl wiyo yangja munje ro koryuksong [Lawsuit between family over adoptee surrounding 200,000 won]," *Tonga Ilbo,* December 7, 1939.

2. Yi Sŭng-il, "1910, 20 nyŏndae Chosŏn ch'ongdokpu ŭi pŏpche chŏngch'aek: Chosŏn minsaryŏng che 11 -cho 'kwansŭp' ŭi sŏngmunhwa rŭl chungsim ŭro."

3. Yi Kwang-su, "Minjok kaejoron [On national reconstruction]," *Kaebyŏk,* May 1922; Michael Robinson, *Cultural Nationalism in Colonial Korea, 1920–1925* (Seattle: University of Washington Press, 1988).

4. Robinson, *Cultural Nationalism.*

5. E. Chen, "Attempt to Integrate," in Myers and Peattie, *Japanese Colonial Empire*, 240–74.

6. Caprio, *Japanese Assimilation Policies*, 123–24.

7. Yi Chŏng-sŏn, "Ilche ŭi naesŏn kyŏrhon chŏngch'aek [Japanese colonial policy on intermarriage between Japanese and Koreans]" (PhD diss., Seoul National University, 2015).

8. Yi Yŏng-mi, "Kankoku kindai koseki kanren hōkyu no seitei oyobi kaisei katei."

9. Yuzawa Yasuhiko, *Taishōki no kazoku mondai: Jiyū to okuatsu ni ikita hitobito* [The family problem in the Taishō period: People who lived between freedom and oppression] (Kyoto: Minerva Shobō, 2010), 179–82.

10. Yuzawa, *Taishōki no kazoku mondai*, 182.

11. "Kaega munje [The problem of widow remarriage]," *Tonga Ilbo*, July 22, 1924.

12. Reports on widow infanticide were both numerous and sensationalized. See, for example, "Kwabu ga san'a apsal hu yugi [Widow kills and abandons infant]," *Tonga Ilbo*, September 11, 1935; "Yŏng'a'si palgyŏn doeja kwabu eksu chasal" [Widow strangles herself to death when infant corpse is found]," *Tonga Ilbo*, February 12, 1935.

13. "Kwabu yŏng'a sarhae sagŏn maenyŏn osip'kŏn [Fifty widow infanticide cases every year]," *Tonga Ilbo*, January 27, 1935.

14. So Hyŏn-suk, "Sujŏl kwa chaega sa'i esŏ: Singminji sigi kwabu tamron" [Between chaste (widowhood) and remarriage: Discourse on widows during the (Japanese) colonial period]," *Han'guksa Yŏngu* 164 (March 2014): 59–89.

15. "Kwabu sar'a munje e taehaya [About the widow infanticide problem]," *Tonga Ilbo*, June 12, 1935.

16. "Konggyu e urbujinnŭn kwabu e salgil ul chura [Rescue widows crying in seclusion]," *Tonga Ilbo*, January 27, 1935.

17. "Hoengsŏl susŏl [Babbling]," *Tonga Ilbo*, January 29, 1935.

18. "Kaega ga sirŏ kwabu aeksa [Widow strangles herself to death, refusing remarriage]," *Tonga Ilbo*, May 8, 1936.

19. "Myŏnŭri kaega sik'yŏttago hyŏngsujip e panghwa [Puts sister-in-law's house on fire for remarrying daughter-in-law]," *Tonga Ilbo*, May 11, 1936.

20. So, "Sujŏl kwa chaega sa'i esŏ."

21. Pŏmnyul komun (Legal advice), *Tonga Ilbo*, December 19, 1929.

22. Pŏmnyul komun, *Tonga Ilbo*, March 1930.

23. Pŏmnyul komun, *Tonga Ilbo*, January 28, 1931.

24. Nagumo Kōkichi, "Matsudera hōmukyokuchō no shijun jikō riyū setsumei [Explanation of the explication of Chief Matsudera of the Legal Department]," *Genkō Chōsen Shinzoku Sōzokuhō Ruishū* [Collection of current family and inheritance law in Korea] (Keijō [Seoul]: Ōsakayagō Shoten, 1935), 605–9.

25. "Chosŏn esŏdo ddal ege sangsokkwŏn ŭl chunda [Daughters will be given inheritance rights in Korea too]," Pu'in [Women], *Tonga Ilbo*, November 15, 1925.

26. Translating Korean difference temporally into Korean backwardness was one of the ways Japan legitimized its colonial rule as a "civilizing mission." As "the pivotal measure of cultural distance between metropole and colony," Korean oppression of women's rights or status was magnified and subjected to colonial reform. Atkins, *Primitives Selves*, 97–98.

27. Son-in-law adoption in Japan did give families more options for family succession and as such strengthened daughters' standing in the family. See Marcia Yonemoto, *The Problem of Women in Early Modern Japan* (Berkeley: University of California Press, 2016).

28. Chōsen Sōtokufu, *Kanshū chōsa hōkokusho*, 343–44.

29. "Tongsŏng tongbon kyŏrhon do inhŏ! Sŏyangja dŭng ch'aeyong [Even intralineage marriage will be allowed! (They) will adopt son-in-law adoption and others]," *Tonga Ilbo*, December 12, 1930. Another article alarmed readers by predicting—erroneously—that son-in-law adoption was to be implemented in Korea imminently. "Chosŏn minsaryŏng kaejŏng: Sŏyangja pŏp silsi [Civil-Ordinances Reform: Implementing son-in-law adoption law]," *Tonga Ilbo*, September 13, 1931.

30. "Minpŏp kaejŏng'an Chosŏn eŭi yŏnjang silsi nŭn yŏha [When will they extend Civil-Code reform proposal to Korea?]," *Tonga Ilbo*, December 30, 1930.

31. "Yŏkwŏn ŭl sinjang hara [Expand women's rights]," *Tonga Ilbo*, December 10, 1933.

32. "Minsaryŏng kaejŏng ŭn puji hasewŏl [No one knows when (they will) reform the Civil Ordinances]," *Tonga Ilbo*, June 29, 1932.

33. Chōsen Kōtō Hōin Shokika, *Hanketsuroku*, 18:133–137.

34. Pŏmnyul komun, *Tonga Ilbo*, April 7, 1934.

35. Chōsen Kōtō Hōin Shokika, *Hanketsuroku*, 20:200–209.

36. Chōsen Kōtō Hōin Shokika, *Hanketsuroku*, 20:205.

37. Yi Sŭng-il, "Chosŏn ch'ongdokpu ŭi pŏpche chŏngch'aek e tehan yŏngu," 215, 217, 223.

38. Hozumi Nobushige, *Ancestor Worship and the Japanese Law* (Tokyo: Maruya, 1901), 41–47.

39. Asami, *Chōsen hōseishi kō*, 34, 391. Brief biographical information on Asami Rintarō is available in Chaoying Fang, *The Asami Library: A Descriptive Catalogue* (Berkeley: University of California Press, 1969), v–vi.

40. Nomura Chōtarō, "Chōsen ni okeru genkōno yōshi seido [Adoption system in practice now in Korea] (1)–(20)," *Shihō Kyōkai Zasshi* 6, no. 6 (1927): 2.

41. Hong Yang-hŭi, "Singminji sigi sangsok kwansŭppŏp kwa 'kwansŭp' ŭi ch'angch'ul," 114, 117.

42. Nomura, "Chōsen ni okeru genkōno yōshi seido," 22.

43. Nomura, qtd. in Aono Masa'aki, "Chōsen sōtokufu no dai sosen saishi seisaku ni kansuru kisōteki kenkyū: 1930 nendai o chūshin ni [A preliminary research on the Government General policy toward ancestor veneration: Focusing on the 1930s]," *Momoyama gakuin daigaku ningen kagaku* 25 (2003): 140.

44. Nomura, qtd. in Aono, "Chōsen sōtokufu no dai sosen saishi seisaku ni kansuru kisōteki kenkyū," 142.

45. Gakubukyoku-chō, "Girei junsoku seitei ni kansuru ken [About promulgating guidelines for rituals]," *Sha Dai-261-go*, November 10, 1934. Copy of "Chungch'uwŏn chosa charyo, Sohwa 9 nyŏn sŏmuchŏl, 167: Ŭirye chunch'ik chejŏng e kwanghan kŏn," Kuksa P'yŏnchan Wiwŏnhoe, accessed July 3, 2018, http://db.history.go.kr.

46. Janelli and Janelli, *Ancestor Worship*.

47. Aono, "Chōsen sōtokufu no dai sosen saishi seisaku ni kansuru kisōteki kenkyū."

48. According to Roger and Dawnhee Janelli, people in some regions continued to follow the higher requirements for ancestral rites from the *Zhu Xi jiali* (Family ritual of Zhu

Xi) for four generations. This rule continued into the 1970s, when the Janellis conducted their ethnographic field work in Suwon, Korea. Janelli and Janelli, *Ancestor Worship*, 99.

49. Chōsen Sōtokufu Chūsūin, *Dai jūkyū kai chūsūin kaigi sangi toshinsho* [Answers sent by Chūsūin members to the nineteenth Chūsūin meeting] (Keijō [Seoul], 1938).

50. Aono, "Chōsen sōtokufu no dai sosen saishi seisaku ni kansuru kisōteki kenkyū."

51. Aono, Chōsen sōtokufu no dai sosen saishi seisaku ni kansuru kisōteki kenkyū," 138.

52. Kim Tu-hŏn, "Chōsen ni okeru dai-kazoku seido hōkai no keikō (1) [The trend of large family dissolution in Korea (1)]," *Chōsa Geppō* [Monthly report on surveys] 11, no. 1 (1940): 3–5.

53. Chōsen Sōtokufu Chūsūin, *Dai nijūnikai chūsūin kaigi sangi toshinsho* [Answers sent by Chūsūin members to the twenty-second Chūsūin meeting] (Keijō [Seoul], 1941), 22:64.

54. Chōsen Sōtokufu Chūsūin, *Dai nijūnikai chūsūin kaigi*, 22:75. Japanese-style names taken by Koreans were read in a variety of ways. Depending on personal preference, the names were pronounced either in Korean or Japanese. If pronounced in Japanese, the household name was usually read in *kunyomi* (Japanese-style reading of Chinese characters) and the given name in *onyomi* (Chinese-style reading of Chinese characters). The pronunciation of Kanemistu Sōemi and Kinoshita Tōei was taken from Nakamura Kentarō, ed. *Sōshi kinen meishi kōkan meibo* [List of exchanged name cards commemorating the new names] (Keijō [Seoul]: Keijō Dōminkai Honbu, 1940). I thank Professor Mizuno Naoki for this information and also for the pronunciations of the remaining Japanese-style names of Koreans cited here.

55. Chōsen Sōtokufu Chūsūin, *Dai nijūnikai chūsūin kaigi*, 22:38.

56. Chōsen Sōtokufu Chūsūin, *Dai nijūnikai chūsūin kaigi*, 22:105; Yi Chŏng-sŏn, "Ilche ŭi naesŏn kyŏrhon chŏngch'aek," 43–44.

57. Chōsen Sōtokufu Chūsūin, *Dai nijūnikai chūsūin kaigi*, 22:26.

58. Chōsen Sōtokufu Chūsūin, *Dai nijūnikai chūsūin kaigi*, 22:163, 114–15.

59. Chōsen Sōtokufu Chūsūin, *Dai nijūnikai chūsūin kaigi*, 22:146.

60. *Shihō Kyōkai Zasshi* 23 (1944): 7, 113–14; and *Shihō Kyōkai Zasshi* 23 (1944): 8, 85–89, cited from Chŏng Kwang-hyŏn, *Han'guk kajokpŏp yŏngu*, 295–302.

4. CONJUGAL LOVE AND CONJUGAL FAMILY ON TRIAL

1. Chōsen Kōtō Hōin Shokika, *Hanketsuroku*, 25:560.

2. "Ch'ukchŏp ŭn ihon chogŏn [Concubinage is grounds for divorce]," *Tonga Ilbo*, December 28, 1938.

3. Chōsen Kōtō Hōin Shokika, *Hanketsuroku*, 30:90–94.

4. Yi Sŭng-il, "1910, 20 nyŏndae Chosŏn ch'ongdokpu ŭi pŏpche chŏngch'aek"; Caprio, *Japanese Assimilation Policies*.

5. Legal precedents that predated formal promulgation and revision of laws were not unprecedented in colonial Korea. For example, the extension of the Japanese Civil Code was in practice in Korea from 1909, before its formal promulgation in 1912. About colonial policy changes following the Second Sino-Japanese War, see Caprio, *Japanese Assimilation Policies*, 145. About the Civil-Ordinances Reform in 1939, see Miyata et al., *Sōshi kaimei*.

6. For the influx and spread of new ideas about love and marriage, see Yoo, *Politics of Gender*, 81–86.

7. Chōsen Kōtō Hōin Shokika, *Hanketsuroku*, 2:349–350, 3:215–225, 4:873–879, 13:213–220, 15:313–319, 16:107–110, 18:76–83, 25: 553–561, 28:36–46, 30:90–94.

8. Harald Fuess, *Divorce in Japan: Family, Gender, and the State, 1600–2000* (Stanford: Stanford University Press, 2004), 55.

9. Vera Mackie, *Feminism in Modern Japan: Citizenship, Embodiment, and Sexuality* (Cambridge: Cambridge University Press, 2003), 17–19, 24, 30.

10. Fuess, *Divorce in Japan*, 56; Mackie, *Feminism and Modern Japan*, 17.

11. Barbara Molony, "The Quest for Women's Rights in Turn-of-the-Century Japan," in *Gendering Modern Japanese History*, ed. Barbara Molony and Kathleen Uno (Cambridge, MA: Harvard University Asia Center, Harvard University Press, 2005), 471–72.

12. Muta Kazue, *Senryaku to shite no Kazoku: Kindai nihon no kokumin kokka keisei to josei* (Tokyo: Shinyōsha, 1996), 58.

13. Michiko Suzuki, *Becoming Modern Women: Love and Female Identity in Prewar Japanese Literature and Culture* (Stanford: Stanford University Press, 2010), 13, 65–66.

14. Chŏng Chi-yŏng [Jung Ji Young], "1920–30 nyŏndae sinyŏsŏng kwa chŏp/che'i pu'in: Singminji kŭndae chayu yŏne kyŏrhon ŭi kyŏllyŏl kwa sinyŏsŏng ŭi haengwisŏng" [New Women and concubinage/second wife in the 1920s and 1930s: The failure of love marriage in colonial modernity and the agency of the New Women], *Han'guk Yŏsŏnghak* 22, no. 4 (2006): 47–84.

15. The legal age of marriage was seventeen for men and fifteen for women, but around 10 percent of Koreans married before the legal age, and 45 percent of men and 80 percent of women married before they turned twenty. Inoue Kazue, "Chosŏn 'sinyŏsŏng' ŭi yŏnegwan kwa kyŏrhongwan ŭi pyŏnhyŏk [The transformation of New Women's perspectives on love and marriage in Korea]," in *Sin yŏsŏng* [New Women], edited by Mun Ok-p'yo et al. (Seoul: Chŏngnyŏnsa, 2003), 161.

16. So, "Singminji sigi kŭndaejŏk ihon chedo wa yŏsŏng ŭi tae'ŭng."

17. Kawashima Takeyoshi, "Nihon shakai no kazoku teki kōsei [Familial construction of the Japanese society]," in *Kawashima Takeyoshi chosakushū* (1983; repr., Tokyo: Iwanami Shoten, 2002), 10:2–17.

18. Ken Ito, *The Age of Melodrama: Family, Gender, and Social Hierarchy in the Turn-of-the-Century Japanese Novel* (Stanford: Stanford University Press, 2008).

19. Ann Laura Stoler, *Carnal Knowledge and Imperial Power: Race and the Intimate in Colonial Rule* (Berkeley: University of California Press, 2002), 12.

20. Clark Sorensen, "The Korean Family in Colonial Space: Caught between Modernization and Assimilation," in *Colonial Rule and Social Change in Korea, 1910–1945*, ed. Hong Yung Lee, Yong-Chool Ha, and Clark Sorensen (Seattle: University of Washington Press, 2013), 321–24. For an examination of the dissemination of ideals of love and gender equality through contact with foreign missionaries, see Hyaeweol Choi, *Gender and Mission Encounters in Korea: New Women, Old Ways*, Seoul-California Series in Korean Studies, vol. 1 (Berkeley: University of California Press, 2009).

21. Ruth Barraclough, "Tales of Seduction: Factory Girls in Korean Proletarian Literature," *Positions* 14, no. 2 (2006): 354–55. For an attempt at challenging this binary, see Kwon Podŭrae, *Yŏnae ŭi sidae: 1920-nyŏndae ch'oban ŭi munhwa wa yuhaeng* [The age of love: Culture and trend in the early 1920s] (Seoul: Hyonsil Munhwa Yŏn'gu, 2003).

22. Deuchler, *Confucian Transformation of Korea*, 232–36.

23. Kyung Moon Hwang notes how the number of sons of concubines *(sŏŏl)* greatly increased by the late Chosŏn dynasty and how they came to embody the complications of the social stratification system of Chosŏn dynasty. *Beyond Birth*, 60, 208–9.

24. In the very rare case where a woman was chosen from the yangban class, her natal family would face the risk of having its family status demoted. See one example in "Yu-ssi pu'in" (Madam Yu), in Kim Kŏn-u, ed., *Nanŭn tangdang hage salgetta* [I will live with pride] (Seoul: Munjahyang, 2003), 127–31.

25. Yi Hyojae, *Chosŏnjo sahoe wa kajok: Sinbun sangsŭng kwa kabujangje munhwa* [Family and society in the Chosŏn dynasty: Upward social mobility and patriarchal culture] (Seoul: Han'ul, 2003), 107–9.

26. Nonregistered marriages were a constant problem in colonial Korea. People also seem to have resisted registering concubines as wives even after the primary wife passed away because of the traditional ban on such practice.

27. Deuchler, *Confucian Transformation of Korea*, 268.

28. Hwang, *Beyond Birth*, 60. The practice of bypassing sons of concubines for adopted nephews followed the distinction between wives and concubines in 1413 and became established practice in the seventeenth century (211–12).

29. Chōsen Kōtō Hōin Shokika, *Hanketsuroku*, 1:475–477.

30. Chōsen Shihō Kyōkai, *Shihō Kyōkai Zasshi* [Journal of the Judicial Association] 1, no. 8 (1922): 153–54.

31. "Kaejŏng minpŏp ch'oan kŏmt'o (11) kyech'ul chu'ŭi ŭi p'yehae [Examining the reform draft of the Civil Code (11), the ills of the registration principle]," *Tonga Ilbo*, February 1, 1934.

32. A similar temporary condoning of concubines happened in Meiji Japan as well. Fuess, *Divorce in Japan*, 11–12, 56–57.

33. "Ihondo yŏnmal seŭm," *Tonga Ilbo*, December 28, 1921.

34. In 1922 concubines did lose the parental rights they had previously enjoyed, as shown in specific court rulings. See Chōsen Kōtō Hōin Shokika, *Hanketsuroku*, 1:402, 4:1178.

35. Daishin'in Civil Matters Division 2, December 19, 1918, case 946, cited from Chōsen Kōtō Hōin Shokika, *Hanketsuroku*, 15:317. In Japan the principle of fidelity in marriage developed in the 1920s to the extent of a declaration that husbands also had the "obligation of chastity." See Michiko Suzuki, "The Husband's Chastity: Progress, Equality, and Difference in 1930s Japan," *Signs* 38 (Winter 2013), 331.

36. One of the *Tonga Ilbo* editorials expressed frustration against the colonial government's lax attitude about reforming evil customs, especially early marriage, which was considered to be the main reason for the continuation of concubinage. "Chohon ŭi p'yehae wa ki ch'aegimja [The evils of early marriage and its culprits]," *Tonga Ilbo*, June 22, 1920.

37. Yun Hwa-sŏn, "Mŏnjŏ ch'ukch'ŏp p'yeji [First abolish concubinage]," *Tonga Ilbo*, May 25, 1923.

38. "Sahak ŭl chinhŭng hara [Expand private schools]," *Tonga Ilbo*, April 19, 1920.

39. "Ch'ŏpse ga saero saeng'gyŏ [Plans for a new concubinage tax]," *Tonga Ilbo*, July 5, 1924; "Mundye ŭi ch'ŏp segŭm [The concubinage tax under debate]," *Tonga Ilbo*, July 6, 1924.

40. Kwon Podŭrae, *Yŏnae ŭi sidae*.

41. Inoue, "Chosŏn 'sinyŏsŏng' ŭi yŏnegwan," in Mun Ok-p'yo et. al., *Sin yŏsŏng*, 161.

42. One newspaper article relayed the story of a deserted wife who ran away to get an education upon hearing that her husband had eloped with a lover while he was studying abroad in Japan. The underlying assumption was that the lack of education on the part of the wife had been partially the reason for the marital discord. "Saenghwallan ŭro mochŏ ch'ukch'ul [Expelled wife and mother-in-law due to poverty]," *Tonga Ilbo*, June 22, 1925.

43. *Sin Yŏsŏng* dedicated a special issue on the "second wife." *Sin Yŏsŏng* 7 (February 1933). The term "second wife" began appearing in Korean newspapers in the early 1920s and referred to concubines of Chinese political leaders. The most famous second wife was Song Mei-ling. "Sarangŭl wihayŏnŭn myŏngmangdo chiwi do p'yeri [Abandoning honor and status for love]," *Tonga Ilbo*, October 4, 1927.

44. Beverly Jo Bossler describes a similar function of concubinage in Song China. In contrast to the reserved feelings expressed toward wives, romantic feelings toward concubines were more openly celebrated in poetry. *Courtesans, Concubines, and the Cult of Female Fidelity: Gender and Social Change in China, 1000–1400*, Harvard-Yenching Institute Monograph Series 83 (Cambridge, MA: Harvard University Asia Center, 2012), 93–99.

45. "Yŏhakkyo rŭl chorŏphago chŏp yi doeŏganŭn saramdŭl [Those who become concubines after graduating from girls' school]," *Sin Yŏsŏng* 1, no. 2 (1923): 48–55

46. Chŏng Chi-yŏng, "1920–30 nyŏndae sinyŏsŏng kwa chŏp/che'i pu'in."

47. "Sunsa namp'yŏn kwa ihon: Ch'injŏng e ponae noko kamanhi chŏp ŭl odŏ [Divorced policeman husband, (who) secretly took in concubine while wife visited with natal family]," *Tonga Ilbo*, September 14, 1921. See also the Pu'in [Ladies] column in November 27, 1925.

48. "Ch'ukchŏp namp'yŏn silso: Sinyŏja ŭi ihon sosong [Doesn't want husband who keeps a concubine: A New Woman's divorce suit]," *Tonga Ilbo*, April 20, 1928; "Pŏmnyul sang ŭrodo ch'ukchŏp ŭn pulga [Concubinage is even legally impossible]," *Tonga Ilbo*, October 6, 1928; "Pŏmnyul komun," *Tonga Ilbo*, May 27, 1932.

49. Kwŏn Hŭi-jŏng, "1920 nyŏndae ihon sosong [Divorce suits from the 1920s]," *Pigyo Munhwa yŏngu* 11, no. 2 (2005): 52–53.

50. Chōsen Kōtō Hōin Shokika, *Hanketsuroku*, 15:316.

51. Litigants in colonial Korea, including Yi Myŏng-rye in this case, commonly employed a lawyer in such proceedings. Both Korean and Japanese lawyers were available (in this particular case, Yi employed a Korean lawyer). It is entirely possible that the strategies were heavily informed by the lawyers, but legal knowledge about divorce was also available through newspapers and novels. Validity of the litigants' personal conviction in such statements, if such a thing can be verified, is inconsequential to the argument at hand. Information about the qualifications and numbers of Japanese and Korean lawyers in colonial Korea can be found in Chŏng Kŭng-sik, *Han'guk Pŏpchesa go*, 273–74.

52. The case that Yi Myŏng-rye cites here as precedent (Daishin'in Civil Matters Division 2, December 19, 1918, case 946) is an earlier case than the one Michiko Suzuki cited on May 17, 1927, for establishing a husband's obligation to chastity. "Husband's Chastity," 331.

53. Chōsen Kōtō Hōin Shokika, *Hanketsuroku*, 15:313–19. In her argument, she mentions that the Japanese Supreme Court has already declared that "men also have the obligation for chastity" (315), showing that she knew of the famous decision that Michiko Suzuki has discussed in "Husband's Chastity." The news about this Japanese Supreme Court decision in 1928 seems to have traveled to Korea at the time and started a debate over chastity among Korean women. This discussion may have affected Yi Myŏng-rye's case, discussed later,

although it is unclear from the legal text if Yi was an educated New Woman. Hyaeweol Choi, ed., *New Women in Colonial Korea: A Sourcebook* (London: Routledge, 1912, 141–44).

54. Chōsen Kōtō Hōin Shokika, *Hanketsuroku*, 15:318.

55. So Hyŏn-suk notes that some figures are available for the number of concubines in Korea in precolonial surveys, but these surveys by newspapers were conducted only locally. "Singminji sigi kŭndaejŏk ihon chedo wa yŏsŏng ŭi tae'ŭng," 224–25.

56. Chōsen Kōtō Hōin Shokika, *Hanketsuroku*, 3:215–225, 13:213–220, 16:107–110.

57. Chōsen Kōtō Hōin Shokika, *Hanketsuroku*, 4:873–879., 18:76–83. For further discussion of the latter 1931 case, see Sungyun Lim, "Women on the Loose: Household System and Family Anxiety in Colonial Korea" in *Mobile Subjects: Boundaries and Identities in Modern Korean Diaspora*, ed. Wen-hsin Yeh (Berkeley: Institute of East Asian Studies, University of California, 2013).

58. For additional examples of discourses on sexuality and conjugal love in colonial Korea, see Choi, *New Women*, 94–166.

59. "Segye kakkuk ŭi rihon pŏpche wa chosŏn rihonpŏp ŭi kwagŏ hyŏnjae kŭp changrae [Divorce Laws in the world and the past, present, and future of the divorce law in Korea]," *Tonga Ilbo*, November 28, December 1, 1933.

60. "Yŏne wa kyŏrhon e daehan na'ŭi chech'ang [My advocacy about love and marriage]," *Tonga Ilbo*, January 26, 1935.

61. Kim Mal-bong, *Millim* [The jungle], *Tonga Ilbo*, January 5, 1938.

62. *Tonga Ilbo* ran a series of editorials exploring the possible effects of the reform on acknowledgments of "engagement." "Minsaryŏng kaejŏng kwa honin yeyak ŭl ronham [Discussing the Civil-Ordinances Reform and engagement]," *Tonga Ilbo*, July 3–21, 1923.

63. "Pŏmnyul komun: Samdo ch'ulga hu saengnyŏ haettago ch'ukch'ul [Legal advice: Kicked out of third marriage for giving birth to a daughter]," *Tonga Ilbo*, November 11, 1933. The article uses the term for marriage *(ch'ulga)* but explicitly notes that there was no registration of marriage. The column writer (lawyer, Kim Pyŏng-ro) answers that depending on the nature of the relationship, the woman may be able to sue the man for not completing the marriage engagement *(honin yeyak)*.

64. "Hojŏngnyŏng silsi chŏne chŏnan hamyŏn kyŏrhon sŏngnip [Marriage legitimate if chŏnan is carried out before the Household Registration Law]," *Tonga Ilbo*, November 4, 1935. For the criteria on Korean marriage customs that the High Court judges must have consulted, see Chōsen Sōtokufu, *Kanshū chōsa hōkokusho;* and *Kankoku heigōshi kenkyū shiryō* (Tokyo: Rōkei Shoten, 1995), 5:301–9.

65. Chōsen Kōtō Hōin Shokika, *Hanketsuroku*, 20:229.

66. Viviana A. Rotman Zelizer, *The Purchase of Intimacy* (Princeton: Princeton University Press, 2005). I thank Hae Yeon Choo for informing me about this book.

67. Chōsen Kōtō Hōin Shokika, *Hanketsuroku*, 3:733–748, 4:102–107.

68. The High Court's statement was in conjunction with the customs surveys carried out in 1913. Three reports that survive from the cities of Chŏnju, Keijō (Seoul), and Chŏngju all acknowledged that sons had the right to own property separate from the household head. Accounts on wives were equivocal. All acknowledged that women traditionally had the right to own separate property, but they differed as to what was to be included and also the extent to which the husband could exercise rights over it. In either case, it is clear from the customs-survey reports that whatever property rights Korean women had or were

believed to have had (by the male interviewees), they were not neatly contained within the separate-property concept outlined in the Japanese Civil Code. "Shinzoku ni kansuru jikō: Keijō, Seishū, Zenshū [Cases concerning kinship: Seoul, Chŏngju, Chŏnju]," manuscript, 1913, East Asian Rare Collection, C. V. Starr East Asian Library, UC Berkeley.

69. Chōsen Kōtō Hōin Shokika, *Hanketsuroku*, 18:76–83.

70. Chōsen Kōtō Hōin Shokika, *Hanketsuroku*, 16:13–16, 18:100–104.

71. "Kujik ch'ilbaek yuksip'yŏmyŏng ch'wijik ŭn pulgwa yibaek [Among over 760 job-seekers only 200 find jobs]," *Tonga Ilbo*, March 8, 1929.

72. Kang Man-gil, *Ilche sidae pinmin saenghwalsa yŏn'gu* [A study of the everyday history of the urban poor in the Japanese colonial period], Ch'angbi sinsŏ 79 (Seoul: Ch'angjaksa, 1987), 379. Additional information on the job market for educated women in the 1920s and 1930s can be found in Kim Sujin, *Sin yŏsŏng: Kŭndae ŭi kwa'ing* [New Women: The excess of modernity] (Seoul: Somyŏng, 2009).

73. "Yŏja mujikcha nŭn namja ŭi yibaena toenŭn hyŏngp'yŏn [The circumstances of female unemployment being double the number of male unemployment]," *Tonga Ilbo*, March 22, 1923.

74. "Yohakkyo chorŏpsaeng dŭrŭi kanŭn got [Where the girls' school graduates are going]," *Sin Yŏsŏng* 1, no. 4 (1924): 56–57.

75. "Chorŏpch'ŏnyŏ dŭrŭi sokt'anŭn kŏkchŏng [Agonizing worries of maiden graduates]," *Sin Yŏsŏng* 1, no. 4 (1924): 32–40; "Yohakkyo chorŏpsaengdŭlgge kinjŏlhan put'ak [Earnest request to girls' school graduates]," *Sin Yŏsŏng* 1, no. 4 (1924): 18–20.

76. Caprio, *Japanese Assimilation Policy,* 156–57.

77. Sabine Frühstück, *Colonizing Sex: Sexology and Social Control in Modern Japan* (Berkeley: University of California Press, 2003), 168–77.

78. Sŏ Yŏng-in, "Kŭndaejŏk kajok chedo wa ilche malgi yŏsŏng tamron [Modern family system and the discourse on women in the late colonial period]," *Hyŏndae Sosŏl Yŏngu* 33 (March 2007): 135–49.

5. CONSOLIDATING THE HOUSEHOLD ACROSS THE 1945 DIVIDE

1. Yi T'ae-yŏng, *Kajokpŏp kaejŏng undong 37-nyŏnsa* [Thirty-seven years of movement to reform the family law] (1948; repr., Seoul: Han'guk Kajŏng Pomnyul Sangdamso Ch'ulp'anbu, 1992), 78.

2. "Chŏryakhalsu innŭn kajŏng yongp'um: Kyŏngsa, Chang Hwa-sun [Things to conserve in the home: Chang Hwa-sun from the capital]," radio schedule, *Tonga Ilbo,* November 13, 1937; "Kajŏng sigan: Pisangsi wa kan'i saenghwal [Home hour: Simple life in the time of emergency]," *Tonga Ilbo,* August 3, 1938.

3. Mizuno Naoki, *Sōshi kaimei: Nihon no Chōsen shihai no nakade* [The Name-Change Policy: From the midst of Japanese rule of Korea] (Tokyo: Iwanami Shinsho, 2008), 59.

4. Minami Jirō, "Shihō jō ni okeru naisen ittai no gugen: Naichijin shiki shi no settei ni tsuite [Embodiment of Japan-Korea unity in the law: About choosing a Japanese-style surname]," in *Shi seido no kaisetsu: Shi towa nanika, ikani shite sadameruka* [Explanation on the (Japanese-style) surname system: What is a surname; how does one choose it?] (Keijō [Seoul]: Chōsen Sōtokufu Hōmukyoku, 1940), 4–6. Listed as appendix in Miyata et. al., *Sōshi kaimei,* 228–259.

5. Sangi Hyŏn Jun-ho, qtd. in Chōsen Sōtokufu Chūsūin, *Dai jūkyū kai chūsūin kaigi sangi toshinsho*, 19:72. Despite such grandiose hopes, the effect the assimilation of family laws had on Japan-Korea unity proved to be minimal. By the end of Japanese colonial rule in 1945, there was only one case of a Japanese son-in-law adopted into a Korean family. Hong Yang-hŭi [Hong Yang-hee], "Chosŏn ch'ongdokpu ŭi kajok chŏngch'aek yŏngu: Ka chedo wa kajŏng ideologi rŭl chungsim ŭro [The family policy of Japanese colonialism in Korea: With a focus on family system and home ideology]" (PhD diss., Hanyang University, Seoul, 2004), 101.

6. Miyata et. al., *Sōshi kaimei*, 78–80.

7. Miyata et al., *Sōshi kaimei*, 14–27.

8. Yang T'ae-ho, cited in Miyata et al., *Sōshi kaimei*, 150–60.

9. Fujitani, *Race for Empire*, 441.

10. Yi Chŏng-sŏn, "Singminji Chosŏn Taeman esŏ'ŭi ka-chedo chŏngch'aek kwajŏng [The process of implementation of the household system in Korea and Taiwan during the colonial period]," *Han'guk Munhwa* 55 (September 2011): 278.

11. Chōsen Kōtō Hōin Shokika, *Hanketsuroku*, 29:112–19.

12. The practice of utilizing eunuchs at the court was modeled on the Chinese practice, began in the Three Kingdoms period, and persisted until the end of the Chosŏn dynasty. About the adoption practices of eunuch families and the genealogical register *(yangse kyebo)* of eunuch families, please see Chang Hŭi-hŭng, *Chosŏn sidae chŏngch'i kwŏllyŏkkwa hwan'gwan* [Political Power in the Chosŏn dynasty and eunuchs] (Seoul: Kyŏngin Munhwasa, 2006), 309–42.

13. Park Yŏng-gyu, *Hwan'gwan kwa kungnyŏ* [Eunuchs and court ladies] (Seoul: Kimyŏngsa, 2004), 99.

14. Chŏng Kwang-hyŏn, *Sŏngssi nongo* [A study of family names] (Keijō [Seoul]: Tong-gwangdang Sŏjŏm, 1940); Nomura Chōtarō, "Chōsen kanshūhō jōno ie to sono sōzokusei [The household and its inheritance in Korean customary laws]," *Shihō Kyōkai Zasshi* 19, no. 1 (1941): 2.

15. Minami Jirō, "Shihō jō ni okeru naisen ittai no gugen," in *Shi seido no kaisetsu*, 4–6.

16. The preservation of Korean names in the household registers was part of the policy's design to preserve the distinction, and thus discrimination, between metropolitan and colonial subjects. Mizuno Naoki argues that the Name-Change Policy was in fact a differentiation policy rather than an assimilation policy. *Sōshi Kaimei*, 43, 144.

17. Helen Kim, qtd. in Mizuno, *Sōshi Kaimei*, 192.

18. Miyata et al., *Sōshi Kaimei*, 138; Hildi Kang, *Under the Black Umbrella: Voices from Colonial Korea, 1910–1945* (Ithaca, NY: Cornell University Press, 2005), 119.

19. Mizuno, *Sōshi Kaimei*, 190–92. Another example of choosing a name to express a Christian identity is found here. In this autobiographical account, the family is said to have chosen "Iwamoto," after Saint Peter, as their name (both mean "rock"). Richard E. Kim, *Lost Names: Scenes from a Korean Boyhood* (New York: Praeger, 1970), 106.

20. Mizuno, *Sōshi Kaimei*, 43.

21. Yang T'ae-ho, cited in Miyata et al., *Sōshi Kaimei*, 131.

22. Mizuno, *Sōshi Kaimei*, 31, 39; Miyata et al., *Sōshi Kaimei*, 51.

23. Yi Kwang-su, "Sōshi to watashi [Name change and me]," *Mainichi shinpō*, February 20, 1940, cited in Miyata Setsuko, "Sōshi kaimei no jisshi katei [Process of Name Change Implementation]," in Miyata et al., *Sōshi Kaimei*, 90.

24. Mizuno Naoki, "Chōsenjin no namae to shokuminchi shihai [The names of the Koreans and the colonial rule]," in *Seikatsu no nakano shokuminchi shugi* [Colonialism in everyday life], ed. Mizuno Naoki (Kyoto: Jinbun Shoin, 2004), 50–52.

25. David Chapman, "Different Faces, Different Spaces: Identifying the Islanders of Ogasawara," *Social Science Japan Journal* 14, no. 2 (2011): 189–212. Also, Sakamoto Shin'ichi, "Haisenzen nihonkoku ni okeru Chōsen koseki no kenkyū: Tōroku gijutsu to chōhei gijutsu wo chūshin to shite [Research on the Korean household registry in Japan before the end of the war: Focusing on the techniques of registry and conscription]," *Seikyū Gakujutsu Ronshū* 10 (1997): 233–93.

26. Nomura Chōtarō, "Chōsenjin aida no engumi no yōken taru shōboku tekigō ni tsuite [About the rule of Somok, which is the condition for adoption among Koreans]," *Shihō Kyōkai Zasshi* 18, no. 1 (1940): 1–8; Nomura, "Shūchū ni kansuru hōritsu kankei [Laws concerning lineages]," *Shihō Kyōkai Zasshi* 18, no. 11 (1940): 1–20; Nomura, "Chōsen kanshūhō jōno ie to sono sōzokusei [The household and its inheritance in Korean customary laws]," *Shihō Kyōkai Zasshi* 19, no. 1 (1941): 9, 12, 13.

27. Cases over widow rights were continuously brought to the High Court. Chōsen Kōtō Hōin Shokika, *Hanketsuroku,* 27:93 (widow's right to adopt heir); 27:204 (widow's right to manage lineage land—duped to allow outsiders to bury their dead in the lineage land); 27:208 (a woman household head, whose property lacked an heir); 28:113 (widow mortgages the land with the consent of the family council), 29:14 (widow sells daughter's land), 29:112 (widow's right to adopt heir); 29:226 (widow sued by daughters over the sale of their father's estate).

28. Hong Yang-hŭi argues that Nomura's position to maintain lineage laws while disposing customary rights of widows is because ancestor-veneration inheritance was useful in implementing the Japanese family system, which was also the patriarchal family system, in Korea. Hong also notes that by using ancestor-veneration inheritance to implement the Japanese family system in Korea, the Japanese managed to disseminate the ancestor-veneration practice to lower levels of Korean society and make it a nationally uniform practice. "Singminji sigi sangsok kwansŭppŏp kwa 'kwansŭp' ŭi ch'angch'ul," 117–19.

29. Yama'uchi Toshihiko, "Chōsen ni okeru kafu no sōzokuken [Widows' inheritance rights in Korea]," *Koseki* 3, no. 6 (1943): 1–10.

30. Iwajima Hajime, "Chōsen minjirei ni okeru muko-yōshi ni tsuite [On son-in-law adoption according to Korean Civil Ordinances] (1)–(3)," *Koseki* 1, no. 1 (1941): 2, no. 1 (1942): 2, no. 5 (1942): 1–5.

31. Chang Sŭng-du, "Dōsei dōhon fukon [The ban on intralineage marriage]," *Chōsa Geppō* 10, no. 10 (1944): 1–15.

32. *Migunjŏng pŏmnyŏngjip* [Collection of codes under the U.S. military occupation] (Seoul: Yŏgang Ch'ulp'ansa, 1983), 358.

33. Kim Tu-hŏn, *Han'guk kajok chedo yŏngu* [Research in the Korean family system], 614.

34. Kim Tu-hŏn, *Chosŏn kajok chedo yŏngu* [Study of the Korean family system] (Seoul: Ŭlyu Munhwasa, 1948), 67–68.

35. Despite the U.S. military government's Ordinance 14, minor changes did happen through Supreme Court decisions, such as the one in 1947 that nullified Japanese Civil Code, article 14, which stated that women had limited legal capacity. Kim Chu-su, cited in Pak Pyŏng-ho, ed., *Han'guk pŏbchesa go: Kŭnse ŭi pŏp kwa sahoe* [Research in the Korean legal system: Law and society in the early modern period] (Seoul: Pŏmmunsa, 1974), 27.

36. Taebŏpwŏn Pŏpwuhoe, "Pong Ha-hyŏng vs. Hwang Kyu-yong," *Taebŏpwŏn minsa p'allyejip* [Collection of precedents in civil cases from the Supreme Court], vol. 2, *1958–1962* (Seoul: Ŏmun'gak, 1963), 154.

37. Myŏng Sun-gu [Soon-Koo Myoung], "Ajikto sarainnŭn pŏp, Chosŏn minsaryŏng: Chosŏn minsaryŏng ŭi sogŭpchŏk p'yeji rŭl che'an handa [The law that still survives, the Civil Ordinances of Korea: Proposing the retroactive abolition of the Civil Ordinances]," *Jŏsŭtisŭ* 103 (March 2008): 220–36.

38. Yi T'ae-yŏng, *Kajokpŏp kaejŏng undong 37-nyŏnsa*, 24.

39. Yi T'ae-yŏng, *Kajokpŏp kaejŏng undong 37-nyŏnsa*, 25–26.

40. Yi T'ae-yŏng, *Kajokpŏp kaejŏng undong 37-nyŏnsa*, 70.

41. Yi T'ae-yŏng, *Kajokpŏp kaejŏng undong 37-nyŏnsa*, 122.

42. The ban on intralineage marriage *(tongsŏng tongbon kyŏrhon)* was lifted only in 1997. Marie Kim, *Law and Custom*, 288–89.

43. Yi T'ae-yŏng, *Kajokpŏp kaejŏng undong 37-nyŏnsa*, 77, 80.

44. Myŏng Sun-gu [Myoung, Soon-Koo], *Sillok taehanmin'guk minpŏp* [Veritable records of the Civil Code of the Republic of Korea] (Seoul: Pŏmmunsa, 2008), 1:32–39.

45. Yi T'ae-yŏng, *Kajokpŏp kaejŏng undong 37-nyŏnsa*, 32.

46. Myŏng Sun-gu, *Sillok taehanmin'guk minpŏp*, 1:58.

47. Kim Chu-su, in Pyŏng-ho Pak et al., *Modernization and Its Impact upon Korean Law* Korea Research Monograph 3 (Berkeley: Institute of East Asian Studies, University of California, 1981), 28.

48. The new penal code promulgated in 1953 made the Adultery Law applicable to both husband and wife; one could press criminal charges on the spouse's adultery only after divorce, so the penal code already assumed the wife's right to sue for a divorce on the ground of adultery or infidelity. A brief history of the Adultery Law and the debate around it can be found in Hŏ Il-t'ae, "Kant'ongjoe ŭi wihŏnsŏng [Constitutional violation of the criminalization of adultery]," *Jŏsŭtisŭ* 104 (June 2008): 118–35.

49. Yi T'ae-yŏng, *Kajokpŏp kaejŏng undong 37-nyŏnsa*, 32.

50. "Sŏyangja nŭn sangsokkwŏn ŏpta, chŏnt'ong sallin taebŏpwŏn sinp'an'gyŏllye [Sons-in-law have no inheritance rights, new decision by the Supreme Court that revived tradition]," *Kyŏnghyang Sinmun*, April 13, 1949.

51. "Wanryo doen ch'injokpŏp ch'o'an kolcha, koyu ŭi mi'p'ung kwa chŏnt'ong ŭl t'odaero kich'o [Finished outlines of the family-law draft, drafted based on unique beautiful customs and traditions]," *Kyŏnghyang Sinmun*, July 7, 1953.

52. "Pong'gŏn chanjae rŭl pŏp ŭro t'ap'a [Law abolishes feudal vestiges]," *Tonga Ilbo*, September 9, 1956.

53. Other reforms in the adoption laws in the new Civil Code included the following: anyone (man or woman) could adopt; the ban on nonagnatic adoption was lifted (but adopted children were not allowed to change their surname); and a family with a daughter was not allowed posthumous adoption (i.e., daughters could not be bypassed by an adoptee for succession). On the surface women made much progress: they could adopt as a woman (or widow), and they could become a household head and continue their natal families by having a husband become an adopted son-in-law.

54. "Sae minpŏp haesŏl (4) [Explanations on the new Civil Code]," *Tonga Ilbo*, January 6, 1960.

55. Yi T'ae-yŏng, "14-nyŏn kwa yŏsŏng haebang [Fourteen years (after liberation) and (finally) the liberation of women]," *Tonga Ilbo*, August 15, 1959.

56. "Sae minpŏp haesŏl (13)," *Tonga Ilbo*, January 17, 1960.

57. "Wŏryo ŭngjŏpsil [Monday salon]," *Tonga Ilbo*, February 17, 1958.

58. "Ddak'han munam dong'nyŏ [Pathetic only daughter]," *Tonga Ilbo*, November 19, 1965; "Komyŏng dd'al kwa chŏlson ŭi komin [The only daughter and the worry of discontinuing the family]," *Tonga Ilbo*, November 25, 1965.

CONCLUSION

1. "Rho taet'ongryŏng e konggae chirŭisŏ: Yŏsŏng tanch'eryŏn hojuje p'yeji dŭng kongyak chik'ilddae [Open inquiry to President Rho: Women's Group Federation says it is time to keep election promises including abolishing household-head system]," *Chosŏn Ilbo*, November 11, 1989. The first organized effort to revise the family law was launched in 1973, as sixty-one women's groups in Korea formed a Pan-Women's Committee for the Expedition of the Amendment of the Family Law and fought for ten reforms, including the abolition of the family-head system, more equal inheritance and property rights for women, and better parental rights for divorced mothers. The women's rights movement was able to achieve a major revision in 1977, which was heralded as "epoch-making" by one Korean legal scholar. The new Family Law came into effect in 1979, with revisions that implemented joint property ownership for married couples, increased the inheritance shares for widows and unmarried daughters, and allowed equal parental authority for both parents. But the law still denied divorced mothers parental rights to their children and birth mothers' rights to a child born out of wedlock (if the child was registered in the father's household). Needless to say, even if the inheritance portion was increased for daughters and widows, it fell short of reaching inheritance amounts equal to those of male descendants. And, most important, this revision did not do away with the household system, which was the main culprit in various kinds of sex discrimination. Pyŏng-ho Pak, "Family Law," in Pyŏng-ho Pak et al., *Modernization and Its Impact*, 8; Kim Chu-su, cited in Pak Pyŏng-ho, *Han'guk pŏbchesa go*, 20.

2. "Kukhoe t'onggwa pŏban: Minpŏp kaejŏng'an [Bills passed in the National Assembly: Amendment draft of the Civil Code]," *Chosŏn Ilbo*, December 20, 1989.

3. "Hojuje p'yeji ch'ujin: Ihon chanyŏ kajŏng ŏmŏni sŏng kanŭng [Pushing for abolition of the household-head system: Children of divorced families can use mother's surname]" and "Hojuje ppuri nŭn ilche? [Is the origin of the household-head system in the Japanese rule?]," *Chosŏn Ilbo*, May 7, 2003. Nationalist sentiment rekindled in the aftermath of the International Monetary Fund takeover in 1998 was kept alive in the Cleaning of Colonial Legacy campaign under the Kim Dae-jung government and the following Roh Mu-hyŏn government. In 2004 the Special Law to Investigate Anti-national Acts under Japanese Colonial Rule (Ilche Kangjŏmha Panminjok Haengwi Chinsang Kyumyŏng e Kwanhan T'ŭkpyŏlpŏp) was passed in the National Assembly to establish a special committee to investigate pro-Japanese collaborators. In 2006 a special presidential Committee to Investigate Property of Pro-Japanese Anti-National Collaborators (Ch'inil Panminjok Haengwija Chaesan Chosa Wiwŏnhoe) was set up to track down and confiscate property owned by those who had collaborated with the Japanese government during the colonial period.

4. Yang Hyun-ah, "Hoju chedo wihŏn sosong e kwanhan pŏpsahoehakchŏk koch'al: Kajok ŭi pyŏnhwa rŭl chungsim ŭro [Considering the legal accusation of the

unconstitutionality of the household-head system from the legal sociological perspective: Focusing on the changing family]," *Hanguk sahoehak* 36. no. 5 (2002): 201–29.

5. Kano Masanao, *Senzen ie no shisō* [Ideology of the family in the prewar era] (Tokyo: Sobunsha, 1983); Kathleen S. Uno, "Women and Changes in the Household Division of Labor" and Miriam Silverberg, "The Modern Girl as Militant," in *Recreating Japanese Women, 1600–1945,* ed. Gail Lee Bernstein (Berkeley: University of California Press, 1991), 22–23, 247–47.

6. Ito, *Age of Melodrama,* 52. Ken Ito argues that the popular melodramatic fiction about family was a literary response to the anxieties about social mobility in the Meiji period. The Meiji family system also was a modern invention created to function as a "bulwark against the social dislocations of the era." Therefore, even though the Meiji family system was also a modern invention, its effect was dependent on the belief in its long history, that is, "through concealing its origins" (24–30).

7. This dynamic is similar to the politics of inclusion of colonial subjects during the wartime, examined by Fujitani in *Race for Empire.*

8. Muta Kazue also argues the same for the Japanese case. She states that, contrary to the dominant understanding that the hierarchical and premodern nature of the family system bolstered the family-state ideology through a forceful implementation of "voluntary submission" *(shihatsu teki fukusō),* the warm intimacy of "home" also provided a basis for the family-state ideology. *Senryaku to shite no kazoku: Kindai nihon no kokumin kokka keisei to josei* (Tokyo: Shinyōsha, 1996), 108.

9. "Dasi pulpunnŭn 'ddaldŭl ŭi chŏnjaeng' [Daughters' war reignited]," *Tonga Ilbo,* October 7, 2001; "'Ch'ulga yŏsŏng chongjungwŏn anida' p'angyŏl [Decision that married-out daughters not members of lineage]," *Yŏnhap News,* March 25, 2001; "Chongjung chaesan namnyŏ ch'adŭng punbae, sŏng ch'abyŏl anida [Unequal distribution of lineage property not sex discrimination]," *Tonga Ilbo,* December 6, 2006.

10. Even though the women lost the cases, they succeeded in having the Supreme Court make some important affirmation on the principle of equality between the sexes. In a decision in July 21, 2005, the Supreme Court proclaimed that daughters should also be given rights of membership to lineages. "P'allye ŭi panran ikkurŏnaen ddaldŭl ŭi panran [Daughter's upheaval that led to the upheaval of the precedent]," *Yŏnhap News,* July 21, 2005; "Taebŏp chongjung chaesan punbae sŏng ch'abyŏl ha'myŏn muhyo [Supreme Court says, 'If lineages commit sex discrimination in property distribution, it will be ineffective']," *Tonga Ilbo,* October 3, 2010.

BIBLIOGRAPHY

COLLECTIONS OF CODES AND LEGAL RECORDS

Chōsen Kōtō Hōin Shokika. *Chōsen kōtō hōin hanketsuroku* [Legal decision of the High Court of Colonial Korea]. 30 vols. Keijō [Seoul]: Daesŏng, 1913–43.

Kankoku heigōshi kenkyū shiryō. Vol. 5. Tokyo: Rōkei Shoten, 1995.

Migunjŏng pŏmnyŏngjip [Collection of codes under the U.S. military occupation]. Seoul: Yŏgang Ch'ulp'ansa, 1983.

Pŏppu sojang [Appeal letters to the Ministry of Legal Affairs]. Vols. 1–7. Seoul: Sŏul Taehakkyo Kyujanggak, 2000–2004.

Taebŏpwŏn minsa p'allyejip [Collection of precedents in civil cases from the Supreme Court]. Vols. 1–3. Seoul: Ŏmun'gak, 1958, 1963, 1969.

GOVERNMENT GENERAL PUBLICATIONS AND MANUSCRIPTS

Abe Kaoru, ed. *Chōsen kōrōsha meikan* [Who's who among *(kōrōsha)* in Korea]. Keijō [Seoul]: Minshū Jironsha, 1935.

Ariga Keitarō. "Kosekini kansuru jikō: Chūwa-gun [Cases concerning household registers: Chunghwa county]." Manuscript. 1913. East Asian Rare Collection. C. V. Starr East Asian Library, University of California, Berkeley.

Cho Pyŏng-jo. "Gogun no kyūkan chōsa hōkokusho [Report of old customs in five counties]." Manuscript. 1919. East Asian Rare Collection. C. V. Starr East Asian Library, University of California, Berkeley.

Chōsen Chūō Keizaikai. *Keijō shimin meikan* [Who's who among Seoul citizens]. Keijō [Seoul]: Chōsen Chūō Keizaikai, 1921.

Chōsen Koseki Kyōkai. *Koseki* [Household registers]. Keijō [Seoul], 1941–45.

Chōsen Shihō Kyōkai. *Shihō Kyōkai Zasshi* [Journal of the Judicial Association]. Keijō [Seoul], 1922–44.

Chōsen Sōtokufu. *Chōsa geppō* [Monthly report on surveys]. Keijō [Seoul], 1930–44.
——. *Kanshū chōsa hōkokusho* [Customs-survey report]. Keijō [Seoul], 1912.
Chōsen Sōtokufu Chūsūin. *Chōsen kyūkan seido chōsa jigyō gaiyō* [Outline of the customs-survey project in Korea]. Keijō [Seoul], 1938.
——. *Dai jūkyū kai chūsūin kaigi sangi toshinsho* [Answers sent by Chūsūin members to the nineteenth Chūsūin meeting]. Keijō [Seoul], 1938.
——. *Dai nijūnikai chūsūin kaigi sangi toshinsho* [Answers sent by Chūsūin members to the twenty-second Chūsūin meeting]. Keijō [Seoul], 1941.
Chōsen Sōtokufu Hōmukyoku. *Genkō chōsen koseki hōreishū* [Collection of current household registration laws in Korea]. Keijō [Seoul]: Chōsen Koseki Kyōkai, 1942.
Chōsen Sōtokufu Hōmukyoku Hōmuka. *Chōsen no shihō seido* [Judicial system of Korea]. Keijō [Seoul], 1936.
Chōsen Sōtokufu Saibansho Kōtō Hōin. *Chōsen shihō teiyō* [Summary explanation of laws in Korea]. Keijō [Seoul]: Ganshōdō Keijōten, 1923.
Andō Shizuka "Shinzoku ni kansuru jikō: Keijō, Seishū, Zenshū [Cases concerning kinship: Seoul, Chŏngju, Chŏnju]." Manuscript. 1913. East Asian Rare Collection. C. V. Starr East Asian Library, UC Berkeley.
Soktaejŏn. 1744. Reprint, Seoul: Pŏpchechŏ, 1965.
Terazawa Tokusaburo. "Kanshū chōsa: Kōkaido chihō [Customs survey: Hwanghaedo region]." Manuscript. 1924. East Asian Rare Collection. C. V. Starr East Asian Library, University of California, Berkeley.

ARTICLES AND BOOKS

Aono Masaʼaki. "Chōsen sōtokufu no dai sosen saishi seisaku ni kansuru kisōteki kenkyū: 1930 nendai o chūshin ni [A preliminary research on the Government General policy toward ancestor veneration: Focusing on the 1930s]." *Momoyama gakuin daigaku ningen kagaku* 25 (2003):135–47.
Asami Rintarō. *Chōsen hōseishi kō* [A study of Korean legal history]. Tokyo: Ganshodo Shoten, 1922.
Atkins, E. Taylor. *Primitive Selves: Koreana in the Japanese Colonial Gaze, 1910–1945*. Berkeley: University of California Press, 2010.
Barraclough, Ruth. "Tales of Seduction: Factory Girls in Korean Proletarian Literature." *Positions* 14, no. 2 (2006): 345–71.
Bernstein, Gail Lee ed. *Recreating Japanese Women, 1600–1945*. Berkeley: University of California Press, 1991.
Bossler, Beverly Jo. *Courtesans, Concubines, and the Cult of Female Fidelity: Gender and Social Change in China, 1000–1400*. Harvard-Yenching Institute Monograph Series 83. Cambridge, MA: Harvard University Asia Center, 2012.
Bourgon, Jérôme. "Rights, Freedoms, and Customs in the Making of Chinese Civil Law, 1900–1936." In *Realms of Freedom in Modern China*, edited by William C. Kirby, 84–112. Stanford: Stanford University Press, 2002.
——. "Uncivil Dialogue: Law and Custom Did Not Merge into Civil Law under the Qing." *Late Imperial China* 23, no. 1 (2002): 50–90.

Caprio, Mark E. *Japanese Assimilation Policies in Colonial Korea, 1910–1945.* Seattle: University of Washington Press, 2009.

Chang Hŭi-hŭng. *Chosŏn sidae chŏngch'i kwŏllyŏk kwa hwan'gwan* [Political Power in the Chosŏn dynasty and eunuchs]. Seoul: Kyŏngin Munhwasa, 2006.

Chang Pyŏng-in. *Chosŏn chŏn'gi honinje wa sŏngch'abyŏl* [Marriage system in the early Chosŏn period and gender discrimination]. Seoul: Ilchisa, 1997.

Chang Sŭng-du. "Dōsei dōhon fukon [The ban on intralineage marriage]." *Chōsa Geppō* 10, no. 10 (1944): 1–33.

Chanock, Martin. *Law, Custom, and Social Order: The Colonial Experience in Malawi and Zambia.* Portsmouth, NH: Heinemann, 1998.

Chapman, David. "Different Faces, Different Spaces: Identifying the Islanders of Ogasawara." *Social Science Japan Journal* 14, no. 2 (2011): 189–212.

Chen, Edward I-te. "The Attempt to Integrate the Empire: Legal Perspectives." In Myers and Peattie, *Japanese Colonial Empire,* 240–74.

Chen Chao-ju. "*Simpua* under the Colonial Gaze: Gender, 'Old Customs,' and the Law in Taiwan under Japanese Imperialism." In *Gender and Law in the Japanese Imperium,* edited by Susan L. Burns and Barbara J. Brooks, 189–218. Honolulu: Hawai'i University Press, 2014.

Cho, Haejoang. "Male Dominance and Mother Power: The Two Sides of Confucian Patriarchy in Korea." In *Confucianism and the Family,* edited by Walter H. Slote and George A. De Vos, 187–207. Albany: State University of New York Press, 1998.

Choi, Hyaeweol, *Gender and Mission Encounters in Korea: New Women, Old Ways.* Seoul-California Series in Korean Studies. Vol. 1. Berkeley: University of California Press, 2009.

———, ed. *New Women in Colonial Korea: A Sourcebook.* London: Routledge, 2012.

Choi, Kyeong-Hee. "Neither Colonial nor National: The Making of the 'New Woman' in Pak Wansŏ's 'Mother's Stake 1.'" In Gi-wook and Robinson, *Colonial Modernity in Korea,* 221–47.

Chŏng Chi-yŏng [Jung Ji Young]. "1920–30 nyŏndae sinyŏsŏng kwa ch'ŏp/che'i pu'in: Singminji kŭndae chayu yŏne kyŏrhon ŭi kyŏllyŏl kwa sinyŏsŏng ŭi haengwisŏng [New women and concubinage/second wife in the 1920s and 1930s: The failure of love marriage in colonial modernity and the agency of the New Women]." *Han'guk Yŏsŏnghak* 22, no. 4 (2006): 47–84.

———. *Chilsŏ ŭi kuch'uk kwa kyunyŏl: Chosŏn hugi hojŏk kwa yŏsŏngdŭl* [The construction of and fissures in order: Women and household registry in the late Chosŏn dynasty]. Seoul: Sŏgang Taehakkyo Chulp'anbu, 2015.

———. "Chosŏn hugi ŭi yŏsŏng hoju yŏngu: Kyŏngsangdo tansŏnghyŏn hojŏk taejang ŭi punsŏk ŭl chungsimŭro [A study of female household heads in the late Chosŏn dynasty: Analysis of census registers from Tansŏng County, Kyŏngsang Province]." PhD diss., Sŏgang University, Seoul, 2001.

———. "Chosŏn sidae honin changryŏch'aek kwa toksin yŏsŏng [Single women and the policy of promoting marriage in the Chosŏn dynasty]." *Han'guk Yŏsŏnghak* 20, no. 3, (2004): 5–37.

———. "Chosŏn sidae 'kajang' ŭi chiwi wa ch'aegim: Pŏpchŏn ŭi kyujŏng ŭl chungsim ŭro [Family head in Chosŏn dynasty: Focusing on the rules in the law codes]." *Kajok Kwa Munhwa* 25, no. 1 (2013): 121–49.

Chŏng Chong-hyu. *Kankoku minpōten no hikakuhō teki kenkyū* [Comparative research on the Korean Civil Code]. Tokyo: Sobunsha, 1989.

Chŏng Kŭng-sik. *Han'guk kŭndaepŏpsa go* [Study of the modern legal history of Korea]. Seoul: Pakyŏngsa, 2001.

———. *Kugyŏk kwansŭp chosa pogosŏ* [Korean translation of the customs survey report]. Seoul: Han'guk Pŏpche Yŏn'guwŏn, 1992.

———. "Singminjigi sangsok kwansŭppŏp ŭi t'adangsŏng e taehan chaegŏmt'o: Kajogin chang'nam ŭi samang kwa sangsogin ŭi pŏmwi [A reexamination of the legitimacy of inheritance customary law from the colonial period: The death of an eldest son who is a family member and the candidates to be heirs]." *Sŏul Taehakkyo Pŏphak* 50, no. 1 (2009): 287–320.

Chŏng Kwang-hyŏn. *Han'guk kajokpŏp yŏngu* [Research on the Korean family law]. Seoul: Sŏul Taehakkyo Ch'ulp'anbu, 1967.

———. *Sŏngssi nongo* [A study of family names]. Keijō [Seoul]: Tonggwangdang Sŏjŏm, 1940.

Chŏn Pyŏng-mu. *Chosŏn ch'ongdokpu chosŏnin sabŏpkwan* [Korean judges in the Korean Government General]. Seoul: Yŏksa kong'gan, 2012.

Cho Ŭn. "Kabujangjŏk chilsŏhwa wa pu'in gwŏn ŭi yakhwa [Establishment of patriarchal order and the weakening of wife rights]." In *Chosŏn chŏn'gi kabujangje wa yŏsŏng* [Patriarchal domination and women in early Chosŏn], edited by Choe Hong-gi, Kim Chu-hŭi, Kim T'ae-hyŏn, Yun T'aek-rim, Yun Hyŏng-suk, Yi Pae-yong, Cho Ŭn, and Cho Hŭi-sŏn, 227–59. Seoul: Ak'anet, 2004.

Cho Yun-sŏn. *Chosŏn hugi sosong yŏngu* [A study of lawsuits in the late Chosŏn dynasty]. Seoul: Kukhak Charyowŏn, 2002.

"Chungch'uwŏn chosa charyo, Sohwa 9 nyŏn sŏmuchŏl, 167: Ŭirye chunch'ik chejŏng e kwanghan kŏn." Kuksa P'yŏnchan Wiwŏnhoe. Accessed July 3, 2018. http://db.history.go.kr.

Conklin, Alice L. *A Mission to Civilize: The Republican Idea of Empire in France and West Africa, 1895–1930*. Stanford: Stanford University Press, 1997.

Deuchler, Martina. *The Confucian Transformation of Korea: A Study of Society and Ideology*. Cambridge, MA: Council on East Asian Studies, Harvard University, 1992.

———. "Propagating Female Virtues in Chosŏn Korea." In *Women and Confucian Cultures in Premodern China, Korea, and Japan*, edited by Dorothy Ko, Jahyun Kim Haboush, and Joan R. Piggott, 142–69. Berkeley: University of California Press, 2003.

Dudden, Alexis. *Japan's Colonization of Korea: Discourse and Power*. Honolulu: University of Hawai'i Press, 2005.

Duus, Peter. *The Abacus and the Sword: The Japanese Penetration of Korea, 1895–1910*. Berkeley: University of California Press, 1995.

Fang, Chaoying. *The Asami Library: A Descriptive Catalogue*. Berkeley: University of California Press, 1969.

Fay, May Ann. "From Warrior-Grandees to Domesticated Bourgeoisie: The Transformation of the Elite Egyptian Household into a Western-Style Nuclear Family." In *Family History in the Middle East: Household, Property, and Gender*, edited by Beshara Doumani, 77–98. Albany: State University of New York Press, 2003.

Frühstück, Sabine. *Colonizing Sex: Sexology and Social Control in Modern Japan*. Berkeley: University of California Press, 2003.

Fuess, Harald. *Divorce in Japan: Family, Gender, and the State, 1600–2000*. Stanford: Stanford University Press, 2004.

Fujitani, T. *Race for Empire: Koreans as Japanese and Japanese as Americans during World War II*. Berkeley: University of California Press, 2013.

Gi-wook Shin and Michael Robinson, eds. *Colonial Modernity in Korea*. Cambridge, MA: Harvard University Asia Center, 1999.

Griffiths, Anne. "Doing Ethnography, Living Law: Life Histories and Narratives in Botswana." In *Practicing Ethnography in Law: New Dialogues, Enduring Methods*, edited by June Starr and Mark Goodale, 160–81. New York: Palgrave Macmillan, 2002.

Hanguk Chŏngsinmunhwa Yŏnguwŏn Yŏksa Yŏngusil. *Yŏkchu kyŏngguk taejŏn: Pŏnyŏkp'yŏn*, Sŏngnam: Hanguk Chŏngsinmunhwa Yŏnguwŏn, 1985.

Hanguk Kojŏn Kugyŏk Wiwŏnhoe, ed. *Kugyŏk taejŏn hoet'ong*. Seoul: Koryŏ Taehakkyo Ch'ulp'anbu, 1960.

Han'guk Minsapŏp Hakhoe. *Minsapŏp kaejŏng ŭigyŏnsŏ* [Opinions on the civil-laws reform]. Seoul: Pakyŏngsa, 1981.

Hŏ Il-t'ae. "Kant'ongjoe ŭi wihŏnsŏng [Constitutional violation of the criminalization of adultery]." *Jŏsŭtisŭ* 104 (June 2008): 118–35.

Hong Yang-hŭi [Hong Yang-hee]. "Chosŏn ch'ongdokpu ŭi kajok chŏngch'aek yŏngu: Ka chedo wa kajŏng ideologi rŭl chungsim ŭro [The family policy of Japanese colonialism in Korea: With a focus on family system and home ideology]." PhD diss., Hanyang University, Seoul, 2004.

———. "Singminji sigi ch'injok kwansŭp ŭi ch'angch'ul kwa ilbon minpŏp [Invention of family customs during the colonial period and the Japanese Civil Code]." *Chŏngsin Munhwa Yŏngu* 28, no. 3 (2005): 121–45.

———. "Singminji sigi sangsok kwansŭppŏp kwa 'kwansŭp' ŭi ch'angch'ul [Customary law on inheritance during the colonial period and the invention of 'custom']." *Pŏpsahak Yŏngu* 34 (2006): 99–132.

Hong Yang-hŭi and Yang Hyun-ah. "Singminji sabŏp kwanryo ŭi kajok 'kwansŭp' insik kwa gendŏ chilsŏ: Kwansŭp chosa pogosŏ ŭi hojukwŏn e taehan insik ŭl chungsim ŭro [The colonial judicial officials' perception of family custom and gender hierarchy: On perception of household-head rights in the *Customs Survey Report*]." *Sahoe wa yŏksa*, September 2008, 161–95.

Huang, Philip. *Civil Justice in China: Representation and Practice in the Qing*. Stanford: Stanford University Press, 1996.

Hwang, Kyung Moon. *Beyond Birth: Social Status in the Emergence of Modern Korea*. Cambridge, MA: Harvard University Asia Center, 2004.

———. *Rationalizing Korea: The Rise of the Modern State, 1894–1945*. Berkeley: University of California Press, 2015.

Inoue Kazue. "Chosŏn 'sinyŏsŏng' ŭi yŏnegwan kwa kyŏrhongwan ŭi pyŏnhyŏk [The transformation of New Women's perspectives on love and marriage in Korea]." In *Sin yŏsŏng* [New Women], edited by Mun Ok-p'yo, Yi Pae-yong, Pak Yong-ok, Song Yŏn-ok, Kim Kyŏng-il, Inoue Kazue, Yi Sang-gyŏng, Yoneda Sayoko, and Ishizaki Shōko. Seoul: Chŏngnyŏnsa, 2003.

Ito, Ken. *The Age of Melodrama: Family, Gender, and Social Hierarchy in the Turn-of-the-Century Japanese Novel*. Stanford: Stanford University Press, 2008.

Iwajima Hajime, "Chōsen minjirei ni okeru muko-yōshi ni tsuite [On son-in-law adoption according to Korean Civil Ordinances] (1)–(3)," *Koseki* 1, no. 1 (1941): 17–23; 2, no. 1 (1942): 2–8; 2, no. 5 (1942): 1–5.

Janelli, Roger L., and Dawnhee Yim Janelli. *Ancestor Worship and Korean Society.* Stanford: Stanford University Press, 1982.

Joseph, Betty. *Reading the East India Company, 1720–1840: Colonial Currency of Gender.* Chicago: Chicago University Press, 2004.

Kang, Hildi. *Under the Black Umbrella: Voices from Colonial Korea, 1910–1945.* Ithaca, NY: Cornell University Press, 2005.

Kang Man-gil. *Ilche sidae pinmin saenghwalsa yŏn'gu* [A study of the everyday history of the urban poor in the Japanese colonial period]. Ch'angbi sinsŏ 79. Seoul: Ch'angjaksa, 1987.

Kano Masanao. *Senzen ie no shisō* [Ideology of the family in the prewar era]. Tokyo: Sobunsha, 1983.

Kawashima Takeyoshi. "Nihon shakai no kazoku teki kōsei [Familial construction of the Japanese society]." In *Kawashima Takeyoshi chosakushū,* 10:2–17. 1983. Reprint, Tokyo: Iwanami Shoten, 2002.

Kim, Jaeeun. "The Colonial State, Migration, and Diasporic Nationhood in Korea." *Comparative Studies in Society and History* 56, no. 1 (2014): 34–66.

Kim, Jisoo M. *The Emotions of Justice: Gender, Status, and Legal Performance in Chosŏn Korea.* Seattle: University of Washington Press, 2015.

Kim, Jungwon. "'You Must Avenge on My Behalf': Widow Chastity and Honour in Nineteenth-Century Korea." *Gender and History* 26, no. 1 (2014): 128–46.

Kim, Marie Seong-hak. "Law and Custom under the Chosŏn Dynasty and Colonial Korea: A Comparative Perspective." *Journal of Asian Studies* 66, no. 4 (2007): 1067–97.

———. *Law and Custom in Korea: Comparative Legal History.* Cambridge: Cambridge University Press, 2012.

Kim, Michael. "Sub-nationality in the Japanese Empire: A Social History of the *Koseki* in Colonial Korea, 1910–45." In *Japan's Household Registration System and Citizenship: Koseki, Identification and Documentation,* edited by David Chapman and Karl Jakob Krogness, 111–26. London: Routledge, 2014.

Kim, Richard E. *Lost Names: Scenes from a Korean Boyhood.* New York: Praeger, 1970.

Kim, Sun Joo, and Jungwon Kim, *Wrongful Deaths: Selected Inquest Records from Nineteenth-Century Korea.* Seattle: University of Washington Press, 2014.

Kim A-yŏng, "Ch'wi'jae p'a'il: Chaehon kajŏng dŭrŭi sogari, 'tong'gŏ'in chiuryŏ p'yŏnpŏp kamsu [Investigation file: Agonies of remarried families; Daring illegal methods to erase 'coresident (marker)']." *SBS News,* March 30, 2015. http://news.sbs.co.kr/news/endPage.do?news_id = N1002903175&plink = ORI&cooper = NAVER.

Kim Kŏn-u, ed. *Nanŭn tangdang hage salgetta* [I will live with pride]. Seoul: Munjahyang, 2003.

Kim Mi-yŏng. *Kajok kwa ch'injok ŭi minsokhak* [Folk studies of family and kinship]. Seoul: Minsogwon, 2008.

Kim Pyŏng-hwa. *Han'guk sabŏpsa* [Judicial history of Korea]. 3 vols. Seoul: Iljogak, 1979.

Kim Sŏnju and Chu Chin-o. *Han'guk yŏsŏngsa kip'i ilki: Yŏksasok mal ŏmnŭn yŏsŏngdŭl ege malgŏlgi* [Reading deep into Korean women's history: Speaking to the voiceless women in history]. Seoul: P'urŭn Yŏksa, 2013.

Kim Sujin. *Sin yŏsŏng: Kŭndae ŭi kwa'ing* [New Women: The excess of modernity]. Seoul: Somyŏng, 2009.

Kim Tong-in. "Yakan jaŭi sŭlp'ŭm." In *Yakan jaŭi sŭlp'ŭm oe* [Sadness of the weak and other works], edited by Kim Yun-sik, 13–77. Seoul: Pŏm'u, 2004.

Kim Tu-hŏn. "Chōsen ni okeru dai-kazoku seido hōkai no keikō (1) [The trend of large family dissolution in Korea (1)]." *Chōsa Geppō* 11, no. 1 (1940): 1–33.

———.*Chosŏn kajok chedo yŏngu* [Study of the Korean family system]. Seoul: Ŭlyu Munhwasa, 1948.

———. *Han'guk kajok chedo yŏngu* [A study on the Korean family system]. Seoul: Sŏul Taehakkyo Ch'ulp'anbu, 1968.

Ko, Dorothy. *Cinderella Sisters: A Revisionist History of Footbinding.* Berkeley: University of California Press, 2005.

Kwŏn Hŭi-jŏng. "1920 nyŏndae ihon sosong [Divorce suits from the 1920s]." *Pigyo Munhwa Yŏngu* 11, no. 2 (2005): 35–62.

Kwŏn Podŭrae. *Yŏnae ŭi sidae: 1920-nyŏndae ch'oban ŭi munhwa wa yuhaeng* [The age of love: Culture and trend in the early 1920s]. Seoul: Hyonsil Munhwa Yŏn'gu, 2003.

Lee, Chulwoo. "Modernity, Legality, and Power in Korea under Japanese Colonial Rule." In Gi-wook and Robinson, *Colonial Modernity in Korea,* 21–51.

Lew, Young Ick. "Minister Inoue Kaoru and the Japanese Reform Attempts in Korea during the Sino-Japanese War, 1894–1895." *Journal of Asiatic Studies* 27, no. 2 (1984): 145–86.

Lim, Sungyun. "Women on the Loose: Household System and Family Anxiety in Colonial Korea." In *Mobile Subjects: Boundaries and Identities in Modern Korean Diaspora,* edited by Wen-hsin Yeh, 61–87. Berkeley: Institute of East Asian Studies, University of California, 2013.

Loos, Tamara Lynn. *Subject Siam: Family, Law, and Colonial Modernity in Thailand.* Ithaca, NY: Cornell University Press, 2006.

Mackie, Vera. *Feminism in Modern Japan: Citizenship, Embodiment, and Sexuality.* Cambridge: Cambridge University Press, 2003.

Minami Jirō. "Shihō jō ni okeru naisen ittai no gugen: Naichijin shiki shi no settei ni tsuite [Embodiment of Japan-Korea unity in the law: About choosing a Japanese-style surname]." In *Shi seido no kaisetsu: Shi towa nanika, ikani shite sadameruka* [Explanation on the (Japanese-style) surname system: What is a surname; how does one choose it?]. Keijō [Seoul]: Chōsen Sōtokufu Hōmukyoku, 1940.

Miyata Setsuko. "Sōshi kaimei no jisshi katei [Process of name-change implementation]." In Miyata et al., *Sōshi Kaimei,* 90.

Miyata Setsuko, Kim Yŏng-dal, and Yang T'ae-ho. *Sōshi kaimei* [The Name-Change Policy]. Tokyo: Akashi Shoten, 1992.

Mizuno Naoki. "Chōsenjin no namae to shokuminchi shihai [The names of the Koreans and the colonial rule]." In Mizuno, *Seikatsu no nakano shokuminchi shugi,* 21–57.

———, ed. *Seikatsu no nakano shokuminchi shugi* [Colonialism in everyday life]. Kyoto: Jinbun Shoin, 2004.

———. *Sōshi kaimei: Nihon no Chōsen shihai no nakade* [The Name-Change Policy: From the midst of Japanese rule of Korea]. Tokyo: Iwanami Shinsho, 2008.

Molony, Barbara. "The Quest for Women's Rights in Turn-of-the-Century Japan." In *Gendering Modern Japanese History,* edited by Barbara Molony and Kathleen Uno, 463–92. Cambridge, MA: Harvard University Asia Center, Harvard University Press, 2005.

Moon, Yumi. *Populist Collaborators: The Ilchinhoe and the Japanese Colonization of Korea, 1896–1910*. Ithaca, NY: Cornell University Press, 2013.

Mun Suk-cha. *Chosŏn sidae chaesan sangsok kwa kajok* [Property inheritance and family in the Chosŏn dynasty]. Seoul: Kyŏng'in Munhwasa, 2004.

———. "Koryŏ sidae ŭi sangsok chedo [Inheritance system in the Koryŏ dynasty]." *Kuksagwan Nonch'ong* 97 (2001): 25–50.

Muta Kazue. *Senryaku to shite no kazoku: Kindai nihon no kokumin kokka keisei to josei*. Tokyo: Shinyōsha, 1996.

Myers, Ramon H., and Mark R. Peattie, eds. *The Japanese Colonial Empire, 1895–1945*. Princeton: Princeton University Press, 1984.

Myŏng Sun-gu [Myoung, Soon-Koo]. "Ajikto sarainnŭn pŏp, Chosŏn minsaryŏng: Chosŏn minsaryŏng ŭi sogŭpchŏk p'yeji rŭl che'an handa [The law that still survives, the Civil Ordinances of Korea: Proposing the retroactive abolition of the Civil Ordinances]." *Jŏsütisŭ* 103 (March 2008): 220–36.

———. *Sillok taehanmin'guk minpŏp* [Veritable records of the Civil Code of the Republic of Korea]. Vol. 1. Seoul: Pŏmmunsa, 2008.

Nagumo Kōkichi. "Matsudera hōmukyokuchō no shijun jikō riyū setsumei [Explanation of the explication of Chief Matsudera of the Legal Department]." *Genkō Chōsen Shinzoku Sōzokuhō Ruishū* [Collection of current family and inheritance law in Korea]. Keijō [Seoul]: Ōsakayagō Shoten, 1935.

Nakamura Kentarō, ed. *Sōshi kinen meishi kōkan meibo* [List of exchanged name cards commemorating the new names]. Keijō [Seoul]: Keijō Dōminkai Honbu, 1940.

Nobushige, Hozumi. *Ancestor Worship and the Japanese Law*. Tokyo: Maruya, 1901.

Nomura Chōtarō. "Chōsenjin aida no engumi no yōken taru shōboku tekigō ni tsuite [About the rule of Somok, which is the condition for adoption among Koreans]." *Shihō Kyōkai Zasshi* 18, no. 1 (1940): 1–8.

———. "Chōsen kanshūhō jōno ie to sono sōzokusei [The household and its inheritance in Korean customary laws]." *Shihō Kyōkai Zasshi* 19, no. 1 (1941): 1–13.

———. "Chōsen ni okeru genkōno yōshi seido [Adoption system in practice now in Korea]." *Shihō Kyōkai Zasshi* 6, no. 6 (1927): 1–28.

———. "Shūchū ni kansuru hōritsu kankei [Laws concerning lineages]." *Shihō Kyōkai Zasshi* 18, no. 11 (1940): 1–20.

Oldenburg, Veena Talwar. *Dowry Murder: The Imperial Origins of a Cultural Crime*. New York: Oxford University Press, 2002.

Pak Pyŏng-ho, ed. "Family Law." In Pyŏng-ho Pak et al., *Modernization and Its Impact*, 1–17.

———. *Han'guk pŏbchesa go: Kŭnse ŭi pŏp kwa sahoe* [Research in the Korean legal system: Law and society in the early modern period]. Seoul: Pŏmmunsa, 1974.

Pak Pyŏng-ho, Chu-su Kim, Kwŏn-sŏp Chŏng, Kim Hyŏng-Bae, and Kwŏn T'ae-jun, eds. *Modernization and Its Impact upon Korean Law*. Korea Research Monograph 3. Berkeley: Institute of East Asian Studies, University of California, 1981.

Pak Ŭn-kyŏng. *Ilcheha chosŏn'in kwan'ryo yŏngu* [Research on Korean bureaucrats under the Japanese colonial rule]. Seoul: Hakminsa, 1999.

Park Yŏng-gyu. *Hwan'gwan gwa kungnyŏ* [Eunuchs and court ladies]. Seoul: Kimyŏngsa, 2004.

Peattie, Mark R. "Japanese Attitudes toward Colonialism, 1895–1945." In Myers and Peattie, *Japanese Colonial Empire*, 80–127.

Peterson, Mark. *Korean Adoption and Inheritance: Case Studies in the Creation of a Classic Confucian Society.* Ithaca, NY: Cornell University Press, 1996.

Poole, Janet. *When the Future Disappears: The Modernist Imagination in Late Colonial Korea.* New York: Columbia University Press, 2014.

Roberts, Richard, and Kristin Mann, eds. *Law in Colonial Africa.* Portsmouth, NH: Heinemann Educational Books, 1991.

Robinson, Michael. *Cultural Nationalism in Colonial Korea, 1920–1925.* Seattle: University of Washington Press, 1988.

Sakamoto Shin'ichi. "Haisenzen nihonkoku ni okeru Chōsen koseki no kenkyū: Tōroku gijutsu to chōhei gijutsu wo chūshin to shite [Research on the Korean household registry in Japan before the end of the war: Focusing on the techniques of registry and conscription]." *Seikyū Gakujutsu Ronshū* 10 (1997): 233–93.

Schmid, Andre. *Korea between Empires, 1895–1919.* New York: Columbia University Press, 2002.

Silverberg, Miriam. "The Modern Girl as Militant." In Bernstein, *Recreating Japanese Women,* 239–66.

Sim Hŭi-gi. "Tongasia chŏnt'ong sahoe ŭi kwansŭppŏp kaenyŏm e taehan pip'anjŏk kŏmt'o [Critical examination of the customary law concept in traditional societies in East Asia]." *Pŏpsahak Yŏngu* 46 (October 2012): 205–46.

So Hyŏn-suk [So Hyun Soog]. "Singminji sigi kŭndaejŏk ihon chedo wa yŏsŏng ŭi tae'ŭng [A study on the modern divorce and women as historical actors during the Japanese colonial period in Korea]." PhD diss., Hanyang University, Seoul, 2013.

———. "Sujŏl kwa chaega sa'i esŏ: Singminji sigi kwabu tamron [Between chaste (widowhood) and remarriage: Discourse on widows during the (Japanese) colonial period]." *Han'guksa Yŏngu* 164 (March 2014): 59–89.

Son Pyŏng-gyu. *Hojŏk, 1606–1923: Hogu kirok ŭro pon Chosŏn ŭi munhwasa* [Household registry: Cultural history of the Chosŏn dynasty seen through census records, 1606–1923]. Seoul: Hyumŏnisŭtŭ, 2007.

Sorensen, Clark. "The Korean Family in Colonial Space: Caught between Modernization and Assimilation." In *Colonial Rule and Social Change in Korea, 1910–1945,* edited by Hong Yung Lee, Yong-Chool Ha, and Clark Sorensen, 314–34. Seattle: University of Washington Press, 2013.

Sŏ Yŏng-in. "Kŭndaejŏk kajok chedo wa ilche malgi yŏsŏng tamron [Modern family system and the discourse on women in the late colonial period]." *Hyŏndae Sosŏl Yŏngu* 33 (March 2007): 135–49.

Spivak, Gayatri. "Can the Subaltern Speak?" In *Marxism and Interpretation of Culture,* edited by Cary Nelson and Lawrence Grossberg, 271–313. Urbana: University of Illinois Press, 1988.

Sreenivas, Mytheli. *Wives, Widows, and Concubines: The Conjugal Family Ideal in Colonial India.* Bloomington: Contemporary Indian Studies, Indiana University Press, 2008.

Stoler, Ann Laura. *Carnal Knowledge and Imperial Power: Race and the Intimate in Colonial Rule.* Berkeley: University of California Press, 2002.

Suzuki, Michiko. *Becoming Modern Women: Love and Female Identity in Prewar Japanese Literature and Culture.* Stanford: Stanford University Press, 2010.

————. "The Husband's Chastity: Progress, Equality, and Difference in 1930s Japan." *Signs* 38 (Winter 2013): 327–52.

Taebŏpwŏn Pŏpwuhoe. "Pong Ha-hyŏng vs. Hwang Kyu-yong." In *Taebŏpwŏn minsa p'allyejip* [Collection of precedents in civil cases from the Supreme Court]. Vol. 2, *1958–1962*. Seoul: Ŏmun'gak, 1963.

Takushokukyoku. *Ōshū rekkoku shokuminchi hōsei gaiyō* [Outline of colonial legal systems of European empires]. 1911.

Uchida, Jun. *Brokers of Empire: Japanese Settler Colonialism in Korea, 1876–1945*. Cambridge, MA: Harvard University Press, 2014.

Uno, Kathleen S. "Women and Changes in the Household Division of Labor." In Bernstein, *Recreating Japanese Women*, 17–41.

Wagatsuma Sakae, ed. *Meiji zenki Daishinin minji hanketsuroku* [Verdicts of the Supreme Court from the early Meiji period]. 12 vols. Kyoto: Sanwa Shobo, 1957–66.

Wells, Kenneth M. "The Price of Legitimacy: Women and the Kŭnuhoe Movement, 1927–1931." In Gi-wook and Robinson, *Colonial Modernity in Korea*, 191–220.

Yama'uchi Toshihiko. "Chōsen ni okeru kafu no sōzokuken [Widows' inheritance rights in Korea]." *Koseki* 3, no. 6 (1943): 1–10.

Yang Hyun-ah. "Hanguk kajokpŏp ŭl t'onghae pon singminjijŏk kŭndaesŏng kwa yugyojŏk chŏnt'ong tamron [Colonial modernity and discourses of Confucian tradition examined through Korean family law]." *Hanguk Sahoehakhoe Hugi Sahoehak Taehoe Palp'yomun Yoyakjip*, December 1998, 342–51.

————. "Hoju chedo wihŏn sosong e kwanhan pŏpsahoehakjŏk koch'al: Kajok ŭi pyŏnhwa rŭl chungsim ŭro [Considering the legal accusation of the unconstitutionality of the household-head system from the legal sociological perspective: Focusing on the changing family]." *Hanguk sahoehak* 36, no. 5 (2002): 201–29.

————.*Han'guk kajokpŏp ilki*. Seoul: Ch'angbi, 2011.

Yi Chŏng-sŏn. "Han'guk kŭndae hojŏk chedo ŭi pyŏnch'ŏn: Minjŏkpŏp ŭi pŏpchejŏk t'ŭkching ŭl chungsim ŭro [Transformation of the modern Korean household registration system: Focusing on the legal characteristics of the Civil Registration Law]." *Han'guksaron* 55 (2009): 275–328.

————. "Singminji Chosŏn Taeman esŏ'ŭi ka-chedo chŏngch'aek kwajŏng [The process of implementation of the household system in Korea and Taiwan during the colonial period]." *Han'guk Munhwa* 55 (September 2011): 253–83.

————. "Ilche ŭi naesŏn kyŏrhon chŏngch'aek [Japanese colonial policy on intermarriage between Japanese and Koreans]." PhD diss., Seoul National University, 2015.

Yi Hyojae. *Chosŏnjo sahoe wa kajok: Sinbun sangsŭng kwa kabujangje munhwa* [Family and society in the Chosŏn dynasty: Upward social mobility and patriarchal culture]. Seoul: Han'ul, 2003.

Yi Suk-in [Lee, Sook-in]. "Kŭndae ch'ogi yŏgwŏn ŭi yuip kwa yugyo ŭi chaegusŏng [Influx of women's rights in the early modern period and the reconstruction of Confucianism]." *Kukhak Yŏngu* 24 (2014): 187–218.

Yi Sŭng-il [Lee Seung-il]. "1910, 20 nyŏndae Chosŏn ch'ongdokpu ŭi pŏpche chŏngch'aek: Chosŏn minsaryŏng che 11 -cho 'kwansŭp' ŭi sŏngmunhwa rŭl chungsim ŭro [Legal policy of the Korean Government General in the 1910s to 1920s: Centering on the codification of custom [shown in] Civil Ordinances in Korea article 11]." *Tongbang Hakpo* 126 (June 2004).

———. *Chosŏn chʼongdokpu pŏpche chŏngchʼaek: Ilche ŭi singmin tʼongchʼi wa chosŏn minsaryŏng* [Legal policy of Korean Government General: Japanese colonial rule and the Civil Ordinances of Korea]. Seoul: Yŏksa pipʼyŏngsa, 2008.

———. "Chosŏn chʼongdokpu ŭi pŏpche chŏngchʼaek e tehan yŏngu: Chosŏn minsayŏng che 11 cho "kwansŭp" ŭi sŏngmunpŏphwa rŭl chungsim ŭro [A study on the legislative policy of the Korean Government General; Focusing on codification of article 11 'customs' of Korean Civil Ordinances]." PhD diss., Hanyang University, Seoul, 2003.

———. "Chosŏn hojŏngnyŏng chejŏng e kwanhan yŏngu [A study about the Household-Registration Law (of colonial Korea)]." *Pŏpsahak Yŏngu* 32 (October 2005): 37–68.

Yi Tʼae-yŏng. *Kajokpŏp kaejŏng undong 37-nyŏnsa* [Thirty-seven years of movement to reform the family law]. 1948. Reprint, Seoul: Hanʼguk Kajŏng Pomnyul Sangdamso Chʼulpʼanbu, 1992.

Yi Yŏng-mi. "Chōsen tōkanfu ni okeru hōmu hosakan seido to kanshū chōsa jigyō: Ume Kenjirō to Oda Mikijirō o chūshin ni (3) [Judicial advisory system of the Resident-General Office and the customs-survey project: Focusing on Ume Kenjirō and Oda Mikijirō, no. 3]." *Hōgaku Shirin* 99, no. 2 (2001): 197–242.

———. "Chōsen tōkanfu ni okeru hōmu hosakan seido to kanshū chōsa jigyō: Ume Kenjirō to Oda Mikijirō o chūshin ni (4) [Judicial advisory system of the Resident-General Office and the customs-survey project: Focusing on Ume Kenjirō and Oda Mikijirō, no. 4]." *Hōgaku Shirin* 99, no. 3 (2002): 183–223.

———. "Kankoku kindai koseki kanren hōkyu no seitei oyobi kaisei katei: 'Minsekihō o chūshin ni [The establishment and demise of the laws concerning household registers in modern Korea: Focusing on the Household-Registration Law]." *Tōyō bunka kenkyū* 6 (March 2004): 1–30.

———. *Hanʼguk sabŏp chedo wa Ume Kenjiro* [Korean judicial system and Ume Kenjiro], translated by Kim Hye-jŏng. Seoul: Iljogak, 2011.

Yonemoto, Marcia. *The Problem of Women in Early Modern Japan.* Berkeley: University of California Press, 2016.

Yoneyama, Lisa. *Cold War Ruins: Transpacific Critique of American Justice and Japanese War Crimes.* Durham, NC: Duke University Press, 2016.

Yoo, Theodore Jun. *Politics of Gender in Colonial Korea: Education, Labor, and Health, 1910–1945.* Berkeley: University of California Press, 2008.

Yūhō Kyōkai, ed. *Chōsen ni okeru shihō seido kindaika no sokuseki: Chōsen shihōkai no ōji o kataru zadankai* [The footprints of modernization of the judicial system in Korea: A roundtable on the past of the judicial association of (colonial) Korea]. Tokyo: Yūhō kyōkai, 1966.

Yuzawa Yasuhiko. *Taishōki no kazoku mondai: Jiyū to okuatsu ni ikita hitobito* [The family problem in the Taishō period: People who lived between freedom and oppression]. Kyoto: Minerva Shobō, 2010.

Zelizer, Viviana A. Rotman. *The Purchase of Intimacy.* Princeton: Princeton University Press, 2005.

INDEX

adoption, 153n52. *See also* son-in-law adoption

adultery, 153n47

affective relationships. *See* conjugal relationships; romantic love, ideal of

alimony, 92, 113

ancestral rites: in Civil Ordinances (*Minjirei*), 68–72; Japanese concept of, 71; daughters' responsibilities for, 22–23, 37–38; effects of, on agnatic kin, 136n24; inheritance of, 20, 23, 38–39, 58, 62, 67–68, 80, 98–99, 105, 115–16, 152n27; widows' responsibilities, 23, 25, 27, 48, 51–52, 119

An Chung-gŭn, 32

Annexation Treaty (1910), 33

Asami Rintarō, 68, 106

assimilation: and the Civil Code (Japanese, 1898–1948), 5–6, 9, 68–69; and civil law, 63; under Cultural Rule, 55–56; definitions of, 6; as desirable, 9; and family law, 4–8; "forced assimilation policy," 6, 77, 96–97, 104; and ideal of romantic love, 79–80; and Japanese distortion of Korean customs, 6–7; of Korean customs, 71; Name-Change Policy, 6, 72, 73, 96–97, 107–8; and notions of progress, 8–9, 72; and perpetuation of difference, 104–5; as reshaping Japanese empire, 6

Borrowed Civil Code (*Ŭiyong Minpŏp*), 95, 108

Bourgon, Jérôme, 138n2

burial sites, 47, 69

Chang Hwa-sun, 95

Chang Kyŏng-gŭn, 109–10, 111

Chang Sŭng-du, 106

Chanock, Martin, 8

Chen Chao-ju, 8

China, 137n46, 138n2

Chŏng Kŭng-sik, 7, 132n16

Cho, Yun-sŏn, 136n20

Chŏng Chi-yŏng, 21, 78, 83

Chŏng Kwang-hyŏn, 110, 111

Chōsen kōtō hōin hanketsuroku, 10, 14–15, 78, 148–49n53, 152n26

Chosŏn dynasty period: civil law in, 24; concubinage in, 80–81; and Confucian ideology, 20–21, 136n22; family-property regime (*kasan*) in, 25–28; legal conflicts of women's property rights during, 24; rise of patrilineal system in, 19–21; widows' status as precarious in, 25–26; women's marginalization in, 19–20; women's property rights in, 27–28, 37

Cho Ŭn, 25

Civil Code (Japanese, 1898–1948): and ancestral rites, 69; application of, in colonial Korea, 4–5; and assimilation policies, 5–6, 8; vs. Civil Code (South Korean, 1960–), 113; and civil law, 32; common-law marriage in, 88, 89; and definition of family, 49–50,

www.ingramcontent.com/pod-product-compliance
Lightning Source LLC
Chambersburg PA
CBHW070338270326
41926CB00017B/3911